A.T.Q. STEWART was born in Belfast, where he was educated at the Royal Belfast Academical Institution and Queen's University. After some years in teaching, he returned to Queen's as a lecturer, and was appointed Reader in Irish History in 1975. He took early retirement in 1990 to devote more time to writing, and he is a frequent broadcaster on radio and television. He was consultant to both BBC Television's *The History of Ireland* and Thames Television's *The Troubles* and was a presenter for the Channel 4 series *The Divided Kingdom*. Since 1970 he has contributed to many encyclopedias and works of reference, prepared sets of questions for the BBC *Mastermind* series, and written articles for newspapers and journals, including the *Spectator*, the *Irish Arts Review*, *History Ireland*, the *Irish Times, Irish Independent, Sunday Tribune* and the *Belfast Telegraph*. His publications include *The Ulster Crisis: Resistance to Home Rule, 1912–1914* (Faber and Faber, 1967; reissued by Blackstaff Press, 1997), *The Pagoda War: Lord Dufferin and the Fall of the Kingdom of Ava* (Faber and Faber, 1972), *The Narrow Ground: Aspects of Ulster 1609–1969* (Faber and Faber, 1977; reissued by Blackstaff Press, 1997), *Edward Carson* (Gill and Macmillan, 1982), *A Deeper Silence: The Hidden Origins of the United Irishmen* (Faber and Faber, 1993) and *The Summer Soldiers: The 1798 Rebellion in Antrim and Down* (Blackstaff Press, 1995). In 1977 he was a joint winner of the first Christopher Ewart-Biggs Memorial Prize for *The Narrow Ground*. He is married with two sons and lives in Belfast.

The Ulster Crisis

A.T.Q. STEWART

The Ulster Crisis

RESISTANCE TO HOME RULE
1912–1914

•

THE
BLACKSTAFF
PRESS

BELFAST

First published in hardback in 1967
and in paperbck in 1969 by
Faber and Faber Limited
This Blackstaff Press edition is a photolithographic facsimile
of the first edition printed by
The University Press, Glasgow

This edition published in 1997 by
The Blackstaff Press Limited
Blackstaff House, Wildflower Way,
Apollo Road, Belfast BT12 6TA, Northern Ireland
Reprinted 1999

Printed by The Guernsey Press Company Limited

A CIP catalogue record for this book
is available from the British Library

ISBN 0-85640-599-X

TO

MY

MOTHER

ACKNOWLEDGEMENTS

While writing this book I have received kindness and encouragement from many people. Mr. Charles Monteith of Faber and Faber, who invited me to undertake it, has been unfailingly helpful during its preparation. Professor J. C. Beckett of the Queen's University, Belfast, to whose inspiration I owe my interest in Irish history, has read several drafts of the typescript and made many detailed comments from which I have been able to benefit. Mr. Kenneth Darwin and Mr. Brian Trainor, of the Public Record Office of Northern Ireland, have been indefatigable in tracing source material for me and making smooth the path of research; my debt to them, and to their colleagues, is considerable.

For permission to quote from papers deposited in the Record Office I wish to thank the Hon. Denis Craig of Priston, Somerset; the trustees of the estate of the late Lieutenant-Colonel F. H. Crawford, C.B.E.; Mr. Roger Hall of Warrenpoint, Co. Down; Lord O'Neill of Shane's Castle, Co. Antrim; and the Ulster Unionist Council. Lady Spender not only allowed me to consult and quote from the papers of her late husband, Lieutenant-Colonel Sir Wilfrid Spender, K.C.B., C.B.E., D.S.O., M.C., and her own diaries (in themselves a most valuable source), but was kind enough to draw upon her recollections of events in order to assist me, and in discussion and correspondence patiently to answer many of my questions.

For help of various kinds in my researches I am grateful to Miss Isabel Agnew; Mr. Norman Canning; Colonel Adair Crawford; Mr. Patrick Crawford; Mr. Peter Grant; the late Lieutenant-Colonel Frank Hall; Mr. R. G. D. Hamilton; Sir Wilson Hungerford; the Rev. C. Brett Ingram; Mr. W. P. Johnston; Mr. John Kerr; the late Rev. R. Kirkpatrick and Mrs. Kirkpatrick; Mr. John H. MacLeod; Dr. D. B. McNeill; and Mrs. Doreen M. Penson. Mr. Noel Clarke carried out valuable research for me in Hamburg, and the *Museum für Hamburgische Geschichte* helped to verify important facts.

ACKNOWLEDGEMENTS

My thanks are due also to Miss Margaret Williamson who typed the manuscript, and to Mr. Ronald Marshall who undertook the reading of the proofs. I am indebted to Mr. J. W. Vitty and the staff of the Linenhall Library, Belfast, and to the staffs of the Queen's University Library and of the University Library, Cambridge, for many courtesies.

In preparing the book I have had much patient and cheerful help from my wife, which no form of words could adequately acknowledge.

Finally I owe a debt of gratitude to the Wiles Trust for enabling me to spend a year at Peterhouse, Cambridge, where the book was completed, to Stranmillis College, Belfast, for generous leave of absence, and to the Master and Fellows of Peterhouse for their hospitality.

Cambridge,   A. T. Q. STEWART
May 1966.

CONTENTS

MAPS

'For as the nature of Foule weather lyeth not in a showre or two of rain; but in an inclination thereto of many dayes together: So the nature of war consisteth not in actuall fighting; but in the known disposition thereto, during all the time there is no assurance to the contrary.'

HOBBES, *Leviathan*

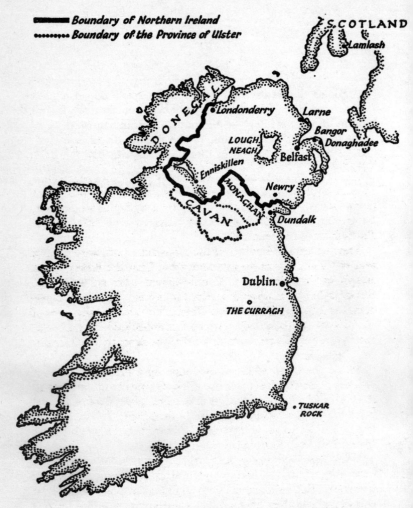

Boundary of Northern Ireland
•••••••• Boundary of the Province of Ulster

S.COTLAND
Lamlash

DONEGAL
•Londonderry   Larne
                Bangor
LOUGH   Donaghadee
NEACH
        •Belfast
Enniskillen
        MONAGHAN   •Newry
CAVAN   •Dundalk

        Dublin.
        ○ THE CURRAGH

                • TUSKAR
                  ROCK

IRELAND; showing places mentioned in the text

1

PRELUDE

Attendance at the House of Commons was unusually low that day, and only sixty members were present when, at ten minutes past noon, the Gentleman Usher of the Black Rod appeared and summoned them to the House of Lords, to hear the royal assent given by commission to Bills agreed upon by both Houses, and, for the first time, to Bills 'duly passed under the provisions of the Parliament Act of 1911'.

The red leather benches of the House of Lords were empty, and not a single peer was present apart from the Bishop of St. Asaph and the five Lords Commissioners who sat below the throne, splendid in robes of scarlet and ermine and black three-cornered hats. While the Lord Chancellor read out the titles of the Bills, the representatives of the Commons stood in silence at the Bar of the House, waiting for the one dramatic moment in the brief ceremony.

At last the Clerk of the Crown took up a printed document and in a loud voice read out 'The Government of Ireland Act'. The Clerk of the Parliament bowed to the Commons and pronounced the ancient formula '*Le roi le veult*'. Instantly from the public galleries, which were crowded in contrast to the House itself, there arose a deafening cheer.

The excited Commons surged back through the corridor to their own Chamber, and as they did so, someone produced a green Irish flag emblazoned with a golden harp and waved it in triumph above their heads. When they had returned, a Labour member asked, in a voice that trembled with emotion, if they might sing 'God Save the King', and without waiting for an answer, began to lead the House in the anthem. Parliament was then prorogued; the members filed past the Deputy Speaker and shook hands with him. The time was twenty-five minutes past twelve, and the date 18 September 1914.[1]

This strange and unprecedented scene brought to a close the most bitter political crisis experienced in Britain since the days of the Long Parliament. The final ceremony, played out on a deserted stage, with most of the principal actors missing, contrasted sharply with the drama which had preceded it. The progress through Parliament of the third Home Rule Bill (to give it the title by which it was generally known) had taken two years, five months and seven days, and every inch of the way had been contested with a bitterness hitherto unknown in public life, and by methods alien to every British tradition.

Long before it reached the Statute Book, the Bill had ceased to be relevant to the Irish situation it was intended to ameliorate, and in any case it was passed subject to the condition that it would not come into force until the end of the war. Yet, to a small group of men present, its passing had profound significance, for on that day the Irish Nationalist members entered the promised land towards which O'Connell had led, and in sight of which Parnell had died. For them it marked the end of more than a century of unavailing agitation to undo the Act of Union of 1801, which had suppressed the Irish Parliament and made Ireland part of the United Kingdom.

The Irish question was, of course, older than the Union. As a problem for British statesmen it began on the May day in 1169 when Robert Fitzstephen, a Norman earl, landed in Wexford with a force of 600 soldiers. From that date until 1922 Irish history is really the history of Anglo–Irish relations. For the Irish it is the story of seven centuries of English oppression, a misleading verdict, if for no other reason, because it suggests an efficiency which has never been an English characteristic. During the long period of their rule in Ireland, the English behaved neither better nor worse than they behaved elsewhere, and the peculiar bitterness of Anglo–Irish discord springs, not from ruthless domination, but from the fact that every attempt to subjugate Ireland was mismanaged or left incomplete. Ireland was linked to England by the accident of geography, and the English could neither anglicize her nor leave her alone.

For seven centuries they allowed Irish hatreds to flourish like weeds in a neglected garden, hatreds engendered by religious persecution, dispossession, insurrection and famine. Not all of these evils were inflicted by the English, but they permitted them to happen, which, in Irish eyes, was infinitely worse.

With the passing of the Act of Union the spirit of Irish distress came to dwell at Westminster, and for over a century it continued to disturb British political life. Whether it appeared in the guise of Robert Emmet or Deirdre of the Sorrows, as the Spectre of Famine or the Fenian dynamiter so familiar to readers of *Punch*, its influence was uniformly malign. For Britain at the zenith of her imperial might, Ireland was a *damnosa hereditas*. It was no use washing the historical bloodstain out of the carpet; it always reappeared overnight. As far back as anyone could remember there had been the sound of keening in the west wing.

During the nineteenth century Irish nationalism manifested itself first by agitation for the repeal of the Union, then after the mid-century by renewed violence, and finally by sustained political pressure exerted upon successive governments by a well-disciplined and troublesome party in the House of Commons. The men of this party with their quicksilver temperaments and Irish wit were popular, even when they wantonly outraged every canon of parliamentary behaviour, for the Irish character eluded English statesmen as much as the Irish question. The English could never understand, when Irish eyes were smiling, why Irish mouths had to be filled with bitter invective. Every time that Ireland was mentioned the temperature in the House rose sharply; tempers were lost, ministries fell, parties crumbled, and all, it seemed, to little purpose. The evil spirit of Ireland that roamed the corridors of Westminster would not rest and could not be satisfied.

Only one man possessed the experience, the prestige and the courage to undertake the task of exorcism. At the beginning of his first ministry in 1868 William Ewart Gladstone had declared that his mission was to pacify Ireland, and this he had striven resolutely to accomplish. After disestablishing the Anglican Church in Ireland he had turned to the intractable problem of the land system and by 1881 had freed it from the worst of its complex iniquities. Yet the core of the political problem remained, and Irish nationalism grew stronger and more militant as the years went by.

It was in August 1885, while on a brief holiday among the

Norwegian fiords that Gladstone decided that nothing short of political independence would ever satisfy the demands of the Irish people.[2] The example of Norway impressed him deeply, and reflecting in those placid surroundings on the long years he had devoted to Ireland's problems, he came to the conclusion that it was his duty and his destiny to give her Home Rule. The ship of state, however, sailed in more turbulent waters than Sir Thomas Brassey's *Sunbeam*, and Gladstone could scarcely have chosen a less propitious moment, since he was temporarily out of office, his ministry having been defeated in the previous June by a combination of Conservatives and Irish Nationalists. Lord Salisbury had formed a caretaker government to last until a general election could be held on the new household franchise created in 1884. The election, fought on a confusing number of issues, gave the Liberals a majority of 86 over the Conservatives. The Irish Nationalist members elected also numbered 86, a compact group ruled with iron discipline by Charles Stewart Parnell.

Gladstone had hoped that the Conservatives might bring in Home Rule on the basis of some kind of party compromise, but any possibility of this had faded by December, when his son Herbert revealed to the newspaper editors the details of his father's political conversion. Gladstone, who characteristically was just then conducting an argument with T. H. Huxley about the literal truth of the Book of Genesis, did not appear to be very disconcerted, and he accepted the challenge almost joyfully when Parnell offered him the support of the Irish votes if he would undertake to introduce a Home Rule Bill.

In January 1886 Gladstone formed a Government which was completely dependent upon the Irish vote, and he at once began to frame a Bill to restore a parliament to Ireland, and give her an independent executive with authority over all matters except defence, foreign policy, trade, and navigation.

His policy met with opposition from both the Whig right and the Radical left of the Liberal party. Nevertheless Gladstone made a superhuman effort to hold the party together, and even persuaded the great Birmingham Radical, Joseph Chamberlain, to accept office in the Government. But Chamberlain soon resigned in protest against Gladstone's Irish proposals, and many prominent Liberals, offended by their leader's secretive methods, followed his example and withdrew their support completely.

On 8 April 1886, with both wings of his party in revolt, Gladstone introduced the Home Rule Bill in the House. In his speech he mentioned, almost in parenthesis, what was rapidly becoming one of the chief obstacles to the Bill's success. Turning aside to refer to 'that wealthy, intelligent, and energetic portion of the Irish community' which predominated in 'a portion of Ulster', he said that while he would pay no attention to threats of violent measures in certain emergencies but treat them as 'momentary ebullitions, which will pass away with the fears from which they spring', he would adopt every means to disarm those fears. 'I cannot allow it to be said', he continued, 'that a Protestant minority in Ulster, or elsewhere, is to rule the question at large for Ireland . . . but I think that the Protestant minority should have its wishes considered to the utmost practicable extent in any form they may assume.'[3]

Gladstone recognized that an Ulster problem existed, and he considered rationally and fairly how it might be solved, but he failed to appreciate its tremendous emotional potential in British politics. It was just this aspect of it which had already been seized upon by Gladstone's sharpest opponent in the House, Lord Randolph Churchill, the son of the Duke of Marlborough.

This young politician, discontented with the leadership of the Conservative party, had formed his own 'Fourth Party', and from below the gangway on the Opposition side had mercilessly attacked Gladstone's Government on every possible occasion. In Gladstone's conversion to Home Rule he saw the possibility of overthrowing the Liberal party, and he deliberately determined to use the Ulster opposition to achieve his purpose. On 16 February 1886, he had written to his friend Lord Justice Fitzgibbon, 'I decided some time ago that if the G.O.M. went for Home Rule, the Orange card would be the one to play. Please God it may turn out the ace of trumps and not the two.'[4]

Six days later Churchill travelled to Ulster. It was obviously political calculation rather than affection which inspired his journey, for only a short time before he had been complaining to Lord Salisbury that the Ulster Conservatives were 'playing the devil in northern Ireland' and that 'these foul Ulster Tories have always ruined our party'. Colonel Saunderson, the leader of the Ulster members, showed equal candour when he told Churchill that they distrusted him more than any of his colleagues.[5]

No trace of these imperfect sympathies was allowed to mar the enthusiasm of Lord Randolph's welcome at Larne. He travelled on to Belfast where further cheering crowds met him at York Street Station, and a reporter noted that from the railway carriage he seemed to be 'looking quietly at the crowd, forming his own impression of what he saw'. Later that evening he spoke for an hour and a half to a huge audience in the Ulster Hall. He reminded them that his ancestor, the first Duke of Marlborough, had been a general of William of Orange. (He did not mention that he had also been a general of James II.) He urged them to wait and watch, organize and prepare, so that the catastrophe of Home Rule might not come upon them 'as a thief in the night' or find them unready. 'I do not hesitate to say,' he continued, '. . . in that dark hour there will not be wanting to you those of position and influence in England who are willing to cast in their lot with you, whatever it may be, and who will share your fortune and your fate.' His speech ended with a spirited paraphrase of *Hohenlinden*:

> *The combat deepens; on ye brave,*
> *Who rush to glory or the grave*
> *Wave, Ulster, all thy banners wave,*
> *And charge with all thy chivalry.*[6]

The roar of applause which greeted these lines showed that Churchill had sounded the precise note to which Orange hearts responded. Not all the inhabitants of Belfast were so appreciative, however, and in some quarters stones were thrown at the bands and processions as they returned home. In England, too, Lord Randolph had his critics, who accused him of unconstitutional incitement to revolt, but he was totally unrepentant. On 9 May, in a public letter to a Glasgow Liberal Unionist, he repeated with emphasis a slogan he had first used at Larne:

'If political parties and political leaders . . . should be so utterly lost to every feeling and dictate of honour and courage as to hand over coldly, and for the sake of purchasing a short and illusory parliamentary tranquillity, the lives and liberties of the loyalists of Ireland to their hereditary and most bitter foes, make no doubt on this point; Ulster at the proper moment will resort to the supreme arbitrament of force; *Ulster will fight, and Ulster will be right.*'[7]

The stormy passage of the Home Rule Bill continued for two

months during which time Gladstone, deserted by a rapidly increasing number of his supporters, held to his lonely course. Late on the evening of 7 June 1886 he rose to wind up the debate, and, white to the lips with fatigue and strain, he ended his speech with a moving plea to the House: 'Ireland stands at your bar, expectant, hopeful, almost suppliant. . . . She asks a blessed oblivion of the past, and in that oblivion our interest is deeper than even hers. . . . Think, I beseech you, think well, think wisely, think not for a moment but for the years which are to come, before you reject this Bill.' The House immediately divided; 93 liberals voted against the Bill, and it was defeated by 343 votes to 313.[8]

The Queen was asked to dissolve parliament and the country gave an unmistakable verdict against Home Rule. 'Well, Herbert,' Gladstone told his son, 'we *have* had a drubbing and no mistake.'[9] The same jaunty tone was adopted in a pamphlet on Home Rule which he published on 22 August 1886. Ireland, he wrote, had only to persevere for a few years of 'constitutional and peaceful action, of steady and free discussion', and the walls of Jericho would presently fall 'not in blood and conflagration, but at the trumpets' peal'.[10]

In fact the walls of Jericho were to remain disconcertingly intact, and the question of the Union was to trouble British politics for the next forty years. After the election of 1892 when the Irish Nationalists once again held the balance of power the indomitable statesman introduced his second Home Rule Bill, and though he was then in his eighty-third year he carried it through the Commons, only to see it heavily defeated in the Lords. The country clearly agreed with the Lords, and ten years of Unionist government followed, during which the Liberals tried hard to forget about Ireland and, in T. M. Healy's words, Home Rule was 'put into cold storage'.

The Irish question played no part in the general election of 1906 which resulted in a Liberal landslide, and the size of the majority made it certain that the skeleton would remain safely locked away in the Liberal cupboard. In all, 396 Liberals were returned, with 51 Labour and 83 Irish Nationalists, against only 157 Conservatives and Unionists. The Conservative rout was one of the worst in parliamentary history; several Cabinet ministers, including Balfour, lost their seats, while the new government, formed by Henry Campbell-Bannerman, had the support of one of the largest and most talented collections of backbenchers ever to assemble under a party banner.

The Liberal ministry was quite independent of the Irish party, and Home Rule was not mentioned until 1909, and then only in an aside which passed almost unnoticed because public attention was taken up with a more immediate controversy. In April of that year Lloyd George had introduced a budget so framed that the House of Lords was certain to reject it, and break a tradition established in the seventeenth century. By this means the Radical Welsh Chancellor hoped to clear the way for a determined onslaught on the privilege of the Lords, and, in particular, their veto on legislation. He also hoped that in rejecting the budget they would incur all the odium of the struggle.

The Finance Bill was duly rejected in November 1909, and the Liberals joined battle with the Lords. Asquith, who had succeeded Campbell-Bannerman as Prime Minister in 1908, appealed to the country, and the Liberals were returned with a reduced majority. In the political storm which was now seething round the House of Lords, they could no longer afford to ignore the votes of the Irish Nationalist members, and hints about Home Rule began to appear in the speeches of the ministers.

In 1910 the conflict moved from Parliament to the conference room. The sudden death of Edward VII in May further complicated the political situation and, out of respect to the new sovereign, both parties observed an uneasy truce until the end of the year. Another general election in December 1910, far from breaking the deadlock, left the Liberals and Conservatives evenly matched, and once more the Irish Nationalists held the balance between the parties.

Their triumph was sweet because between 1906 and 1910 they had been supporting a Government which they could not influence, while under attack from those of their fellow-countrymen who demanded a more active policy. The issue was now quite clear: if the Liberals were to bring down the House of Lords, they would need the votes of the Irish party, and the price would be Home Rule for Ireland. In December 1910, in answer to a heckler in his constituency of East Fife, Asquith had admitted that he intended to introduce a Home Rule Bill in the next session of parliament. By that time five hundred contests had been decided and the election almost over. The Unionists subsequently claimed that the electorate had not had an opportunity to express its opinions on the Irish question.

The excitement over the Parliament Bill became a frenzy by the summer of 1911. In July the Government announced that the King had consented to create whatever number of peers would be necessary to pass the bill, and the majority in the House of Lords submitted under protest rather than suffer this indignity. The Parliament Act, carried in August, restricted the Lords' veto on legislation to three sessions, after which bills would become law without the consent of the Upper House. Thus the last obstacle to Home Rule was removed. The time had come, it seemed, for the trumpets to sound, and the walls of Jericho would fall down of their own accord.

2

THE ORANGE CARD

Lord Randolph Churchill's Orange card had a curious history. The least disputable statement which can be made about the distinctness of Ulster from the rest of Ireland is that it had always existed. Even in prehistoric times, the culture patterns of Neolithic settlers in the north of Ireland differed significantly from those of the south; and at the point where prehistory shades into history, Gaelic legend tells of the confused battles of the Red Branch Knights of Ulster and the faithful Cuchulain against Queen Maeve and the 'Men of Ireland'.

These distinctions were almost certainly the result of geography. Mountains and forests made Ulster inaccessible from the central plain, a factor which remained important until the seventeenth century. Although the Normans established themselves strongly in eastern Ulster in the twelfth century, building the great castle of Carrickfergus which still stands, Ulster held out longer than the rest of the island in the later stages of the English conquest. The determination of the Tudors to replace the old Gaelic structure of society, based on the Brehon law, was resisted most successfully in the north, and in the last years of Elizabeth I's reign we find the great Hugh O'Neill of Ulster leading the final and most dangerous of the Gaelic rebellions against English authority. Not until his defeat, a few days after the Queen's death, was the Tudor conquest of Ireland complete.

When in 1607 O'Neill and his ally Red Hugh O'Donnell suddenly left Ireland and went into exile on the continent, James I took the opportunity of the political vacuum to draw up plans for the plantation of Ulster with English and Scottish settlers. The counties of Armagh, Cavan, Coleraine (now Londonderry), Donegal, Fermanagh and Tyrone were given over to 'undertakers' and 'servitors', and in the case of Coleraine to certain of the London companies, on the condition that they undertook to settle them with English and Scots. Antrim and Down were not included in the scheme. Scots from the Western Isles, mostly of the Macdonnell clan, had long been settling in the Glens of Antrim, and in 1603 Sir Randal Macdonnell was granted a large part of the county for colonization. In Down Sir Hugh Montgomery, the Laird of Braidstane in Ayrshire, established in 1606 a flourishing colony of Lowland Scots in Clandeboye and the Ards. In time the population of the two eastern counties came to be predominantly Scottish in speech, custom and outlook.[1]

Although the Ulster Plantation was never completed as originally planned, it was by far the most successful of the attempts to colonize Ireland, and its pattern can still be traced to-day. Perhaps too much emphasis has been placed on the difference in 'race' between the planters and the native Irish, for settlers in Ireland have always tended to become quickly more Irish than the Irish themselves, but the difference in religion was of incalculable importance. The failure of the English Reformation in Ireland, which is closely linked with the English failure to subjugate all Ireland at any given time, lies at the root of Anglo-Irish troubles. The Ulster planters were Protestants, either Anglicans or adherents of the Presbyterian Church of Scotland. It is true that the first wave of Scots in Antrim had been Catholic and Gaelic, but they were followed by Lowlanders who brought with them the doctrines of Calvin and Knox.

During the reign of Charles I those Ulster Scots who showed Presbyterian leanings were persecuted by the Laudian Church, as the Puritans were in England, and to such a degree that in 1636 some of them built a ship called the *Eagleswing* and attempted to sail from Belfast Lough to Massachusetts. After two months contrary winds forced them to return to their starting point.[2] These Ulster Scots turned in sympathy to the followers of the National Covenant who were resisting the rule of Charles and Archbishop Laud in Scotland, and during the next few years their Presbyterianism was hardened in the fires of the 1641 Rebellion and the Civil War.

In seventeenth century England religion and politics were still inseparable; they began to diverge only with the Toleration Act and the constitutional settlement which placed William III and his wife securely on the English throne. In Ireland this separation has never occurred, and, indeed, the constitutional struggles at the end of James II's reign had consequences in Ireland which were the opposite of those produced in England. When the deposed King James decided to continue to resist William III on Irish soil, he was acting within his constitutional rights, for he was also King of Ireland; he had moreover the loyal support of the great majority of his Irish Roman Catholic subjects. In Ulster, however, the Protestants of two small towns, Enniskillen and Londonderry, declared their adherence to William, and prepared to defend themselves. Derry, where many refugees had gathered, was in a state of confusion, but when it was learned that the Governor, Lundy, intended to surrender to the Catholic forces the apprentices shut the gates and the town was besieged. A boom was constructed across Lough Foyle, and no supplies were allowed to enter for fifteen weeks, during which the starving defenders repulsed every attack on the walls. On 1 August 1689 an English ship, the *Mountjoy*, broke through the boom and the siege was lifted. The apprentices are heroes of Protestant legend, and Lundy has become the prototype of all traitors.

The interval thus gained was very valuable to William, and in 1690 he landed in Ireland at the head of a large army. On 1 July 1690 he joined action with the Irish and French armies of James II on the line of the River Boyne, and James was decisively defeated. The Battle of the Boyne, probably the most important battle ever to be fought in Ireland, is more real to some Ulstermen than events of the twentieth century, and, in the words of one historian, 'the instinct which has kept its memory alive in Irish politics is a true one, for the Boyne was the critical moment of a long struggle between the Roman Catholic and Protestant interests.'[3] Its result was to establish securely in Ireland the Protestant Ascendancy which lasted until recent times.

Yet the view which sees the north of Ireland as the last stronghold of this Protestant garrison, continually resisting the struggle of the Irish nation towards independence, is misleading, for, as Professor Mansergh reminds us, there is 'an ever-present temptation to explain the very complex forces which mould the political life of Ulster in terms of a false simplicity'.[4] The last quarter of the eighteenth century, perhaps the most stimulating period in Irish history, refuses to fit into the picture which is generally painted of Ulster. Nevertheless it is critically important.

In those years the Protestant north produced the most ambitious attempt yet made in Ireland to separate religion from politics, and to unite all Irishmen in a purpose at once liberal and patriotic. During the eighteenth century there had been a massive emigration from Ulster to America, and the Ulster-Scots had taken a very active part in the War of Independence. The Declaration of Independence itself is in the handwriting of an Ulsterman, and it was first printed by an Ulsterman. Washington once said, 'if defeated everywhere I will take my last stand for liberty among the Scotch-Irish of my native Virginia,' and at least ten of his successors as President of the United States have been of Ulster descent.[5]

The American War had an unsettling effect in Ireland. Most of the English troops were withdrawn, and when there was a threat of invasion by the French, volunteers were raised to take their place. The first company was raised in Belfast in 1778. Soon 40,000 Ulstermen were enrolled, nine-tenths of them Presbyterians, and their example was followed by the other provinces. Ostensibly the Volunteers were to defend Ireland from foreign invasion, but as the representatives of a middle class with economic and political grievances, they succeeded in forcing the British Government to grant independence to the Irish parliament in 1782.

After 1790 the Volunteer movement lost its impetus, but from it sprang a radical group which, inspired by the French Revolution, advocated more revolutionary methods of redress. The Society of United Irishmen was formed in Belfast in 1791, and its founders with the exception of the two best-known, Wolfe Tone and Thomas Russell, were Presbyterians. Although the Synod of Ulster condemned such revolutionary courses, many thousands of Presbyterians were implicated in the Rebellion of 1798, and among those subsequently executed, transported or exiled were nearly a score of Presbyterian ministers. It is not surprising to find Lord Castlereagh describing Belfast as 'the headquarters of disaffection in the north', and the Presbyterians as people who had 'partaken so deeply first of the popular and since of the democratic politics of the country as to be an object much more of jealousy than of support to the Government'.[6]

Why then, in less than a century, did the northern Protestants abandon their radical and nationalist opinions and become conservative and fervently loyal to the British connection? One reason undoubtedly was the Union itself. In uniting the two parliaments Pitt hoped to provide a drastic cure for the ills which had caused the Rebellion, yet the north was the only part of Ireland to benefit economically from the Union. In 1792 Belfast could have been described as a market town with harbour facilities, but by 1825 it had already assumed its modern status as an industrial port. As its position in relation to the rest of Ulster changed, its economy became more closely linked with that of Great Britain.

After 1800 the energy which had gone into politics was diverted into commerce and philanthropic work. There was an inevitable reaction from the horrors of 1798, when the middle-class intellectuals had seen in action the mobs they had inflamed with elevated sentiments of liberty and the rights of man. The course of events in France, leading to the Jacobin terror and the rise of Napoleon, added to their disillusion.

Underlying all these changes was something even more important for the future, the hardening of sectarian feeling. While they shared some of their legal disabilities, the Presbyterians had sympathised with their Roman Catholic fellow-countrymen, but once these were removed they drew closer to the conservative Anglicans. They had never, of course, approved of Roman Catholic doctrine, and distrust, persisting from earlier times, strengthened especially after the killing of some Protestants by the Wexford rebels in 1798. When Catholic emancipation came about in 1829, the increased threat to the Ascendancy caused Irish Protestants of all denominations to close their ranks, a process made easier by the growth of evangelical religion.

But even before the insurrection there was evidence of a very sharp change of opinion in areas like Armagh where the Protestants and Catholics were almost equal in numbers. Here the rivalry was basically economic, for it was most acute where there was considerable pressure of population on the land. Such an atmosphere was favourable to the creation of secret societies, which tended to take the law into their own hands; in Armagh the Protestant peasantry produced the Peep O'Day Boys, in retaliation the Catholic peasantry organized themselves as

Defenders. It was following a skirmish between these two on 21 September 1795 at the Diamond, near Loughgall, that the Orange Society was formed to perpetuate the 'pious and immortal memory' of William III.

To begin with it was simply one more secret society whose members were frequently involved in agrarian outrage, and its early history was unsavoury. Rabidly sectarian, it worked to divide the peasantry at the same time that the United Irishmen were striving to unite them. Within a few years, however, it developed in a remarkable way, which to some extent reflected the changes in the outlook of Ulster Protestants. It grew with a rapidity which astonished contemporaries, and soon worked its way upward through the strata of Protestant society. The first Orange processions in Belfast took place on 12 July 1797, on the anniversary of the Battle of the Boyne. The Presbyterian liberals resented this invasion of their stronghold, as this account by a prominent citizen shows: 'We had a display here yesterday morning of the whole force the Orange boys, Orange wenches, and Orange children could muster, for miles around; it was supposed there might have been three thousand of the motley crew, including the various corps of yeomen. I do not understand the nature of the Orange boy establishment, but it seems to be an establishment *divide et impera*.'[7] To the Government indeed, faced with the threat of rebellion and foreign invasion, the Orange Society must have seemed like the intervention of Providence.

The collapse of the United Irish rebellion and the passing of the Union left the Orange Order stronger than ever. Until then it had recruited its members from the Church of Ireland, but early in the nineteenth century it began to attract Presbyterians in large numbers, particularly the tenant farmers, by stimulating their fear of popery. Towards the middle of the century it began to decline and fell into disrepute, but when Gladstone made known his conversion to Home Rule in 1885 it experienced a dramatic revival. Its character changed and it was taken up by 'huge numbers of men of a solid and superior type and became for the most part, highly respectable, and a very powerful political organization working for the maintenance of the Union'.[8]

Orangeism became a strong element in Irish Unionism, though it was never, as is often assumed, its sole ingredient.

After 1885 several organizations were formed to make the Unionist cause better understood in the British constituencies, the most successful being the Ulster Loyalist and Patriotic Union founded by Lord Ranfurly, and following the second Home Rule crisis in 1893, a network of Unionist clubs in the small country towns was created by Lord Templetown. In June of that year 12,000 representatives from the constituencies of Ulster attended a convention in Belfast, accommodated in a large pavilion, which was constructed in three weeks and just as quickly dismantled.

It was at this convention that the Duke of Abercorn asked the audience, with hands solemnly raised, to repeat after him 'We will not have Home Rule'. Another speaker, Thomas Andrews, was wildly cheered when he declared: 'As a last resort we will be prepared to defend ourselves.' Some young Ulstermen, indeed, were already thinking along those lines. Arms were being illegally imported, rifle clubs were springing up everywhere, and sextons of church halls were moulding bullets in their furnaces.

With the defeat of the Liberals in 1895 the danger passed, and during the ten years of Conservative government, the excitement in Ulster subsided. The Anti-Home Rule organization remained intact, however, and became part of the Unionist electoral machinery. In 1905 the Ulster Unionist Council was formed to unite all the Unionist associations, and provide a central authority to determine Unionist policy in Ulster. It had at first 200 members, of whom 100 represented the local associations, 50 the Ulster members of Parliament and 50 the Orange lodges. Later it was considerably enlarged, and by 1911 it had 370 members. The first Secretary to the Council, T. H. Gibson, retired in 1906 because of ill-health, and a Belfast solicitor, Richard Dawson Bates, was temporarily appointed at a nominal salary of £100 a year, out of which he paid the clerical expenses. This temporary appointment lasted for fifteen years and Bates became the grey eminence of the Ulster movement.

The Ulster Unionist Council was concerned only with the North. Unionists in the other provinces were represented by the Irish Unionist Alliance, and from 1908 the two bodies co-operated smoothly with each other, and with the Union Defence League founded and directed in London by Walter

Long. Much of the overlapping between the various Unionist associations had been reduced, and thus by 1911 the machinery existed for a formidable political resistance to the passing of Home Rule.

Shortly after the election of December 1910, the Ulster Unionist Council observed with much surprise 'the singular reticence as regards Home Rule maintained by a large number of Radical candidates in England and Scotland during the recent elections, and especially by the Prime Minister himself, who barely referred to the subject till almost the close of his own contest'. Since Home Rule had not therefore been placed as a clear issue before the electors, the Council judged that the country had given no mandate for it, and that any attempt by the Government to enact it would be 'a grave if not criminal breach of constitutional duty'.[9]

3

DRAMATIS PERSONAE

There was no one in the Liberal Government who approached the Irish question with enthusiasm, let alone the burning zeal of Gladstone, to whom Home Rule had been 'a debt owed by man to God'. The Liberals tackled the Irish Hydra only because they were kept in office by the 84 Irish Nationalists and the 42 Labour members who wanted the question settled so that attention could be paid to their own demands. Home Rule was a pledge which had to be redeemed; it had been left for as long as possible, and now Asquith, whom some of his admirers called 'the last of the Romans', squared his shoulders and prepared to face Parliament. It would, he knew, be an unpleasant experience. He had entered the Commons in 1886, and he recalled only too vividly the political commotion of that year and of 1893. Now, however, the situation was different in one important respect, for the House of Lords no longer had the power to hold up a Home Rule Bill indefinitely, and no matter how acrimonious the battle might be in the Commons, the Government, while it still had a majority, was bound to win. That the conflict might develop in terms other than parliamentary did not seem to have occurred to him.

One point was never in doubt. The Prime Minister and his colleagues did not lack ability. Indeed it often seemed to contemporaries that Henry Herbert Asquith had drawn more than his fair share of the best prizes in the lottery of life; he was handsome, brilliant, cultivated and, most important of all for a politician, he possessed an exceptionally even temperament. His looks were patrician, and he would have liked to have been thought a scion of the aristocracy, though his forebears were in fact Yorkshire wool manufacturers, a circumstance which left him with a lifelong distaste for trade. The milestones on his road to No. 10 Downing Street were a Balliol scholarship, a first in Classical Greats, a large legal practice and entry to the Commons (with the assistance of his friend Haldane) as the member for East Fife. His second marriage to Margot Tennant, the brewery heiress, carried him into the world of high society, which was apparently very congenial to him.

He had been a successful Home Secretary and Chancellor of the Exchequer, and in 1911, after three years as Prime Minister, he was at the zenith of his prestige and reputation. The secret of his parliamentary adroitness lay in his tactics, which were modelled on those of the Roman general Fabius Cunctator. Asquith never made a decision to-day which he could put off until to-morrow. Invariably dignified, never losing his temper even under the bitterest personal attacks, he waited quietly for his opponents to exhaust themselves or events to turn in his favour. Procrastination had given him victory over the House of Lords, and he hoped that it would serve him as well over Ireland. From his lips an admonition to 'wait and see' sounded like the rebuke of a man whose nerves were of steel, and it was only gradually that the Opposition began to perceive that what they took for strength was the skilful exploitation of a weakness.

Two of Asquith's older colleagues, John Morley the disciple and biographer of Gladstone, and the Marquis of Crewe, a former Lord Lieutenant of Ireland, had first-hand knowledge of the treacherous climate of Irish affairs, although in 1911 they were both more immediately concerned with India. At the other extreme two young members of the Cabinet, David Lloyd George and Winston Churchill had misgivings about Ulster and felt that it should be excluded from the Home Rule Bill right at the beginning. But this compromise was repugnant to Asquith and most of his advisers, except as a last resort, and the Bill as prepared did not differ essentially from Gladstone's. No special provision was made for Ulster, and indeed it was inconceivable that the Irish Nationalists would have permitted it. For them Ireland was one land and one nation.

For the present that nation was governed, in the King's name, by John Campbell Gordon, the seventh Earl of Aberdeen. It was he whom Gladstone had appointed Lord Lieutenant of Ireland in 1886, so that for the second time he found himself at the head of an Administration preparing the way for Home Rule. In 1886 the Chief Secretary had been Morley, now he was Augustine Birrell, a figure remembered more for his wit and literary gifts than for his political acumen. Nevertheless Birrell was an able man who achieved much in Ireland in the less spectacular fields of housing, agriculture and education. Unfortunately both Aberdeen and Birrell exuded an aura of complacency which the Irish situation did nothing to justify. The Lord Lieutenant might claim that it was his duty to keep above politics and always to put the best face on things, but Birrell had no such excuse; throughout the months of crisis which followed no turn of events in Ireland could dismay him; the Opposition treated him with scorn, and on occasion even Asquith seemed irritated by his flippancy. His optimism was finally shattered by the Easter Rising in 1916.

The leader of the Irish Nationalist Party in the Commons was John Redmond, 'a dignified, handsome man with the nose of a Roman senator.'[1] A Southern Catholic of good family, Redmond had been elected leader to heal the divisions which had weakened the party since the fall of Parnell in 1890, as a result of the O'Shea divorce case. He was an effective speaker, though not so eloquent as some of his followers, and although in the United States and in Ireland itself he often spoke the language of extremism, he was in fact far too decent and gentlemanly an opponent ever to abandon the rules of the parliamentary game. By 1911 he and his colleagues were already growing dangerously out of touch with political feeling in Ireland.

As is the way with revolutionaries, many of the Irish Nationalist M.P.s had mellowed and become part of the parliamentary establishment. Men who had been the gadflies of late Victorian governments, whose filibusters had so often brought the business of the Commons to a standstill, were now regarded as old hands and reliable entertainers. The most accomplished of them was Timothy Healy, who was to survive to become the first Governor-General of the Irish Free State. Warily respected for his sharp and witty tongue, he was personally well-liked and, in the Irish fashion, a great individualist. 'There are two United Irish parties in this House', he once told the Commons, 'and I am one of them.'[2] Two of Redmond's other lieutenants were John Dillon, a less attractive figure than Healy but just as formidable in debate, and Joseph Devlin, a Belfast publican who was affectionately known as

'Wee Joe'. A splinter group of two or three members led by William O'Brien frequently quarrelled with the main party. Even in appearance Healy, Dillon and O'Brien, with their beards and *pince-nez*, had a decidedly *fin-de-siècle* air, and there was stirring in Ireland a new kind of nationalism, an ardent patriotism nourished by the literary and artistic revival then taking place.

In contrast to Asquith and Redmond, the leaders of the Conservative and Unionist Party seemed to grasp at once the realities of the Irish situation. Above all they discerned that the Liberals had provided them with a political weapon of great power, and that they had merely to decide on the best tactical use to be made of it. Even if this had not been so, the Conservatives would have been emotionally involved, for they were prey to deep and ancient prejudices.

In the first place the Protestant Ascendancy in Ireland was an integral part of the landed aristocracy which had governed England until the close of the nineteenth century and was still immensely powerful. Home Rule, coming hard upon the heels of the extension of the franchise and the overthrow of the House of Lords, would further weaken what was left of their political influence. Moreover it would inevitably be followed by the expropriation of their Irish property. In addition to this selfish aim, the aristocracy and the upper middle class who were the strength of the Conservative Party had an instinctive sympathy with Ulster whose only crime was loyalty to the Crown. To thrust Ulster out of the British Empire against her will was to attack the idea of Empire at its very heart. This sentiment was not by any means confined to the stately homes; it was held as a self-evident truth by half the nation.

After the rout of the Lords, the Conservatives regrouped to oppose Home Rule. The last struggle had divided them into 'Hedgers' and 'Ditchers', adding a new division to that which already existed on the question of Tariff Reform. Party morale was low following two successive election defeats, and the discontent of the backbenchers expressed itself in an attack on the leadership. Balfour's handling of the crisis, though sane and prudent, had provoked bitter recriminations, and when, after some months of vigorous campaigning against him in one section of the Conservative Press, he announced his intention of resigning, a further split developed over the leadership. The two main contenders, Austen Chamberlain and Walter Long were on terms of personal hostility, and each was supported by a substantial section of the party. As so often happens in such circumstances, the succession went to an outside candidate, Andrew Bonar Law.

Few more extraordinary events can have occurred in English politics than the elevation to the Conservative leadership of this Canadian Presbyterian who had spent a great deal of his life as an iron merchant in Glasgow. Cautious in triumph and stoical in adversity, Bonar Law might have been the man for whom Kipling wrote 'If'. Yet as a young man he had read a paper to the Helensburgh Eclectic Society entitled 'Is life worth living?'[3] and at critical times throughout his career he was liable to lapse into moods of profound pessimism. In his nature diffidence was oddly mingled with high aspiration; Asquith once described him in a damning phrase as 'meekly ambitious'.[4] Even so he might have withdrawn from the contest in 1911 had it not been for the loyal encouragement of his fellow-Canadian, Max Aitken (later Lord Beaverbrook).

With some misgivings the party patched up its differences and fell in behind the new leader. The defence of the Union was at least a platform on which all could agree, even if Bonar Law seemed unlikely to lend it the fervour of a crusade. But as it happened the Home Rule struggle involved Bonar Law in an immediate and personal way, for he was the son of a Presbyterian minister who had been born in Ulster and who had died there. Although he himself was born in New Brunswick, and brought up by an aunt in Scotland, Bonar Law knew Ulster well, and during the last five years of his father's life he visited it almost every week-end.* His brother was a popular and respected physician in Coleraine. There can be no doubt that these family connections profoundly influenced Bonar Law's attitude to the Ulster question, and led him to give outspoken approval to the views of the Ulster Unionist members.[5]

They did not form a separate party in the Commons, though they had been led as a group for many years by Colonel Saunderson. When he died in 1906, Walter Long, who had been a Conservative Chief Secretary for Ireland, became the leader

* The Rev. James Law was born at Coleraine in 1822 and emigrated to New Brunswick in 1845. He returned to Ulster in 1877 and died there in 1882.

of all the Irish Unionists in the House. In the elections of 1910, however, Long was returned for a London seat and the Unionists were obliged to seek a new leader just when the Home Rule question was reviving. The ablest of the Irish Unionist members were the two barristers who represented the University of Dublin — Sir Edward Carson and J. H. Campbell. Carson, who had been the last Conservative Solicitor-General, was able to hold his own as an orator with the best of the Liberals and the Nationalists, and it was to him that the leadership was offered. He accepted it in February 1910, after much careful thought. To put himself at the head of the Irish opposition to Home Rule (which meant in effect the resistance movement in Ulster) involved risks and considerable sacrifice for a man who by sheer determination had risen from a humble practice on the Leinster circuit to the supreme place at the English bar, and who in his fifty-seventh year saw the highest legal and political prizes almost within his grasp. The decision proved far more fateful for Carson and for Ulster than anyone could have foreseen at the time.

So much has been said and written about Carson that at this distance it is not easy to see him in perspective. He has become part of the Irish legend, and most Irishmen, whether they adore or revile his memory, see him as the symbol of partition — he is either the man who saved Ulster, or the man who sabotaged his country's independence. Inevitably, too, he has been misrepresented through popular association with attitudes he in fact mistrusted.

His character was rich in contradictions, and more complex than either his friends or his enemies realised. The world saw an austere fighter who made no concessions, the leader of a zealous Protestant crusade who was utterly convinced that his cause was right. So uncompromising was his demeanour, so unswerving his devotion, that he was respected even by those who sneered at 'King Carson' and his subjects. His height and powerful frame, and the determination of his features, gave an impression of immense strength and energy. His public face was set permanently in a scowl of righteous defiance.

There is evidence that this persona was deliberately cultivated, and his correspondence reveals a different, more vulnerable, figure. There was nothing of the fanatic in his composition, and his mind was not narrow — religious intolerance he despised. He had a shrewd insight into human nature and surveyed the world and its follies with detachment. Frequently he expressed doubts and second thoughts in private about issues on which he was adamant in public.

The same contradictions were to be found in his physical constitution, for behind the granite exterior was a man who worried continually about his health; his pale saturnine features and deep-set eyes were the mirror of his hypochondria. As a schoolboy he had developed a dislike for athletic pursuits which remained with him throughout his life. He never believed his health to be robust, and his letters to friends usually contained gloomy references to his ailments. Yet he lived to be over eighty, and it is hard to believe that a man who in his late fifties undertook such an exhausting political campaign, in addition to heavy legal work, could have been physically unfit.

Carson was born in Dublin of Protestant parents, and before 1911 he had had no connection with the north of Ireland. All his early legal practice had been in southern courts, and he never completely lost his Dublin brogue. His paternal ancestors were Scots Presbyterians, and his mother belonged to an Anglo-Irish family long established in Co. Galway. At first sight it seems strange that he should have thrown himself heart and soul into leading the Ulster resistance, and stranger still that he should have gained so complete a hold on the affection of the Ulster loyalists. He knew that they trusted him absolutely, and the knowledge added immeasurably to the weight of responsibility he felt throughout the crisis.

He once told Lloyd George that he had always been a lawyer first and a politician afterwards, and some of the contradictions are resolved when it is remembered that Carson was above all else a brilliantly successful King's Counsel, one of the last of the great advocates in the old, flamboyant style. Before accepting a brief he always made sure of his client, and then of his case. If he thought that he could get a verdict he went for it to the limit of his resources. Sir Patrick Hastings said that he never knew anyone at the Bar who succeeded so well in convincing the court of the merits of his case; he believed so passionately in his client's cause that he made the judge and jury believe it too.[6] The relentless cross-examination which had humbled Oscar Wilde, and forced the Admiralty to vindicate the innocence of an Osborne cadet accused of stealing a five-shilling postal order, proved equally effective in the House of Commons. Eloquent in a blunt, unadorned way, Carson made no claim to the wit of his friend F. E. Smith. The cutlass, not the rapier, was his weapon, and on occasion he could use it to devastating effect.

About his devotion to the union there can be no question; it was, he said, the guiding star of his political life, and he sincerely believed that Ireland could not prosper if she were separated from Great Britain. In the early stages of the campaign he regarded the Ulster opposition as the most effective way of thwarting the Government, but as it emerged that Asquith would not drop the bill, he became more and more the champion of Ulster, perhaps to a greater degree than he ever intended. Once his mind was made up, it was essential to his purpose that no one should doubt his determination; nor was he deterred by the prospect of a long and hard fight — both as an advocate and an Irishman he regarded it with a certain relish.

If Carson was the accepted leader of the Ulster resistance, its real organizer was Captain James Craig. The sixth son of a self-made Co. Down man, who entered the whiskey firm of Dunville's as a clerk and became a millionaire director before he was fifty, Craig was born at Sydenham, near Belfast, in 1871. Believing that his sons should make their way in the world as he had done, the distiller sent each of them to a different school, and none to a university. James was educated at Merchiston in Edinburgh, where his career was unremarkable, for he was not a scholar, and though fond of games he was not particularly good at them.[7] Some business experience followed, in London and Belfast, and then, on the outbreak of the South African war, he took a commission in the Royal Irish Rifles, being later seconded to the Imperial Yeomanry. After a disastrous action at Lindley, in which Craig, under the most trying conditions, behaved with great coolness and bravery, he was taken prisoner by the Boers. Bitterly ashamed of the surrender, and of the sheer incompetence of his superiors,[8] he hid until the officers were conveyed away in ox-carts, and then marched two hundred miles with his men to the prison camp at Noight-gedacht. The Boers chivalrously put him across the border of Portuguese Mozambique to seek medical attention for an injured ear-drum, and eventually he made his way back to Durban. When the war ended he was railway staff officer at Kroonstadt, a post in which he displayed a flair for meticulous organization.[9]

Unsettled by his military experiences, Craig turned from a business career to politics, and, after one unsuccessful attempt in 1903, he was elected to Parliament in 1906 as the member for East Down. He soon established himself as an expert in tactics, who could 'talk at any length on a subject, and yet remain in order'.[10] Craig was a tall, red-faced man with a massive frame, and features which might have been hewn from the granite of his native county. He looked like a bluff soldier or a country squire, and, expecting him to be slow in the uptake, the Irish Nationalist members tried to catch him in the cross-fire of their wit, only to discover that his mind was alert and incisive. They shouted and jibed at him when he wasted the time of the House with tiresome questions, but they liked him because he was courteous and imperturbable. His equanimity, indeed, was his greatest strength; always an easy man to talk to, he was quite impossible to frighten, and in a crisis he was as steady as a rock. He was well aware that his appearance was misleading, and, on occasion, even used this to his advantage.

Craig identified himself completely with the attitude of his own people, and, to some extent, interpreted it for Carson, who before 1911 had little experience of the north. That attitude was, not surprisingly, misunderstood and misrepresented in England, for English people refused to believe that in Ireland the issues of the Reformation were still alive. Yet much that was baffling about the Irish dispute became clear when this simple fact was remembered. At the time of the Home Rule controversy, religious passion in Ireland still burned with a white-hot intensity; religion was not, as in England, simply a matter for a man's own conscience; it shaped the whole society in which he lived, and dictated his politics and his civic behaviour.

George Bernard Shaw, who understood the emotions at work better than any English observer, had this to say about his co-religionists in the north:

'We must also bear in mind that political opinion in Ulster is not a matter of talk and bluff, as it is in England. No English Home Ruler has the faintest intention, in any event, of throwing

actual paving stones at any English Unionist. . . . The Ulsterman is not like that. He is inured to violence. He has thrown
stones, and been hit by them. He has battered his political
opponent with fist and stick, and been battered himself in the
same manner. . . . He has to avenge not only the massacre of
St. Bartholomew and the wrongs of Maria Monk, but personal
insults, injuries and bloodlettings of quite recent date and
considerable frequency. Consequently, when he sings O God our
help in ages past, he means business. And there is a strength in
his rancor which lifts it above rancor.'[11]

That strength was derived from a frontier tradition, from the
memories of plantation and a Scots covenanting past. It made
the Ulsterman obstinate, hardy, self-reliant and direct. Those
who found his combination of Calvinist morality and Celtic
temper uncongenial often tried to dismiss him simply as a dour
and unattractive bigot. Bigotry certainly flourishes in Ireland,
but no fair-minded person, knowing the facts, would claim a
monopoly of it for any one section of the Irish community. The
Irish are easily moved to anger and violence, but they are
not obsessed by theology, and are much maligned in this
respect. What was often not appreciated in England was that
the religious rancour arose, not so much from difference in
doctrine, as from fear and mistrust which had their roots far
back in Ireland's past.

It is doubtful if the Ulster Protestant had much desire to
persecute his neighbour because of the way he worshipped, but
he certainly had an excessive fear of being persecuted by him,
or, to be more accurate, by his Church. He did not fear his
fellow Ulsterman, but the powerful and world-wide organization behind him. Much of this suspicion arose from ignorance,
for ordinary people had wildly exaggerated ideas of papal
influence in Ireland, and thought of the Pope as a personal and
inveterate enemy, who spent all his time scheming to get his
hands on the Belfast shipyards. But even better-informed
Protestants believed the society of southern Ireland to be
priest-dominated, and feared that an independent Irish
administration would be dictated to by the bishops and that
consequently their civil and religious liberty would in some way
be curtailed.

Sectarian bitterness had been increased in 1908 by the pro-
mulgation of the *Ne Temere* decree, which declared that

43

marriages between Roman Catholics and Protestants not solemnized according to the rites of the Roman Catholic Church were null and void, and by its application in a particularly distressing case in Belfast in 1910. One Alexander McCann, instigated it was alleged by his priest, had suddenly left his Protestant wife and taken away her children. On the other hand Roman Catholics claimed that the Orange Order, despite its apparently defensive character, was, by its very existence, a threat to religious liberty.

The Protestants' fears about a Dublin Parliament may have been exaggerated, and the history of Ireland since independence has, on the whole, tended to suggest that they were, but they did not think so at the time, and it was upon that belief that they acted. Home Rule, they declared, would be Rome Rule, and that was all there was to it. 'It may seem strange to you and me,' Bonar Law told Lord Riddell, 'but it is a religious question. These people are ... prepared to die for their convictions.'[12]

Religion was not, of course, the only factor at work in the north. The Ascendancy had undoubtedly chosen Ulster as the ditch they would make their last stand in; and it may well be, as Alice Stopford Green wrote, that in a changing world Ulster required that the guarantees of its commercial interests should remain unchanged. Nevertheless, religion was the dynamic in Ulster, and not merely a cloak for other motives: historians have sometimes underestimated it, but politicians never.

Craig, like Carson, was not personally much concerned with religious issues, but he knew what they meant for his people, and he appreciated the peculiarities of the Ulster situation. He knew also that the Ulsterman was thrifty, industrious and reliable, proud of his heritage and of his city, that monument to Victorian self-help.

Belfast was not an old city, as cities go, and its phenomenal development after 1800 was the more remarkable because the act of Union had arrested economic growth elsewhere in Ireland. It owed its prosperity largely to the short-lived cotton boom which ended in 1830, but the much older linen industry, which Huguenot settlers had consolidated in the Lagan valley during the late seventeenth century, returned to take over the looms and remained pre-eminent until a short time ago. The second pillar of Belfast's commercial success was shipbuilding, introduced almost fortuitously in 1853, after a major re-construction of the harbour. Although all the coal and iron had to be imported from England, the vast force of cheap labour available made it a success, and by 1911, when the *Titanic* was built there, Belfast had the largest shipyards in the world. The sinking of the *Titanic*, at the height of the Home Rule crisis, was a staggering blow to Belfast's pride in her craftsmanship, and one, perhaps, from which she has never quite recovered. Round these twin giants grew up all the subsidiary industries of a great port, engineering, rope-making, flour-milling and the manufacture of tobacco, whiskey, chemicals, soap and glass.

Economically, Belfast belonged to the industrial complex of the English north, and this offspring of industrial England and rural Ireland grew up lacking affection from both its parents. English visitors were repelled by its rainswept streets and joyless Sundays, its harsh accent and reputation for civil commotion, while to the southern Irish it was the Presbyterian citadel of the Black North, a city of theological gloom and hard-faced businessmen. Both these views omitted so much on the credit side, and were so often inspired merely by political animus, that the Belfastman developed a silent, almost sullen, pride, which for the most part ignored jibes as the crackle of thorns under a pot, and got on with his work, though when he did condescend to reply to criticism, it was usually with crushing effect. Both Catholic and Protestant shared this pride, and regarded their love-hate relationship as something peculiar to themselves, and not the business of any brash outsider.

One aspect of the industrialization of Belfast had important social consequences. In 1800 very few of its citizens were Roman Catholic, but the rapid expansion of industry created a demand for workers far beyond the Protestant hinterland, and even beyond the province of Ulster itself. Consequently the Roman Catholic population increased considerably, and the great famine of 1845–47 accelerated the drift to the town. This process coincided with changes in the religious and political outlook of the Protestants, who became alarmed when by 1850 the proportion of Roman Catholics had reached thirty-five per cent. The majority of the Roman Catholics, for reasons of safety and convenience of worship, settled in one area in the west of the city, along the line of the Falls Road. It was unfortunate that the Shankill Road, which ran parallel to it, was the axis of a very large settlement of Protestant workers, and the proximity of these two communities divided by religion was the chief cause of the sporadic rioting, which was the worst blot on the city's good name. An invisible but sharply-defined frontier ran through the maze of streets, and although people lived together amicably for most of the time, small provocations, like the waving of a flag or the singing of a party song, could lead to large-scale disorders.

The danger was most acute in the long days of summer, before and after the 'Twelfth' of July, when the Orange parades were held. On that day the grey city burst into a strangely partisan festival of colour, as, to the incessant throb of drums and the shrill tunes of flutes, legions of Orangemen in dark suits, bowlers, Orange sashes and white gloves, marched past under huge banners of blue and gold. The banners depicted such scenes from Scripture, English or Irish history, or more recent events, as were likely to support the combined cause of Protestantism and the Union, along with a variety of encouraging quotations. To these the Orangemen in 1911 added another, the appeal of Ruth the Moabite:

'Intreat me not to leave thee, or to return from following after thee: for whither thou goest, I will go; and where thou lodgest, I will lodge: thy people shall be my people, and thy God my God.'

4

STORM WARNING

'What I am very anxious about', Carson wrote to Captain Craig towards the end of July 1911, 'is that the people over there really mean to resist. I am not for a mere game of bluff, and unless men are prepared to make great sacrifices which they clearly understand, the talk of resistance is of no use. We will . . . be confronted by many weaklings in our own camp who talk very loud and mean nothing and will be the first to criticise us when the moment of action comes.'[1]

Carson the advocate was making sure of his ground. Personally he was prepared to give up time, business, money or even his liberty if he was assured that the Ulstermen would not draw back. Since 1886 they had been saying that they would fight; now that the last obstacle to Home Rule had gone did they still mean it?

To prove that they did, Craig undertook to organize a demonstration of loyalists, at which the rank and file would be able to meet their new leader, and hear from him what form their resistance was to take. On Saturday, 23 September, 50,000 men from every part of the Province, representing the Orange lodges and Lord Templetown's Unionist clubs, marched from the centre of Belfast to Craigavon, Craig's residence on the outskirts of the city, where thousands of spectators were already gathered. Altogether it was an impressive display of solidarity by the ordinary people of Ulster and in the planning Craig had revealed a distinct flair for this kind of popular organization.

Craigavon was ideally situated for the purpose. The solid, rather ugly house commanded lawns and meadows which sloped to the shores of Belfast Lough and formed a wide natural amphitheatre. To heighten the effect Craig had had a platform constructed at the top of the hill, and when Carson rose to speak, even those out of earshot could see the determined set of his features. The vast crowd which had been cheering and singing fell silent, and Carson, whose every fibre responded to the appeal of the situation, allowed the pause to lengthen dramatically. 'I know the responsibility you are putting on me to-day,' he told them, 'In your presence I cheerfully accept it, grave as it is, and I now enter into a compact with you, and every one of you, and with the help of God you and I joined together . . . will yet defeat the most nefarious conspiracy that has ever been hatched against a free people.' He described the Liberal ministers as men who were prepared to play with loaded dice, who had deceived the electorate and evaded public opinion, and who intended to present Home Rule to the country as a *fait accompli*. In such circumstances it was not enough to reject it. 'We must be prepared . . . the morning Home Rule passes, ourselves to become responsible for the government of the Protestant Province of Ulster.'[2]

The Craigavon demonstration determined both the policy and the methods to be followed during the next three years. On the following Monday, at a meeting of delegates of the Unionist associations and the Orange institution, the first move was made to give effect to the policy when a 'Commission of Five' was appointed to frame a constitution for a provisional government of Ulster, 'having due regard to the interests of loyalists in other parts of Ireland'. This Commission, which was to work in consultation with Carson, consisted of Captain Craig, Colonel Sharman Crawford, Colonel R. H. Wallace, Thomas Sinclair and Edward Sclater.[3]

On the Tuesday Carson spoke again, this time at Portrush, where he declared that unless the Unionists were in a position to take over the government of those places they were able to control, the Ulster people, if let loose without that organization, might come to a condition of antagonism with consequences which even the present Government would lament. When he denied that they had any intention of fighting the Army and Navy, a voice from the crowd shouted, 'They are on our side'.[4] These events created a sensation on the other side of the Channel. Overnight, and for the first time since 1895, the Irish question had become the leading topic in British politics.

On 3 October Winston Churchill told a meeting at Dundee

that the Government would introduce a Home Rule Bill in the next session 'and press it forward with all their strength'. 'We must not attach too much importance to these frothings of Sir Edward Carson,' he told his listeners, 'I daresay when the worst comes to the worst we shall find that civil war evaporates in uncivil words. . . .' Churchill pointed out that Carson had been 'elected Commander-in-Chief' of only half of Ulster, a line which the Liberal press and the Nationalists took up with enthusiasm. Jerry MacVeagh assured a congress of Liberals at Westminster that the majority of the people of Ulster wanted Home Rule and would not be deterred by the pantomime war which Carson was threatening. He did not think that Sir Edward would ever discard his wig and gown for a spiked helmet and a khaki suit.[5]

There was just enough semblance of truth in all this to allow Liberal observers to deceive themselves into thinking that Carson and his followers were engaged in an outrageous bluff. It was undeniable that three counties of Ulster, Monaghan, Donegal and Cavan had large Nationalist majorities, and two others, Fermanagh and Tyrone, had very slight Nationalist majorities. At most the Unionists predominated only in the four counties of Antrim, Down, Londonderry and Armagh. The total population of the whole Province of Ulster was evenly divided between Protestants and Roman Catholics, and at Westminster the Unionists had a majority of only one, seventeen members as against sixteen. This position was actually reversed when a Home Ruler was returned in a by-election in the city of Londonderry early in 1913, and the Unionists found themselves in a minority of one. Since the Unionists did not, until a very late stage in the struggle, relinquish the demand for separate treatment for all nine Counties of the historic province, there was some justification for the Liberal view that such a claim was preposterous. Nevertheless, no one who understood the real nature of the Ulster situation would have been so deluded, and it turned out to be a fatal error.

It was also true that a strong tradition of liberalism, in the wider sense, had persisted in Ulster since the end of the eighteenth century, particularly among the Presbyterians, although Gladstone's conversion to Home Rule had changed most Ulster Liberals into Conservatives overnight. Nevertheless the tradition survived (and does even still) and it was epitomised in a redoubtable Presbyterian clergyman, the Rev. James Armour of Ballymoney, who was for many years a thorn in the side of his co-religionists. It would be a mistake to assume that the Unionists, and still less the Orangemen, spoke for all the Protestants of Ulster.

Armour was a prominent member of the Ulster Liberal Association, which early in 1912 invited Churchill to speak at a Home Rule meeting in Belfast along with Redmond and Devlin. Churchill, who almost certainly was deceived about the strength of this organization, promptly accepted in order to show that he, at least, did not take Carson too seriously. The Association's following was in fact small, and, what was perhaps a greater weakness, its leading members had little in common beyond a distaste for the Unionists. They included, besides Armour, Lord Pirrie, a brilliant Belfast engineer who was now a director of the shipbuilding firm of Harland and Wolff, and Captain White, a Ballymena man and the son of General Sir George White, V.C., who was besieged at Ladysmith in 1899. White's passionate support for the underdog involved him at one time or another in every Irish row of any consequence.[6]

With something less than tact the Association announced that the meeting would be held in the Ulster Hall, on 8 February, with Lord Pirrie in the chair. Pirrie was just at that period very unpopular with his fellow-citizens, since, according to *The Times* correspondent, he had 'deserted Unionism about the time the Liberals acceded to power, and soon afterwards he was made a peer; whether *propter hoc* or only *post hoc* I am quite unable to say, though no Ulster Unionist has any doubts on the subject'.[7]

The Unionist reaction was swift and sharp. On a motion of Craig, the Standing Committee of the Council observed 'with astonishment the deliberate challenge thrown down by Mr. Winston Churchill, Mr. John Redmond, Mr. Joseph Devlin and Lord Pirrie in announcing their intention to hold a Home Rule meeting in the centre of the loyal city of Belfast, and resolves to take steps to prevent its being held'. The statement provoked an immediate accusation in the Liberal press that free speech was being suppressed, and embarrassed some of Ulster's friends. 'We cannot pretend to rejoice in the decision of the Standing Committee,' stated *The Times*, 'As a matter of political ethics their action is hard to justify, and even from the point of view of mere political tactics its wisdom is open to question.' To such criticisms the Unionists replied that Churchill was free to express his opinions anywhere except in the building which his father had consecrated to the loyal cause.[8]

Clearly Churchill did not then appreciate how intense was the hostility which he had roused; to cross the floor of the House was, in Ulster eyes, bad enough, but to speak in favour of Home Rule in the Ulster Hall was sheer filial impiety. Beyond announcing that they had hired the hall for the evening of 7 February, and that they would pack it with a solid mass of men who would resist all efforts to eject them next day, the Unionists kept their plans secret.

From the Government's point of view the whole situation was becoming decidedly awkward, and the demands of Lord Pirrie and his friends for extra troops and police did nothing to reassure them. If the crowd defied the soldiers there would be bloodshed; if on the other hand they submitted to force it would merely serve to prove the argument that Home Rule could only be imposed on Ulster by bayonets. In such circumstances Churchill was persuaded, not without difficulty, to trail his coat in some less controversial place. On 25 January he wrote to Lord Londonderry: 'If, as I now gather from the newspapers, the main objections of yourself and your friends are directed against our holding our meeting in the Ulster Hall, then, although such claims are neither just nor reasonable, I will ask the Ulster Liberal Association to accede to your wish. There will thus be no necessity for your friends to endure the hardships of a vigil, or sustain the anxieties of a siege.'[9] It now mysteriously transpired that no other hall in the city was available,* and at length Churchill agreed to speak at the Celtic Park football ground in the Nationalist quarter, in a marquee which had to be imported specially from Scotland for the purpose.

By this time Dublin Castle was thoroughly alarmed by the prospect of serious rioting in Belfast. Five battalions of infantry

---

* The proprietor of the Opera House subsequently asserted that he had been offered a knighthood as well as a substantial fee for the use of his theatre. (Interview with F. W. Warden in The *Standard*, 8 Feb. 1912, qtd. McNeill p. 72.)

and two companies of cavalry as well as a considerable body of police were moved into the city. The Unionists, too, were worried about possible disorder, which could only discredit their cause. At the very outset Colonel Wallace, the Grand Master of the Belfast Orangemen, and a man of considerable influence with all classes in the city, had warned the Standing Committee that if they did not find a way of stopping the Ulster Hall meeting, the people would take matters into their own hands. Even with the change of venue, the danger remained acute and at last Carson and Lord Londonderry agreed to remain in Belfast on the 8th as a guarantee of order. Their appearance with Craig and Lord Templetown on the balcony of the Ulster Club did help to calm the huge crowd which surged around Churchill's hotel; it also, of course, turned the episode into yet another demonstration of Unionist solidarity.

The 15th Infantry Brigade stationed in Belfast had been since July 1911 under the command of Brigadier-General Count Gleichen,* a grand-nephew of Queen Victoria. Gleichen, a shrewd and experienced soldier, who was very conscious of his responsibility to assist in preserving order in the city, now acted on his own initiative, and incidentally discovered why the Unionists were being so taciturn. 'Finding myself about the only person in some authority with no axe to grind', he writes in his memoirs, 'I communicated with the Roman Catholic Bishop, Tohill, a man of some character, with the Liberal Association, with one or two Nationalists in authority, and with the Chiefs of the Unionists, Lord Londonderry and Colonel Wallace (Grand Master of the Orangemen) — all with a view to getting them to restrain their different flocks from making disturbances on the day. From all of these, except the Unionists, I got assurances that they would do their best. I was much disconcerted at receiving a polite note from Lord Londonderry (with whom I had been shooting at Mount Stewart only a month before) saying that he regretted he could not meet me on the matter. I caught, however, Colonel Wallace, but he would not promise anything. At last he said that if I would guarantee the presence of a large number of troops he would see what he could do. I guaranteed him 3500; but he did not move until they arrived on the 6th. Then he got to work.

'There was more method in this than I suspected at the time.

* In 1917 he took the style of Lord Edward Gleichen.

The fact was that the Unionist chiefs refused to give any guarantee or promise for this reason, that they thought that if Dublin Castle were to hear that the Orangemen had promised to keep order, they (the Castle) would countermand the troops coming and would throw the whole blame of any disturbances which might occur on to the Orangemen. Hence they waited.'[10]

On the morning of 8 February Churchill stepped ashore at Larne to face the forbidding spectacle of a large and menacing crowd singing the National Anthem. In Belfast itself the excitement was intense; from early morning masses of people had been gathering in the principal thoroughfares, and by noon Royal Avenue and High Street were densely packed with people singing, cheering and waving flags. To reach the hotel where luncheon had been arranged Churchill had to run the whole gamut of this popular demonstration, from the Midland railway station to the city centre. When he left the hotel in the early afternoon, a group of shipyardmen closed in upon his car with the evident intention of turning it over, but they desisted with cries of 'mind the wumman' when they saw that Mrs. Churchill was by her husband's side. A reporter in the car behind noted that throughout this ordeal Churchill 'never flinched ... and no harm befell him'.[11]

On his way to Celtic Park he crossed the invisible boundary that runs through Belfast dividing Roman Catholic from Protestant. Boos and catcalls gave way to cheers, effigies of Carson replaced those of Redmond and Lundy, and the throng of people eager to shake his hand pressed so close about the car that Hamar Greenwood (who was destined to have an even closer connection with Irish troubles) had to stand on the footboard to relieve the pressure. Even so, the meeting was less than a success, largely because of a change in the weather. A heavy downpour flooded the football ground and damped the tent, which was barely two-thirds full. At least there was no disturbance, and the only interruption was made by a woman who asked Churchill, in a broad Belfast accent, 'Will you give the suffrage to women?' On the rainswept Falls Road the police and three battalions of soldiers kept watch; and Gleichen had taken the precaution of having four more battalions 'lying doggo at different points in the town'.[12]

The Protestant demonstrators endured the rain, confident that Churchill would return to his hotel, but as soon as the meeting was over he was taken by a circuitous route through nationalist streets to the station, and dispatched to Larne by special train before Royal Avenue realized that it was to see him no more. The Unionists were quick to point out that his departure was uncomfortably like that of the 'thief in the night' about whom his father had so eloquently warned them. The first round had gone to Ulster. A move intended to expose the weakness of Carson's case had produced exactly the opposite effect, and this impressed moderate Liberal opinion. The Unionist Council clearly had the confidence of the majority of the Protestant community, and the resources to meet any crisis likely to develop in the future.

Parliament opened amid speculation on 14 February. Faced with serious labour troubles, the Government would not expand the statement in the King's Speech that the Home Rule Bill would be introduced in that session. The Opposition continued to wage a vigorous campaign in the country. In Ireland the Bill was awaited with impatience, and the Unionists, believing that it would be introduced before Easter, planned a huge demonstration at Belfast during the recess, at which Bonar Law, the new Conservative leader, promised to speak. As it happened, the Bill was delayed until the end of March, and the Government tardily announced that it would not be brought in until Parliament had reassembled. The Unionists were thus able to get their demonstration in first.

It was held on Easter Tuesday, traditionally a holiday in northern Ireland, at the Agricultural Society's show grounds at Balmoral, a suburb of Belfast. The pattern was the same as at Craigavon, but this was a more solemn occasion, no less than the wedding of Protestant Ulster with the Conservative and Unionist Party, represented by Bonar Law and seventy English, Scottish and Welsh members of Parliament. For good or ill, the Opposition had espoused the cause of the defiant loyalists. Against the backcloth of the blue Antrim hills more than 100,000 men marched past the several platforms; seventy trains had been needed to bring in the provincial demonstrators, and the city's tram-car service was stopped from 8.30 a.m. until 6 o'clock in the evening. The solemn proceedings opened with prayers by the Primate of All Ireland and the Moderator of the Presbyterian Church, and the singing of the 90th Psalm. The spectacular aspect of the meeting had been planned with great care. On entering the grounds the main column divided into two streams passing on either side of the saluting base, and in the centre of the enclosure there was a tower with a 90-foot high flagstaff, on which was broken, at the instant of passing the resolution against Home Rule, a giant Union Jack measuring 48 feet by 25 feet, said to be the largest ever woven.

Inspired by this drama Bonar Law assured his hearers that their cause was not Ulster's alone, but that of the Empire. 'Once again you hold the pass', he told them, 'the pass for the Empire. You are a besieged city. The timid have left you; your Lundys have betrayed you; but you have closed your gates. The Government have erected by their Parliament Act a boom against you to shut you off from the help of the British people. You will burst that boom. That help will come, and when the crisis is over men will say to you in words not unlike those used by Pitt — you have saved yourselves by your exertions, and you will save the Empire by your example.'[13]

Across the Irish Sea the reactions of the Press to what was happening in Ulster became sharper. While *The Times* endeavoured to explain to English readers just why the Ulstermen would not accept Home Rule unless it was forced upon them by arms, the *Morning Post* printed 'Ulster 1912', an angry poem by Kipling which put the Unionist argument in its most extreme form.

> *The dark eleventh hour*
> *Draws on and sees us sold*
> *To every evil power*
> *We fought against of old.*
> *Rebellion, rapine, hate,*
> *Oppression, wrong and greed*
> *Are loosed to rule our fate,*
> *By England's act and deed.*
>
> *The faith in which we stand*
> *The laws we made and guard,*
> *Our honour, lives, and land*
> *Are given for reward*
> *To murder done by night,*
> *To treason taught by day,*
> *To folly, sloth, and spite,*
> *And we are thrust away.*

The blood our fathers spilt
Our love, our toils, our pains,
Are counted us for guilt,
And only bind our chains.
Before an Empire's eyes,
The traitor claims his price.
What need of further lies?
We are the sacrifice.

We know the war prepared
On every peaceful home,
We know the hells declared
For such as serve not Rome —
The terror, threats, and dread
In market, hearth, and field —
We know, when all is said,
We perish if we yield.

Believe, we dare not boast,
Believe, we do not fear —
We stand to pay the cost
In all that men hold dear.
What answer from the North?
One Law, one Land, one Throne.
If England drive us forth
We shall not fall alone.

No Orangeman could have stated his case more forcefully, but not all the newspapers took the answer from the north so seriously, and the Liberal *Westminster Gazette* published a cartoon which showed Carson, Londonderry and Bonar Law, refreshed by 'Orangeade' taking 'an Easter jaunt in Ulster'.

The Balmoral demonstration marked an important stage in the Ulster crisis. By implying that Ulster could expect nothing more from Parliament, and that Conservative support for Ulster did not necessarily depend on her opposition being kept within the law, Bonar Law committed his party to an extreme course. He was to make his position even clearer in July 1912, at another great Unionist rally at Blenheim Palace, the seat of the Duke of Marlborough. After defining the Government as 'a Revolutionary Committee which has seized upon despotic power by fraud', he said: 'I can imagine no length of resistance to which Ulster can go in which I should not be prepared to support them, and in which, in my belief, they would not be supported by the overwhelming majority of the British people.'[14]

Bonar Law, in these speeches, did not hesitate therefore to attack the conventions upon which British parliamentary democracy was based. At Blenheim he bluntly declared that if Home Rule were passed by a majority in the Commons it would not be binding on the British people; and that if the Ulstermen resisted it by force they would have the wholehearted support of the Conservative Party. Such language had not been heard in English politics since the days of the Long Parliament, and it is clear that Asquith and Redmond were shocked beyond the normal attitudes of pained surprise assumed by politicians under attack. The Conservatives, however, could advance a two-fold justification for their appeal to force: first, that parliamentary democracy must depend on due respect for the convictions of minorities, and this convention had been flagrantly ignored by the Liberals in the case of Ulster; and secondly, that by the destruction of the House of Lords' veto, the Opposition had been deprived of the means of compelling the Government to hold a general election. Bonar Law argued that the Liberals had made a bargain with the Irish Nationalists to destroy the power of the Lords, but had concealed from the electorate that the price was the destruction of the Union, and much of the Conservative bitterness sprang from the belief that if an election were held on the Home Rule issue, they would be certain to win it.

5

THE COVENANT

In retrospect, it seems strange that a measure as limited as the Home Rule Bill should engender such political passion, for it merely granted Ireland local government powers under the Crown, and its federal basis was an attempt to win over those members of the Conservative Party who had all along advocated such a solution. Ireland was still to be ruled by the King and defended by British forces. The Irish Parliament was to be allowed to make its own laws for peace, order and good government, but the Royal Irish Constabulary was to remain, for six years at least, under British control. In the vital spheres of finance, law and education there were checks and safeguards limiting her autonomy.

Yet, for all its reservations, the Bill was to Redmond the fulfilment of a lifelong dream. 'If I may say so reverently,' he told the House, 'I personally thank God that I have lived to see this day.'[1] Congratulations poured in from the Irish community in America, including those of the Mayor of New York and Judge Keogh of the United States supreme court, who assured Redmond that he had 'the race at home and abroad solidly, sincerely, and almost unanimously' with him.[2] The next few years were to prove that that was just what Redmond did not have.

No account need be taken here of the tedious debates which accompanied the measure on every stage of its progress through Parliament. The first and second readings were carried by the usual Government majority of about a hundred Liberal, Labour and Irish Nationalist votes, and the committee stage had been reached on June 11 when Agar-Robartes, the Liberal member for the St. Austell Division of Cornwall moved an amendment to exclude the four counties of Antrim, Armagh,

58

Down, and Londonderry from the Bill. 'I have never heard', he said, 'that orange bitters will mix with Irish whiskey.'[3]

This proposal resulted in a conference of Unionist members and peers at Londonderry House to consider what attitude they would take towards it. There were sharp differences of view, because until then the opposition had been directed against Home Rule for any part of Ireland, and officially at least there had been no suggestion of separate treatment for Ulster. Nevertheless no one really supposed, from a practical point of view, that Ulster could forcibly resist Home Rule being established elsewhere in Ireland. The Agar-Robartes amendment placed the Unionists in a dilemma: if they supported it, they would seem to be abandoning the loyalists in other parts of Ireland; on the other hand, if they opposed it, they might well be accused later of turning down the offer of the peaceful exclusion of 'those districts which they could control'. Carson persuaded the conference to support the amendment, and in doing so, he opened the way for the recognition in the autumn of the following year that only the six counties with a Protestant population could make an effective resistance. After three days of debate in the Commons, during which the Ulster question was exhaustively discussed, the amendment was defeated by sixty-nine votes. The Unionists had every reason to be satisfied; they had avoided a trap, and at the same time forced a discussion of what the Government least wanted to discuss. Carson now chose to regard Asquith's attitude to the amendment as a declaration of war. 'We are not altogether unprepared,' he told an audience in the Albert Hall. 'I think it is time we should take a step forward in our campaign, and I will recommend that to be done.'[4]

The step forward was to take the form of a further series of demonstrations at which the Ulster loyalists might enter into some solemn undertaking to resist Home Rule to the last breath, and to impose upon themselves the discipline of a crusade. Even while all this was being planned, the need for it was sharply underlined by an increase in civil disorder in Ulster. Already minor incidents had occurred, like flickers of lightning on the summer horizon, but on 29 June a more serious affray took place. On that day a Sunday school excursion set out from Whitehouse, near Belfast, to spend the day in the country at Castledawson in Co. Londonderry. The party had its own band,

and the children carried flags and banners with Scripture texts, but the outing had no political significance. In the evening a procession of the Ancient Order of Hibernians, a society revived by Joe Devlin to balance the Orange Order, met the Sunday school party on the road to the station. The Hibernians, provoked by the sight of Union Jacks in the children's hands, attacked the procession, wounding several people and creating such terror among the children that some of them were later found almost a mile away crouching in ditches and under hedges. Protestants from Castledawson quickly arrived on the scene and a general mêlée ensued until the small number of police available managed to separate the groups and get the Sunday school party on board the train.

The affray occurred on a Saturday, and the minister involved, the Rev. Mr. Barron, told his congregation next morning not to talk about it and create ill-will against their Roman Catholic neighbours.[5] But on the Monday the story was in the Belfast newspapers, and on Tuesday the inevitable reprisals began in that most sensitive area, the shipyards. Roman Catholic workmen found themselves surrounded by knots of hostile Protestants who ordered them to put on their coats and leave the yards, and when they did so, some of them were knocked down and beaten, or pelted with 'Belfast confetti', the steel discs punched out of the plates by the riveters. During July there were twenty-five assaults inside and fifty-five outside the yards, 'five of the most dangerous character'. All the Roman Catholics were terrorized into leaving, with consequent distress to their families, and weeks passed before they dared to come back.[6]

Once kindled, the age-old fire of sectarian hatred burst out sporadically, and despite every effort to damp it down, smouldered through the summer and into the autumn, when the Falls Road took its long meditated revenge. On 14 September ten thousand spectators were watching a football match at Celtic Park between the Celtic team and Linfield, their Protestant rivals, when a scuffle developed at half-time in the unreserved space. Within minutes the ground had become a battlefield for two well-prepared factions, who hoisted their flags and banners and clashed furiously with fists, knives, and revolvers. After a police baton charge the rioters disengaged and left the ground, where fortunately a large part of the crowd had remained steady. A running battle then developed outside which ended only when the last of the Protestants had been driven into their own part of the city. Some sixty casualties were treated in the nearby Royal Victoria Hospital.[7]

Such signs of coming trouble weighed heavily on Carson's mind. He understood, no less than Craig, the nature of the ancient prejudices at work, and the now urgent need to impose on the Protestant side a discipline which would direct their feeling against Home Rule and away from their Roman Catholic neighbours, and so avert any premature and disastrous outbreak of civil war. In Tim Healy's words, he needed 'a safety-valve for the Orangemen', and by the time of the Celtic Park riots it had already been found.

Ever since the Easter meeting at Balmoral Carson had been discussing with Craig and one or two others whether some means might be found for their followers to enter into a solemn and binding oath to resist Home Rule. The credit for the form which it eventually took must go to the Belfast businessman B.W.D. Montgomery, who one day discovered Craig musing in his London club with paper and pencil before him. Craig told him that he was 'trying to draft an oath for our people at home', and that it was no easy matter 'to get at what will suit'. 'You couldn't do better', said Montgomery, 'than take the old Scotch Covenant. It is a fine old document, full of grand phrases, and thoroughly characteristic of the Ulster tone of mind at this day.'[8] The two men then consulted the club librarian who found for them a History of Scotland which contained the full text of the Covenant originally drawn up in 1580.

The idea was taken up, and a special commission was appointed to alter the wording to suit the situation of the Ulster Protestants of 1912; but it was soon realized that its phrasing was too involved and orotund for the purpose, and a much shorter, and completely original Covenant was drafted by Thomas Sinclair. In its final form even this was cut by half, and one important change made when it was submitted to the Protestant Churches for approval. The Presbyterians, advised by Alexander McDowell, insisted that the obligation on the signatories should be confined to the present crisis, as no one could foresee what circumstances might arise in future, a most prudent qualification as later events were to prove.[9]

As early as 17 August it had been announced in the Press that

Saturday 28 September was to be 'Ulster Day', when the loyalists would dedicate themselves to a solemn Covenant, the terms of which had not then been made public, or indeed settled. Craig, to whom Carson always left the detail of the political campaigning in Ulster, planned a programme of meetings beginning in the West and sweeping inwards to Belfast, with Carson as the principal speaker to explain the purpose of the Covenant.

It began on 18 September at Enniskillen, which was the western gateway to Ulster and a frontier town of the Plantation. Carson was met at the station by two squadrons of mounted volunteers raised among the gentry and farmers of Fermanagh, who escorted him to Portora Hill, where 40,000 members of the Unionist clubs marched past him in military order. Next day he returned specially to Craigavon to make public the terms of Ulster's Solemn League and Covenant. At four o'clock in the afternoon, bareheaded and smoking a cigarette, he came out on the steps to read it to the assembled journalists.[10] The text was as follows:

'Being convinced in our consciences that Home Rule would be disastrous to the material well-being of Ulster as well as the whole of Ireland, subversive of our civil and religious freedom, destructive of our citizenship, and perilous to the unity of the Empire, we, whose names are underwritten, men of Ulster, loyal subjects of His Gracious Majesty King George V, humbly relying on the God whom our fathers in days of stress and trial confidently trusted, do hereby pledge ourselves in solemn Covenant throughout this our time of threatened calamity to stand by one another in defending for ourselves and our children our cherished position of equal citizenship in the United Kingdom, and in using all means which may be found necessary to defeat the present conspiracy to set up a Home Rule Parliament in Ireland. And in the event of such a Parliament being forced upon us we further solemnly and mutually pledge ourselves to refuse to recognize its authority. In sure confidence that God will defend the right we hereto subscribe our names. And further, we individually declare that we have not already signed this Covenant. God save the King.'

That evening at Lisburn Carson watched a huge procession of men carrying wooden dummy rifles and torches, while the fifes and drums played 'The Boyne Water' and 'Protestant Boys'. The torchlit multitudes seemed to *The Times* correspondent like the sea with a storm brooding over it,[11] but the storm was merely metaphorical, for the next nine days were days of perfect autumn weather, with the September sunlight gilding the parades and bands in a dozen provincial towns. Carson spoke at six of the meetings, F. E. Smith at five, and Lord Charles Beresford, Lord Salisbury, James Campbell, Lord Hugh Cecil, and Lord Willoughby de Broke all lent a hand. A single resolution was carried at every one of these meetings, the reaffirmation of the Duke of Abercorn's words in 1892: 'We will not have Home Rule', and the slogan, abbreviated to 'We won't have it', soon came to be heard with monotonous regularity.

The campaign ended with a great eve of the Covenant rally in the Ulster Hall in Belfast, where Colonel Wallace put into Carson's hands a faded yellow silk banner which, it was claimed, had been carried before William III at the Battle of the Boyne.[12] It had been obtained by Craig, and this masterstroke created an atmosphere of deep emotion as Carson unfurled the flag, and holding it aloft exclaimed 'May this flag ever float over a people that can boast of civil and religious liberty'. Then Craig presented his friend with a silver key, symbolizing Ulster as the key to the situation, and a silver pen to sign the Covenant.

Already the most elaborate arrangements had been made to enable thousands of Ulstermen to do the same. The specially appointed Ulster Day committee was headed by an energetic triumvirate, Dawson Bates, Col. T. V. P. McCammon and Captain Frank Hall representing the Unionist Council, the Orange Order and the Unionist clubs respectively. On Wednesday 25th they had sent off from the Old Town Hall 700 large cardboard boxes containing the forms for signatures and copies of the Covenant. The forms were in books of ten sheets of foolscap size, each providing spaces for ten signatures, with the text of the Covenant printed above. The boxes also contained copies of the Covenant printed on cardboard in large, bold, type for display in the halls, and parchment copies in old English type headed with the Red Hand of Ulster to be given to the signatories. Hundreds of these copies are preserved in Ulster homes to the present day.

Despite a forecast of a break in the weather, the Covenant

Day dawned fine and clear, with the hills around Belfast blue in the sunshine. The morning began with an impressive act of dedication in religious services throughout the city, for the Protestant Churches had given the anti-Home Rule campaign their solemn blessing. The industrial heart of Belfast was still; the great shipyards were silent, the looms idle in the linen factories, the rope-works and foundries deserted, while in a hundred churches the congregations sang, as in a time of national crisis, 'O God, our help in ages past'.

When the religious services ended about noon, Carson and the Unionist leaders walked along Bedford Street from the Ulster Hall to the City Hall, preceded by the Boyne standard, and a smartly turned-out guard of men wearing bowler hats and carrying walking sticks, part of a force of 2,500, drawn from the Orange lodges and the Unionist clubs, which all day long marshalled the huge crowds through the City Hall and protected the gardens and statuary. On this brief progress there was no cheering; for once the throng of spectators stood silent and bareheaded as Sir Edward passed by.

At the entrance of the City Hall, which the city fathers found no difficulty in allowing to be used for this purpose, Carson was received by the Lord Mayor and the Corporation, wearing their robes of office, and by the Harbour Commissioners, the Water Board, and the Poor Law Guardians. Inside, in the circular entrance hall opposite the marble stairway, stood a round table draped with the Union Jack, and on it the Covenant, with an inkstand and the silver pen. Sunlight streamed through the stained glass windows, dappling the marble with glowing colours as the Press cameras and cinematographs went into action, and Carson bent forward to sign. He was followed by Lord Londonderry, then by the representatives of the Protestant Churches. Craig, who more than anyone was responsible for the whole *mise en scène*, was, characteristically, not among the first to sign, though in one photograph he stands, a massive and defiant figure, by Carson's side.

As they signed, the leaders could hear the murmur of the human sea which surged around the building. J. L. Garvin, the editor of the *Observer*, who was watching from the topmost outside gallery of the dome, saw that the square below and the street striking away from it were black with people. 'Through the mass, with drums and fifes, sashes and banners, the clubs marched all day. The streets surged with cheering, but still no disorder, still no policemen, still no shouts of rage or insult. Yet no-one for a moment could have mistaken the concentrated will and courage of these people. They do not know what fear and flinching mean in this business, and they are not going to know. They do not, indeed, believe it possible that they can be beaten, but no extremity, the worst, will ever see them ashamed.'[13]

The marshals admitted them in batches of four or five hundred at a time. Lines of desks, stretching for a third of a mile along the corridors of the City Hall, allowed 540 signatures to be taken simultaneously, and the signing went on until 11 p.m. At the Ulster Hall the women signed a Declaration, similar in words to the Covenant, associating themselves with the men 'in their uncompromising opposition to the Home Rule Bill now before Parliament'.

All over Ulster the same scenes were enacted. The Duke of Abercorn, whose health was failing, signed the Covenant under an oak-tree at Baronscourt, Lord Templetown signed it at Castle-Upton on the old drum of the Templepatrick Infantry, and at Londonderry, Enniskillen, and Armagh it was signed with ceremony by bishops and peers.

In the one-street villages and hamlets, the country people turned out to sign in their Sunday go-to-meeting clothes. 'There was no excitement whatever, and no hesitation', wrote Martin Ross (co-author of *Some Experiences of an Irish R.M.*) about one such village, 'four at a time the men stooped and fixed their signatures and were quickly replaced by the next batch. Down the street in a market house, the women were signing, women who had come in flagged motors, and on bicycles, and on foot . . . In the City Hall of Belfast the people were signing at the rate of about a hundred and fifty a minute; here there was no hypnotic force of dense masses, no whirlwind of emotion, only the unadorned and individual action of those who had left their fields, and taken their lives and liberties in their hands laying them forth in the open sunshine as the measure of their resolve.'[14]

In Dublin the Covenant was signed by two thousand men who gave proof of their birth in Ulster, in Edinburgh it was signed on the 'Covenanters' Stone' in the old Greyfriars church-yard, and signatures were collected in London, Glasgow, Manchester, Liverpool, Bristol, and York. When, some days after Ulster Day, the lists were closed the signatures were checked and counted in the Old Town Hall, and it was found that in Ulster 218,206 men had signed the Covenant and 228,991 women had signed the Declaration. Another 19,162 men and 5,055 women had signed elsewhere, and the grand total of signatories was 471,414.

The climax of Covenant Day came when Carson left the Ulster Club to go on board the Liverpool steamer. The docks were only a few minutes' walk away, but it took an hour for the wagonette, drawn not by horses but by men, to reach its destination. More than 70,000 people had managed to jam themselves into Castle Place, all of them intent upon getting near enough to shake Carson's hand, and at the quayside they would not let him go. 'Don't leave us,' they shouted. 'You mustn't leave us.' When at last he got on board the steamer, aptly named the *Patriotic*, they called for yet another speech from him as he stood in the beam of a searchlight at the rail of the upper deck. He left them with the message they never tired of hearing, and promised to come back, if necessary to fight. Then as the steamer cast off he heard the vast crowd in the darkness begin to sing 'Rule Britannia' and 'Auld Lang Syne', and then 'God Save the King'; and as she moved into the channel rockets burst in red, white, and blue sparks above her, and bonfires sprang up on either shore of the Lough.

In Belfast the day had been marked by exemplary conduct and sobriety. Apart from a little unpleasantness after the football match between Distillery and Celtic (and why it was allowed to be played at all defeats speculation) there were no breaches of the peace. *The Times* correspondent paid the city a left-handed compliment by noting that it had had one of the lowest of its Saturday records for drunkenness and disorder, and the police reported that the number of arrests had been 'nothing beyond normal'.[15]

But for Carson the Covenant celebrations were not yet over. As he went ashore at Liverpool next morning he was greeted by Alderman Salvidge and a crowd of 150,000 people singing the now familiar battle-hymn, 'O God, our help in ages past', and conducted in procession to the Conservative Club, where an admirer seized his hand and shouted: 'It's been marvellous, sir. Nothing like it has been seen at Liverpool landing-stage since Crippen was brought back from America!' Liverpool, with its large Irish population divided between Orange and Green, was perhaps the only city in Britain where the case of the Ulster loyalists was thoroughly understood. Nevertheless, that such a multitude should assemble at 7.30 a.m. on Sunday morning was an astonishing proof of enthusiasm, as well as a personal triumph for Salvidge. On Monday night an even more impressive demonstration took place under brilliant arc lamps at Sheil Park; torchlit processions of demonstrators from all the railway termini converged upon the park to the accompaniment of bands and fireworks.[16]

There were fireworks, too, in the House of Commons when Parliament reassembled and Asquith made it clear that the Home Rule Bill was to be forced through by the ruthless use of the guillotine. Tempers were already frayed when, on 11 November, the Government was defeated on a snap division by 228 votes to 206. Something very like hysteria swept the Opposition benches, and two days later when Asquith declared that the defeat did not represent the considered judgment of the House, Sir William Bull rose and shouted 'Traitor'. Called upon to withdraw the expression, he refused and walked out of the House. The rhythmical chanting of 'resign, resign' and 'civil war, civil war', prevented any other member of the Government from being heard, and the Speaker, giving his opinion that grave disorder had arisen, adjourned the House under Standing Order 21. When it reassembled an hour later, uproar broke out afresh, and the Speaker left the chair after ten minutes. As the members of the Front Bench walked out Churchill waved his handkerchief first at the Liberals and then tauntingly at the Opposition, whereupon Ronald McNeill, an Ulster Unionist, seized a small bound copy of the Orders and threw it at him, striking him on the forehead. Churchill was with difficulty restrained from retaliation and persuaded to leave the Chamber.

Next day McNeill made a full apology, which Churchill accepted, and everyone began to feel that the legislature was quite itself again. But November 13 had been a bad day for parliamentary democracy, though even at the worst moment the traditional British safety-valve had operated, when, after the assault on Churchill, the Labour member Will Crooks had called out, 'Should auld acquaintance be forgot?' and tension dissolved in laughter. The Speaker, who had threatened to resign, kept the book as a souvenir, pointing out that 'a bent corner of the leather binding bears evidence of the improper use to which it had been applied'.[17]

In contrast to these autumn storms, the new year opened quietly, and after fifty-two days of tedious debates the Bill passed the Commons and went up to the Lords, who threw it out at the end of January by 326 votes to 69. In Ulster the Commission of Five presented its draft scheme for a provisional Government; the basis for this rebel administration was to be an ordinance 'enacted by the Central Authority in the name of the King's Most Excellent Majesty'.[18] The Unionist cause suffered a setback at this time by the death of the Duke of Abercorn, for the Home Rulers just managed to win the resulting by-election at Londonderry by 57 votes in a poll of 95 per cent of the electorate. The loss of the Maiden City was a humiliating blow to Unionist pride, but by then something was happening in Ulster which more than compensated for it.

6

AN ARMY WITH BANNERS

Among the thousands of Orangemen who paraded in Craig's grounds on 23 September 1911 was a contingent from Co. Tyrone who by their smart appearance and the precision of their marching caught the interest of the spectators. It was discovered that they had, on their own initiative, been practising military drill, and soon Orange lodges all over Ulster were following their example.[1] Thus, almost by accident, the political leaders were made aware of an effective means of resistance to Home Rule, for the Orange Order provided a framework for a citizen army totally opposed to Ulster's exclusion from the United Kingdom, and the zeal for military training soon spread to the Unionist clubs and ultimately to men who belonged to neither organization.

In 1911 the secretary of the Grand Orange Lodge of Ulster was Colonel R. H. Wallace, a lawyer turned soldier who had commanded the 5th Royal Irish Rifles in South Africa. Wallace learned, in consultations with J. H. Campbell, K.C. (later Lord Glenavy) that some anomaly of the law permitted any two Justices of the Peace to authorize drilling and other military operations within the area of their jurisdiction provided that (and the condition was in itself a delicious irony) the object was to render citizens more efficient for the purpose of maintaining the constitution of the United Kingdom as now established and protecting their rights and liberties thereunder. To this condition the Orangemen were only too ready to assent, and the first application was made by Wallace himself to two Belfast magistrates on 5 January 1912.

More licences were issued during the months which followed, and, although not much publicity was given to them, activities such as drilling, route-marching and semaphore signalling were carried on with considerable enthusiasm. In September, during the week which preceded the signing of the Covenant, Carson reviewed Orange and Unionist volunteers in various parts of Ulster. At Enniskillen and at Portadown farmers on horseback, wearing slouch hats and carrying bamboo lances with Union Jack pennons, escorted him through the streets, followed by Red Cross ambulances and detachments of nurses in uniform. At Lisburn columns of men had marched past him armed with batons and rifles fashioned in wood, a sufficient indication of what was to come. By the end of the year the whole province seemed in a fever of military preparation.

At their annual meeting in January 1913 the Ulster Unionist Council decided that the volunteers should be united into a single body to be known as the Ulster Volunteer Force, and recruitment limited to 100,000 men who had signed the Covenant and were between the ages of seventeen and sixty-five.[2] The military committee then drew up a scheme of organization on the framework of the Unionist associations. The nine counties of Ulster were marked off into divisions and districts. Each county division was to consist of a variable number of regiments, according to the strength of the volunteers, and each regiment was to be divided into a variable number of battalions, companies and sections. Belfast was to raise four regiments, one from each parliamentary constituency.[3] In each county a committee was set up, and divisional and district representatives chosen,[4] circular letters were sent out to the Orange lodges and Unionist clubs, and it soon became clear that there was boundless enthusiasm for the work.

We can see the early progress of the organization in the correspondence of Captain Roger Hall, who was appointed divisional representative for South Down. On 20 January one district leader wrote to him: 'I got your letter brought before the Newry district loyal Orange lodges and they appointed the Worshipful Master in each lodge to confer with your humble [servant]. We had a meeting and divided the district into six localities. . . . I am arranging for each locality being drilled weekly and once a month having a combined drill in Newry if I can get a suitable place.'[5] A few days later another wrote: 'we are getting on well in raising the volunteer force and I am sending you herewith forms from three locality leaders. I want you to send me by return 130 declaration forms.'[6]

The membership form demanded only essential information, the volunteer's name, age, address, occupation, whether he was married or single, and a declaration that he had signed the Covenant and was willing to serve in the force 'throughout the crisis created by the passage into law of the Home Rule Bill at present before Parliament, or in any previous emergency for the mutual protection of all loyalists and generally to keep the peace'.

Most of the drilling was done in the Orange halls, or, when the weather permitted, in parks and demesnes of sympathetic landowners. Each company drilled once or twice a week, and often more than one company would use the same hall. The standard of attendance, at a time when the working week still consisted of six long days, was high, and the difficulty was not to find recruits but to find enough instructors for them, for the most part ex-N.C.O.s who had served in the South African war. Wooden batons were provided for the drilling, and already some of the volunteers were using the 'dummy rifles' which caused so much mirth in the cross-channel Press. One enterprising Belfast firm offered to supply a wooden rifle 'shaped as nearly as possible like a service weapon, at one-and-eightpence each in pitch pine and one-and-sixpence in spruce'.[7]

The licences for drilling issued by the Justices of the Peace specifically included training in the use of arms. As the law then stood, it was quite legal to import arms into Ireland for this purpose, for the Liberal Government had allowed the Peace Preservation Act to lapse in 1907. Ever since the first Home Rule commotions of the 1880s, rifle clubs, which enjoyed a great popularity, had provided cover for training in the use of arms, and in 1913 the U.V.F. used many of the ranges for this purpose. All that the law required was that the owner of a rifle should possess a firearms licence, which could be obtained for ten shillings in any post office.

A trickle of rifles purchased in England, of varying makes and patterns, began to flow into the north, and some well-to-do noblemen and businessmen took action on their own initiative to increase the supply. In March Charles Craig, the Member of Parliament for South Antrim, and the brother of James Craig, said publicly that while Ulstermen should do their best to educate the electorate, he believed that, as an argument, ten thousand pounds spent on rifles would be a thousand times stronger than the same amount spent on meetings, speeches and pamphlets.[8] How the running in of rifles was organized during 1913 is narrated in chapter VIII.

It is not surprising, in view of their obvious interest in maintaining the Union, to find the landowners of Ulster well represented among the U.V.F. commanders. Unreservedly they placed their wealth, their time and their property at the service of the Force. The extent to which they were involved is well described by Count Gleichen who, although he was in command of the Crown forces in the area, was a frequent and popular guest at their tables. 'The large landowners, almost to a man Unionists, and many of them ex-officers of the Regulars or late Militia, peers and commoners, rich men and well-to-do farmers, held local meetings and enrolled nearly all their men in the Volunteer Force. They went round their properties night after night, superintending the organization and attending at the drill-halls to see that all was going well. Some had given up their parks to batches of men for a week or more's training at a time.'[9]

In May Carson came to Ulster to open a new drill hall, specially built for the U.V.F. in the Willowfield district of Belfast. 'Why are we drilling?' he asked. 'We seek nothing but the elementary right implanted in every man: the right if you are attacked, to defend yourself.' Referring to rumours that the government might take some form of legal action against the volunteers, he went on: 'Let them not attack humble men. I am responsible for everything, and they know where to find me.' 'Go on, be ready,' he enjoined his listeners, 'You are our great army. It is on you we rely. Under what circumstances you will have to come into action you must leave with us . . . You must trust us that we will select the most opportune methods, or if necessary, take over ourselves the whole government of this community in which we live.'[10]

By the summer the military organization of the U.V.F. was well advanced. From Fair Head to the Mountains of Mourne and from Belfast to the shores of Donegal, recruiting was going on at a rate which exceeded the most sanguine expectations. After a hard day's work in the fields or in the factories men walked for miles to attend parades and drills; the accent was on self-sacrifice and the clear call of duty, so familiar to, and so well understood by, hearts set in a Calvinist mould. Social distinctions were forgotten in the volunteer ranks; the gentry cheerfully took orders from their tenants, and company directors from their employees. Before the autumn some of the volunteers had reached the 'extended order' stage of drill, and most of them had had some practice on the ranges with the few rifles then available. Outside Ulster these military preparations were regarded with amusement, but within the province itself there reigned, in Gleichen's words 'a stern and disciplined atmosphere and a serious spirit of unity and organization'.[11]

The next step was to find a soldier of suitable rank and experience who was willing to become the U.V.F.'s commander-in-chief, and to solve this problem the political leaders turned for help to their allies in England, where there were already encouraging signs of support. On 27 March a letter in the London newspapers had announced the formation of the 'British League for the support of Ulster and the Union' with an office at 25 Ryder Street, St. James's. The moving spirit was Lord Willoughby de Broke, and he was supported by the Duke of Bedford and 100 peers and 120 members of Parliament, all of whom signed their names to the letter. Thomas Comyn-Platt, a friend of Carson's, was appointed secretary, and one of the members of the executive most active on Ulster's behalf was the M.P. for South Wolverhampton, Colonel T. E. Hickman. He now agreed to seek the advice of Lord Roberts of Kandahar.

For a brief moment it seemed possible that Roberts, the most distinguished British soldier alive, might himself take command of the Ulster host and throw his enormous prestige into the balance against the Government. 'Bobs' had made no secret of his sympathy for the Ulster cause, and he was growing very restive as the political crisis became more acute. But if the old war-horse smelt battle afar off, it was in an entirely different direction; his preoccupation with the menace of Germany had induced him, at the age of eighty, to undertake a strenuous campaign for a scheme of national service, a campaign he felt he could not give up. Nevertheless he undertook to find the right man, and on 4 June he wrote from Englemere as follows:

'Dear Hickman,
    I have been a long time finding a senior officer to help in the Ulster business, but I think I have got one now. His name is Lieut.-General Sir George Richardson, K.C.B., c/o Messrs.

Henry S. King & Co., Pall Mall, S.W. He is a retired Indian officer, active and in good health. He is not an Irishman, but has settled in Ireland . . . Richardson will be in London for about a month, and is ready to meet you at any time.

I am sorry to read about the capture of the rifles.*

Believe me,

Yours sincerely,

Roberts'[12]

Sir George Lloyd Reily Richardson was sixty-six in 1913. He belonged to a Devon family with a long tradition of service in India. His grandfather had been a captain in the old East India Company, and his father had fought through the Mutiny. His own connection with the Indian Army went back to 1869, and he had served with distinction under Roberts in the Afghan campaign. Much of his active service had been taken up with colonial forays now almost forgotten, the Waziri, Tirah, Zhob Valley and Kunnan Valley expeditions, but in 1900 he had been put in charge of the British force sent to China during the Boxer rising, and when Gaselee's column finally reached the Peking Legations, it was Richardson, at the head of the Cavalry Brigade, who stormed the great feudal stronghold of the Temple of Heaven. For the last four years before his retirement in 1908 he had commanded a division at Poona.

Small and wiry like his old chief, though rather stouter in build, Richardson possessed considerable tact and a sense of humour. He was to require both in the months ahead, and despite his wholehearted approval of the Ulstermen's cause, there were times when he was to be bewildered and alarmed by their actions. In July he moved quietly to Belfast, and soon (in Colvin's somewhat ambiguous phrase) he was as completely at home with the Ulster volunteers as with the tribesmen of the Tirah or Zhob Valley. He found himself in command of some 50,000 men of no military experience but limitless enthusiasm. His officers had no statutory powers of discipline, but so strong was the *esprit de corps* that the threat of dismissal was the severest possible punishment.

During the early part of 1913 Carson, who always insisted that he was a barrister first and a politician afterwards, was

* See p. 94 below.

occupied with two very important cases. In March he and F. E. Smith appeared for Sir Rufus Isaacs and Sir Herbert Samuel in the *Le Matin* libel case, which arose out of the many allegations directed at members of the Government in connection with the scandal over shares in the Marconi Company. Since the Conservatives were squeezing every ounce of propaganda out of the Marconi affair, and since Carson and Smith felt obliged to desist from speaking on the Commons motion attacking the Government, their action puzzled and angered many of their supporters, both in England and in Ulster.[13]

In June, Carson also appeared in the 'million pound lawsuit' arising out of the will of a wealthy bachelor, Sir John Scott, who had left much of his money to Lady Sackville of Knole in Kent. The will was disputed by Sir John's family. At the end of the case Carson collapsed with acute neuritis, so that he missed the third reading of the Home Rule Bill on its introduction for the second time in the Commons.* Barely recovered, he crossed over to Belfast to review the annual parade of the Orangemen on 12 July. That year the rallying point was Craigavon, and the uneventfulness of the occasion, after the disturbances of the previous year, was a heartening sign of the discipline achieved through the U.V.F.

The 'Twelfth' safely past, Carson, in a letter to Edward Sclater, the chairman of the executive committee of the Unionist clubs, expressed appreciation of the way in which their members had enrolled in the U.V.F., and of the improvement in discipline and determination since the signing of the Covenant. 'As leader', he wrote, 'my responsibility compels me to point to the danger of ANYONE holding aloof at this juncture, when it is necessary to perfect final arrangements. My request is that ALL our men should join the Ulster Volunteers. Even old men can help to guard their property. . . . Victory comes to those who are organized and united. Those who are unorganized cannot help and may hinder our efforts.'[14]

The strain and responsibility were beginning to tell on Carson, and he privately told Lady Londonderry that he thanked God the time for speaking was nearly over. As soon as the Commons rose for the summer recess, he went to the

* This was a difficult and gloomy time for Carson, for the death of his wife Annette coincided with immense pressure of legal work and a critical phase of the Ulster resistance.

Rhineland Spa of Homburg that had become his annual refuge. 'I was overworked in Ulster', he wrote home, 'and my doctor thinks I want a long rest to set me up.' But on 9 September he was back in London, in time for the sensation created by Lord Loreburn's letter to *The Times*. Loreburn, better known to his friends as Bob Reid, had been Lord Chancellor until June 1912 when he was succeeded by Haldane, and was the man who had rebuked Churchill and Lloyd George for suggesting that Ulster, or part of it, should be treated separately from the rest of Ireland. Now in the autumn of 1913 he unexpectedly came forward with a plea for an accommodation on the Ulster question, suggesting that a conference should be held behind closed doors and a settlement reached by consent. No alternative seemed feasible to him, for if the Bill as it stood became law in 1914 civil war would ensue, or at the very least serious rioting in the north of Ireland. Even if the riots were put down, a spirit of bitterness and resistance would remain permanently.

Like a good many other observers Loreburn had been much impressed by the formation and rapid growth of the U.V.F., but in the explosive atmosphere of that September his rational and realistic proposals simply ignited new controversies. To Redmond, who like Carson was taking a much-needed rest, this time in the Wicklow mountains, they seemed like a stab in the back — Loreburn had run up the white flag before the battle had begun. Carson's reaction was guarded. In so far as it indicated a weakening of the Liberal position he welcomed the letter, but he deprecated any suggestion of a scheme of devolution which would put Ulster outside the Union. The English Unionists, for their part, were in a mood of resistance to the utmost. Nevertheless, as we shall see, the Loreburn letter marked a turning point in the crisis.

Meanwhile Carson had gone back to Ulster where there was little evidence of a spirit of compromise. On 23 September 500 delegates of the Ulster Unionist Council assembled in the Ulster Hall and approved the setting up of the Provisional Government if Home Rule should become law. Before the meeting Carson had tried to persuade Lord Londonderry not to involve himself and his family in this undertaking. 'They can do little to me,' he told him, 'therefore I have little to fear. But you have great possessions, a great title, friendships at court, a seat in the House of Lords. You have to consider also the future of your son

Charley. The Government, when they grow vindictive, as they will, may strike at you — and him.' With tears in his eyes the peer replied: 'My dear Edward, if I was to lose everything in the world, I will go with you to the end.'[15]

The Council, with Londonderry in the chair, delegated its powers to a Provisional Government of seventy-seven members, with Carson as chairman of the Central Authority. A Military Council was set up, and departmental matters entrusted to special sub-committees dealing with finance and business, education, law, publications, and customs, excise and post office.[16]

At the same meeting an indemnity guarantee fund was opened to compensate members of the U.V.F. and their dependants for any loss or disability they might suffer in the service of Ulster. Carson proposed a fund of £1,000,000 and headed the list with a guarantee of £10,000. Londonderry, Craig, Sir John Lonsdale, Sir George Clark and Lord Dunleath put their names down for the same sum and a quarter of a million pounds was guaranteed before the meeting ended. By the end of the week the figure was £387,000 and on 1 January 1914 it stood at £1,043,816.[17] In this way the business community of Belfast underwrote the U.V.F. and provided for anticipated casualties if the worst came to the worst.

Later in the year, in November, the businessmen had their own meeting, at which they expressed complete approval of all that Carson had done, including the formation of the Volunteer Force, and declared that they would refuse to pay 'all taxes they could control'.[18] This form of resistance had been under consideration for some time. At a preliminary meeting on 2 September it had been stated that the total income tax paid in Belfast was about £90,000 and it was argued that refusal to pay it would be useless as the amount was so small. Mr. Alexander McDowell explained that non-payment was not intended as a financial menace, but as a protest against Home Rule. Someone drew attention to the difficulties of directors of limited liability companies, whose shareholders might not be in sympathy with their views, and no decision was reached on this point. Duties on liquor and tobacco were considered next, but it was agreed that refusal to pay them would not help the Provisional Government, and any form of action which would mean stoppage of business was firmly ruled out. One director gave his opinion that it was absurd to talk about not doing this or that because it was illegal. All that they were doing was illegal, and the non-payment of income tax was a very mild way of acting up to the conditions of the Covenant.[19]

The public announcement of the plans for the Provisional Government was accompanied by a series of U.V.F. parades throughout the province, inspected by General Richardson with Carson and F. E. Smith. Two days before the Unionist Council meeting, Carson made headlines in the British Press by declaring that he had 'pledges and promises from some of the greatest generals in the army, who have given their word that, when the time comes, if it is necessary, they will come over and help us to keep the old flag flying'. Watching the volunteers that day, an English reporter compared them with the finest class of the national reserve. 'Led by keen, smart-looking officers, they marched past in quarter column with fine swinging steps as if they had been in training for years.'[20]

The climax of these parades came on Saturday 27 September with a review of the Belfast Division at Balmoral. It was on this occasion that F. E. Smith acquired his famous nickname by acting as 'galloper' to Richardson, although the other members of the party were irritated by his failure to keep in line. At this time the four Belfast regiments comprised fourteen battalions; North, South and East Belfast had each four battalions, but West (Joe Devlin's constituency) mustered only two, drawn mostly from the area in and about the fiercely Orange Shankill Road. When these two battalions were led in to the grounds by their commanding officer, Major F. H. Crawford, they received a tremendous ovation from the crowd. General Richardson called for three cheers for the Union; once again the giant Union flag was unfurled, the band played 'Rule Britannia', and then the whole vast concourse joined in singing the National Anthem.[21]

7

THE OLD TOWN HALL

While these belligerent preparations were going forward in Ulster, important events were taking place behind the scenes in England. Even before the announcement of the plans for the Provisional Government, the Loreburn letter had provided Asquith with a pretext for a new approach to the party leaders, and now a new and powerful factor was coming into play. The growing seriousness of the political situation had greatly distressed the King, who during 1913 received thousands of letters from his subjects calling upon him to intervene. But, as a constitutional monarch, that was precisely what he could not do. The Conservative leaders, and some eminent Conservative lawyers, argued that the King would be within his rights if he insisted on the dissolution of Parliament or on a referendum, while the Liberals advised him that, if he forced an election the only issue at it would be, 'Is the country governed by the King or by the people?'

Perplexed to discover where his duty lay, George V spent long hours listening to the counsel of the elder statesmen, but without finding the answer. Everybody was prepared to offer advice except Asquith, who scrupulously refrained from involving the Crown in the controversy. On 11 August, however, the King sent for the Prime Minister and handed him a memorandum of his thoughts. They were, in short, that there ought to be a general election before Home Rule was passed, and that Asquith would probably prefer to resign rather than agree to the dissolution. The King asked if it would not be possible to secure a settlement by consent. 'Whatever I do, I shall offend half the population,' he had written, 'I cannot help feeling that the Government is drifting and taking me with it.'

In his considered reply Asquith maintained that if the veto of the Crown were used to force an election it would be a 'constitutional catastrophe', and he minimized the danger of an Ulster revolt. He feared that the 'unbridgeable gulf of principle' between the two sides made a conference unlikely.[1]

The King was far from being satisfied, and writing from Balmoral on 22 September he put some further embarrassing questions before his chief minister. Did he propose to employ the Army to suppress disorders in Ulster? Would it be wise, or fair to the Sovereign as head of the Army, to subject the discipline and loyalty of his troops to such a strain? 'You will, I am sure, bear in mind that ours is a voluntary Army,' the King continued, 'our soldiers are none the less citizens; by birth, religion and environment they may have strong feelings on the Irish question; outside influence may be brought to bear on them; they see distinguished retired officers already organizing local forces in Ulster; they hear rumours of officers on the active list throwing up their commissions to join this force.'[2] And once again the King advocated that some basis should be found for a conference.

These dedicated efforts now began to bear fruit, though of a somewhat meagre kind. For those in the know there were unmistakable signs that the antagonists were not so intransigent as they had recently appeared in public. Whatever they might say, Asquith and his colleagues were seriously alarmed at the prospect of an Ulster rebellion. Bonar Law had, for his part, while staying at Balmoral, dropped a hint of uneasiness at the lengths to which Carson seemed prepared to go. After a game of golf with some of his Liberal fellow-guests, he had explained to Churchill that as soon as Home Rule was passed Carson would set up his Provisional Government, mobilize the volunteers, take over the functions of the police and create a situation which would compel the intervention of troops. The whole Unionist party would then be obliged to support him, and there was every reason to believe that the Army would not obey if ordered to intervene in Ulster.

'Bonar Law recoils from these desperate measures,' Churchill reported to Asquith. 'I must admit that the remarkable conversation of which I have given you some account has altered my views about a conference considerably. . . . I have always wished to see Ulster provided for, and you will remember how Lloyd George and I pressed its exclusion upon the Cabinet (and how Loreburn repulsed us in the most bloodthirsty manner).'[3] Bonar Law also sent an account of this conversation to Carson, who was just then inspecting the U.V.F. in Co. Down. 'As you know,' he wrote, 'I have long thought that if it were possible to leave Ulster as she is, and have some form of Home Rule for the rest of Ireland, that is on the whole the only way out. . . .'[4]

In his reply, penned on the very day of the Unionist Council's meeting, Carson revealed that his private opinion was very much more moderate than his public utterance. 'As regards the position here I am of opinion that on the whole things are shaping toward a desire to settle on the terms of leaving "Ulster" out. A difficulty arises as to defining Ulster. My own view is that the whole of Ulster should be excluded but the minimum would be the six plantation* counties, and for that a good case could be made.' If Home Rule were inevitable, that would be the best settlement to make, though he felt that personally he might not be able to abandon the southern Unionists. Then follows a very revealing sentence: 'I have such a horror of what may happen if the Bill is passed as it stands and the mischief it will do to the whole Empire that I am fully conscious of the duty there is to try and come to some terms.'[5]

However strong the case might be for the exclusion of Ulster, the difficult question remained of the Unionists in the rest of Ireland. The matter was considered at a meeting in Carson's house in London, and when Craig asked the delegation of southern Unionists to join the north under one leadership,† they refused. After some inconclusive discussion Carson pulled an envelope and a pencil from his pocket, and asked: 'Is it your decision that I am to go on fighting for Ulster?' The southern representatives answered 'Yes'. He made a note and went on: 'Will my fight in Ulster interfere in any way with your fight in the south?' 'No.' Carson made another note, and then, pointing out that if the Ulstermen were asked to fight only to surrender in the long run, it would take the whole heart out of the Ulster

---

* Carson apparently meant the six counties of the present Northern Ireland, i.e., those which had large Protestant populations, and not the actual six counties of the Ulster Plantation, which did not include Antrim and Down. Cf. p. 27 above.

† Carson was not at any time the leader of the southern Unionists. He was the leader of the Irish Unionist Party in the Commons, but all its members, except for Carson and Campbell, came from northern constituencies.

movement, he put a final question: 'If I win in Ulster, am I to refuse the fruits of victory because you have lost?' The logic was inexorable, and the southerners again said 'No'. Carson put the envelope back in his pocket; the decisive step had been taken, and henceforward Ulster went on alone.[6]

It was from this point that the Government began to acknowledge that Ulster was a distinct community and refer openly to the possibility of special treatment. Churchill observed on 9 October that the Ulster claim, if put forward with sincerity, could not be ignored, but, as Carson had anticipated, Redmond and his followers remained adamant. At Limerick three days later Redmond declared that they could never assent to the mutilation of the Irish nation. 'Ireland is a unit ... the two-nation theory is to us an abomination and a blasphemy.'[7]

Nevertheless on 14 October Asquith secretly met Bonar Law at Sir Max Aitken's house at Cherkley near Leatherhead. The atmosphere was chilly, and when Asquith ventured a comment on the beauty of the surrounding countryside it met with no response. As Aitken sadly recorded, Bonar Law 'was not a scenery man'.[8] The talks were not a success, for without breaking his pledges to Redmond, Asquith could not agree even to the exclusion of Carson's six counties. He met Bonar Law twice more, on 6 November and 10 December, but neither was prepared to make any significant concession. Both men felt themselves to be the prisoners of their extremists, and both expressed alarm at the increasing gravity of the situation as the winter drew on.

In Ulster the signs of war advanced. The task of organizing the Ulster Volunteer Force had now been assumed by the Military Council, assisted by subsidiary boards constituted to deal with personnel, finance, intelligence, railways, supplies and medical aid.[9] The Old Town Hall in Belfast, a sombre red-brick building which had been the headquarters of the Unionist campaign against Home Rule,[10] now housed Richardson's staff, presided over by another Indian Army officer, Colonel George William Hacket Pain.

A file among the U.V.F. records contains the enrolment forms of all the Headquarters personnel, identifying each with the letter Z followed by a number. After Richardson and Hacket Pain the key figure among the Z men was T. V. P. McCammon, who was described as 'Lieutenant-Colonel in charge of Administration'. During the next year his duties, particularly with regard to arming the U.V.F., were to be very onerous.

Craig was Political Staff Officer with four political secretaries including R. Dawson Bates and Wilson Hungerford. Lloyd Campbell was appointed the first Director of Intelligence, and Major Frederick Crawford Director of Ordnance, a position for which he was more than usually well qualified. But by far the most interesting appointment was that of Captain Wilfrid Bliss Spender, who a year earlier had been the youngest staff officer in the British Army.[11]

Spender belonged to a family distinguished in journalism and politics. His father, Edward Spender, was the founder of the *Western Morning News* and wrote its daily London letter until 1878, when, with his two eldest sons, he was drowned in Whitesand Bay in Cornwall.[12] Breaking with family tradition, Wilfrid Spender chose to make the Army his career, and after Winchester he went through the Staff College at Camberley, joined the Devon Artillery and was soon afterwards transferred to the Royal Artillery. Most of his service was with a mountain battery on the North West frontier of India. In 1911, however, he became the youngest officer on the General Staff, marked for accelerated promotion, and secretary to one of the sub-committees of the Committee of Imperial Defence, that which was concerned with home defence. While helping to draw up the plans for the United Kingdom defence scheme his attention was drawn to the strategic importance of Ireland. Haldane had directed that on mobilization the fourth and sixth regular divisions were to be earmarked for Ireland, leaving only four divisions for the expeditionary force to France. The defence of Great Britain itself was to be left to the Militia and the new Territorial Army.

Astonished by this state of affairs, Spender began to take an active interest in the Home Rule question, financing Crichton Milne of the Conservative Central Office in getting up a petition to the King, and signing the Covenant in England in 1912. He decided to go forward as a candidate for Parliament and applied to the War Office to be allowed to retire from the Army. This request was refused, and as the result of his actions, he was sent back to regimental duty in India, and told that he could never again hold a staff appointment. In April 1913 he returned to England, having persuaded the Commander-in-Chief in India to allow him home leave in order to put his case before the War Office.[13]

At this point he was sent for by the Secretary of State for War, Colonel Seely, who informed him coldly that he had committed a very grave military offence by signing the Covenant while still one of His Majesty's servants. He was offered the appointment of G.S.O.2 to Sir Douglas Haig at Aldershot if he withdrew his signature. This he declined to do, and on 25 April he was told that the Army Council had decided to allow him to resign. Fearing that resignation might imply a slur on his name, Spender asked leave to be permitted to retire, giving up his pension if necessary, but Seely, alarmed lest other officers might imitate him, had determined to make him an example. He was ordered to rejoin his battery in India forthwith. If, on his return to duty, he applied for permission to retire, 'in a proper and soldierlike manner' his request would receive consideration.

This ultimatum was delivered to him at 11.15 at night by a special messenger whose instructions were to take the reply back to Seely's house and give it to him personally.[14] Spender now considered sending a petition to the King, and inquired of Clive Wigram, the King's private secretary and a fellow Wykehamist, if it would cause embarrassment. Wigram told him to go ahead, but in the event his leave was extended and finally on 7 August 1913 the War Office gave way and allowed him to retire with pension. Spender's case was followed with avid attention by the Press, and discussed throughout the country. The air was thick with rumours of the resignations of officers who intended to fight for Ulster if Home Rule passed.[15]

Since it has been alleged that Carson may have tampered with the loyalty of Army officers, though he repeatedly denied this, his correspondence with Spender is of considerable interest. Spender first wrote to him in December 1912, and Carson's reply was guarded, though sympathetic. 'I felt very grateful indeed to know that there were men like yourself who were prepared to make sacrifices for the cause to which I am devoting so much time, and I am in hopes that there may be many, if it comes to the worst, who will adopt a similar course. I think, however, that isolated action at the present moment would probably not have the same effect as the concentrated action of several would have later on.'[16]

It would appear that Spender sought Carson's advice in May 1913 when he was preparing a statement of his case to send to the War Office, and that he sent the draft to Carson for his approval. Pressure of work prevented Carson from replying in full until 9 June. With a lawyer's caution he gave no advice on paper ('I do not think I can improve upon your own letter') but suggested that he should meet Spender, 'and discuss with you the possibility of our making use of the facts of your case, if you see no objection to that course.' Again he scrupulously warned Spender of the sacrifice he was making.[17]

As soon as Spender left the Army, Carson invited him to Ulster and offered him a place on the Headquarters Staff. Spender had just married, and he and his young wife came to Belfast from their honeymoon, unaware that it was to be their home for so many years to come. Besides being a member of the policy-making Central Authority, Spender was appointed secretary to the three committees concerned with supplies, equipment and transport. He became in fact A.Q.M.G. of the Volunteer Force, and its efficiency in later months reflected both his Staff experience and his complete dedication to the work, which often kept him in his office for sixteen or seventeen hours a day.[18]

One of the problems he had to tackle concerned supplies of food for the civilian population. Even the most determined resistance by the U.V.F. would be futile if the province could be starved out, and so plans had to be drawn up for the secret storing of large stocks of wheat, sugar and other commodities. The equipment committee dealt solely with military stores for the U.V.F., except the supply of arms, which was organized by a special committee appointed for that purpose alone. In the early stages the volunteers had no uniforms; they paraded in their ordinary clothes with the additions of belts, bandoliers and haversacks. Much of the equipment could be supplied locally, and many firms in Belfast showed alacrity in combining business with politics. In 1914 when the U.V.F. was regularly holding camps of instruction and carrying out field manoeuvres the supply problems increased enormously and there was a great deal of frustration about shortages of everything from boots to mattresses.[19]

The transport committee compiled a register of farmers throughout Ulster who were prepared at short notice to allow the U.V.F. to requisition their carts and wagons, and it made a complete list of the very few motor lorries operating at that time. Quite apart from the motor car corps, which will be considered later, the transport section of the U.V.F. was extremely efficient and was a vital factor in the events of the following spring. Spender also paid a good deal of attention to communications, especially the railways and the postal, telegraph and telephone services. Towards the end of the year it became clear that the latter could not be relied upon, since the U.V.F. had proof that a special Government branch was collecting evidence about the movement and its leaders by this means, and that Nationalist sympathizers in the post office were passing information to Dublin Castle.[20]

The U.V.F. therefore began to organize its own communications system, which also came under the control of Spender's committee. From 22 September 1913 the Headquarters Staff issued weekly printed orders to all divisional, regimental and battalion commanders. To make this possible, it set up an entirely independent post office service. The clerical work was done at the Old Town Hall, mostly by women, and the orders were delivered to their destination by an enthusiastic body of motor-cycle dispatch riders. In addition to printed orders, vast numbers of typed and duplicated messages, relating to every aspect of U.V.F. organization, were sent out from the Old Town Hall during the next two years, providing work for a permanent staff of typists, all of whom had, of course, to be Unionists and completely reliable.[21]

The part played by women in the Volunteer movement was considerable, and of some interest to the social historian of the early twentieth century. An Ulster Women's Unionist Council had been formed in 1911, and had recruited over 40,000 members within a year. On 18 January 1912, at a demonstration in the Ulster Hall, the women enthusiastically declared that they would stand by their husbands, brothers and sons in whatever steps they might be forced to take to defeat 'the tyranny of Home Rule'.[22] As soon as the drilling began, thousands of women and girls volunteered to become part-time nurses, giving up their leisure, after long hours in mills, shops and offices, or looking after farm households, to learn first aid and the rudiments of military discipline. From 1912 onwards, every volunteer parade of any consequence was brightened by the presence of sturdy girls in white starched uniforms and caps. All this was in the Florence Nightingale tradition, but a few more adventurous women trained as signallers, or, strangely attired in windproof jackets and trousers, became motor-cycle dispatch riders. Over a year before the war, Ulsterwomen were driving cars and ambulances and acting as clerks, messengers and signallers, and at the Old Town Hall a small group was engaged in intelligence work which included the deciphering of police messages intercepted by the U.V.F.

In October 1913 the Volunteer Medical Board became responsible for all the medical, surgical and nursing organizations connected with the U.V.F., and by the end of the year the signallers and couriers had been brought under a central command as the Ulster Signalling and Dispatch Riding Corps.[23]

While these ancillary forces had already created their own uniforms, the ordinary volunteer still paraded in his working clothes. On enrolment he was given a small bronze badge which depicted a red hand with the legend: 'For God and Ulster,' and a canvas armband on which were printed the name of his regiment and the number of his battalion. Officers wore armbands of red canvas.[24] The volunteer's minimum equipment in the field was to consist of a haversack, a mess tin (infantry pattern with canvas cover), a knife, fork and spoon, a towel and a piece of soap, a pair of socks, bootlaces, a greatcoat and a tin of rifle oil. The greatcoat was to be 'carried either *en banderol* by braces over the shoulders, attached to the waist belt, or worn on the man'.[25] He was strongly urged always to keep in his possession some food 'such as tinned meat, sardines, chocolate, or potted meat, tea, etc.', which in addition to bread or biscuits would provide him with two days' rations.[26] His rifle and ammunition would be issued to him on mobilization. Meanwhile he had to be trained to use them, and just how to acquire sufficient arms for this purpose was posing a serious problem for the Headquarters Staff.

8

THE GUN-RUNNERS

One day in the summer of 1913 a man with an American accent, calling himself John Washington Graham, went to Vickers House in London to inquire about machine-guns. To Mr. Owen, one of the firm's directors, he explained that he wished to purchase six Maxim guns of the very latest design, costing £300 each, but that he was worried on one point. 'You Britishers are so conscientious that if I buy a few guns you will tell your grandmotherly Government what you have done. I shall be kept under observation and have to leave my toys behind when I sail from England.'[1] Mr. Owen assured him that once he took delivery of the guns the firm had no further interest in them. Privately, however, he had a shrewd idea of their destination, for Mexico was in the grip of revolution and civil war, and his suspicions were confirmed when the stranger asked if it would be possible to have the instruction manuals printed in Spanish.

The next step was to arrange for the guns to be tested. Graham, who evidently knew his business, went down to Woolwich and saw the works manager. He tested the guns on the range, and suggested a slight but very important improvement to the elevating spindle. Next day he took the first of the Maxims away, covering the regulation Army grey case with green baize cloth to suggest that it contained band instruments.

His movements thereafter would have been of considerable interest to Mr. Owen. He drove at once to Euston Station where he arranged for the box to be put on board a train. When it was being weighed for surcharge, the weighman demanded to know the contents. Graham said that they were instruments and offered to pay for any excess weight, but the weighman insisted that he open the box. Suspecting that he had been betrayed, Graham protested that he had not got the keys; if the official was not satisfied he would have to break open the box. Grumbling, the man accepted payment, and the box went on its way. The destination on the label was BELFAST.

For Graham was not an American, though he could claim to belong to the race which had formed the backbone of Washington's army and provided the United States with at least ten of her Presidents. His real name was Frederick Hugh Crawford, and he was shortly to be appointed Director of Ordnance on the U.V.F. Headquarters Staff.[2] At fifty-three this ex-Artillery officer with smoothly brushed red hair and light blue eyes of childlike innocence already had behind him a varied and colourful career in many parts of the world, but the best was yet to be.

Crawford was intensely proud of having sprung from what Lord Rosebery had called 'that branch of our race which is grafted on the Ulster stem'[3] and his family was in itself an epitome of Ulster history. The first of his forebears to settle in Ireland was the Rev. Thomas Crawford, a Scots Presbyterian minister who was buried at Donegore in Co. Antrim in 1670. His son, grandson and great-grandson were all ministers, and the last, William Crawford, who died in 1800, founded an academy at Strabane which has an important place in the history of Irish education.

William Crawford was the eldest of four remarkable brothers. The other three were all physicians: John was a surgeon with the East India Company; Adair made his name by his scientific studies on the nature of animal heat, and was reputed to have received a gold medal for curing Napoleon's horse before an important battle; Alexander, the youngest, discovered a formula for chlorine bleach, and founded a bleachworks at Lisburn. The Crawfords shared the views of most northern Presbyterians at that time; William was prominent in the Volunteer movement and Alexander was a friend of the United Irishman Henry Joy McCracken, who was executed in 1798.[4]

Alexander's son took over the bleachworks and about 1836 transferred it to Belfast and established a chemical manufacturing firm which became the family business. He also deserted the faith of his ancestors for Methodism, and it was into a 'solid Methodist' home that his grandson Frederick was born in 1861. He was educated at the Methodist College, Belfast, and University College School in Gower Street, London, where he distinguished himself as an athlete and a rifle shot. His father then sent him to serve as a premium apprentice with the shipbuilders, Harland and Wolff.

One frosty morning in December 1881 a gangway collapsed and threw several hundred men into the dock. 'I was the means of getting some of them out', Crawford wrote, 'with a certain amount of inconvenience to myself and a good ducking which I did not relish as the dock was partly frozen over.' For this plucky feat the Royal Humane Society gave him a bronze medal, and the men presented him with a solid silver cup and an address. A year at sea followed, as an engineer with the White Star Line, and then a spell of wandering about the world which fired his romantic imagination.

In 1892 he came home from Australia to settle down in the family business, and found his native heath ablaze with the Home Rule controversy, into which he threw himself heart and soul. He immediately decided that if the resistance of Ulster were to be successful, it must eventually be armed resistance. To this end he formed a secret society called 'Young Ulster', the condition of membership being the possession of one of three carefully specified firearms. Single-handed, he began those activities which the U.V.F. were to undertake twenty years later — drilling, importing and concealing rifles, and even manufacturing his own ammunition.

An even more daring scheme occurred to him. He worked out an elaborate plan to kidnap Gladstone on the promenade at Brighton and convey him by fast yacht to a lonely Pacific island, where he was to be marooned with a supply of writing material, a few axes, a grindstone, 'and a really good library of the best classics'. When that staunch Unionist Lord Ranfurly declined to advance the £10,000 necessary for the enterprise, Crawford was deeply disappointed.

In 1894 he joined the Artillery Militia as a second lieutenant, and the outbreak of war in South Africa took him abroad again for two adventurous years. He was mentioned in Lord Roberts's last dispatch, and gained a great deal of valuable information about guns of all kinds including Maxims.[5]

When the Liberals returned to power in 1906, Crawford, now on the Reserve and once more a businessman, was Secretary of the Ulster Reform Club. A short time later the members of that respectable establishment were pained to discover that one 'Hugh Matthews' of 'the Reform Club, Belfast' had advertised in French, Belgian, German and Austrian newspapers for 10,000 second-hand rifles and 2,000,000 rounds of ammunition. There was no Hugh Matthews among their number, and they were even more upset when the Secretary freely admitted that he was the culprit.

Having failed to explain to the committee the necessity of 'making the voters think', he considered it best to resign. He had however, many replies to his advertisements, and he learned much about the international market in second-hand rifles. Crawford was at a loss to understand the milk-and-water attitudes of his compatriots, but he persevered with his own preparations. 'I felt', he wrote, 'as Noah must have done all the time he was building the Ark.'

When the rains of Home Rule came, Crawford had the satisfaction of seeing others take up his ideas. From 1911 he was a member of the Ulster Unionist Council, and he was actively concerned in raising the Belfast volunteers. It was he who led the men of West Belfast into the Balmoral grounds at Easter, 1912; he was the commander of the Praetorian Guard in bowler hats who escorted Carson on Covenant Day, and he signed the Covenant in his own blood, claiming that his ancestors had done so in 1638. He rejoiced when at last the Council set up a secret committee to consider the question of resistance by force of arms.

But even yet there were some who were not converted; it was one thing to preach the use of force, and quite another to make the necessary practical preparations. This Crawford was to realize when, after a meeting of the committee, he asked the members to step into an adjacent room to inspect some rifles and bayonets which he had obtained. When they actually saw the cold steel of the bayonets, the rows of cartridges, and the business-like rifles, some of them turned pale and protested that they had no idea he meant 'that sort of thing'. After that the attendance of these fainthearts became rare, and some even resigned, much to Crawford's satisfaction.

When Colonel Wallace and he had tested rifles of various patterns they recommended a particular design, and Crawford was instructed to purchase 1,000 of them in Germany. Since the

Government had repealed the Peace Preservation Act in 1907, it was perfectly legal to import arms into Ireland, but both police and Customs kept an eye on such transactions. Months passed and the rifles did not arrive. First McCammon and then Crawford travelled to Berlin to speed delivery, but without success. Not only did the firm make endless excuses for the delay; they also took the precaution of informing the British Government. The arms trade, having in the nature of things a delicate relationship to maintain with governments and police forces, is notoriously wary of enthusiastic amateurs.

In disgust Crawford went to another Berlin firm owned by a Jewish businessman called Bruno Spiro,[6] who listened sympathetically and at once offered to recover the rifles and forward them himself. This he faithfully did, dispatching them from Hamburg to Belfast in heavy crates labelled 'zinc plate', and Crawford lost only £20 on the whole transaction. He soon decided that Spiro was to be relied on completely, and never had any reason to revise that opinion.

When several hundred of the rifles had arrived safely in Belfast, one of the crates was opened by Customs officers, and the contents seized on the grounds that they were consigned to a fictitious firm, John Ferguson and Co. This was a game which two could play and Crawford persuaded Spiro to write to the authorities, saying that there had been a mistake and requesting the return of the arms at his expense. There was no legal justification for refusing such a request, so the rifles duly returned to Hamburg. The arrangement now was for Spiro to repack them in batches of one hundred, and send them to an agent in West Hartlepool. From there they were smuggled to Belfast on a ship owned by the Antrim Iron Ore Steamship Company.

This scheme worked very successfully for some weeks until the Customs authorities got wind of it. Then the packer in West Hartlepool was threatened with prosecution, and was unable to help again. Crawford switched his operations to Leith, but here too the Customs were alert. They saw one consignment arrive and decided to keep it under continuous observation. The rifles were temporarily stored in the yard of a public house, which the officials watched during the hours of daylight. At night Crawford's men substituted cases with similar markings, and they had got the rifles safely to Aberdeen, when the barmaid told the Customs men. At first they refused to believe her, until they opened one of the cases and found it to contain only boiler ashes. Then they telephoned to Aberdeen, and once more Spiro had politely to ask for his rifles back.

Crawford was not the only amateur in the field. From the beginning of 1913 Lord Leitrim of Carrigart, the commander of the Donegal regiment of volunteers, had been operating his own gun-running system. One day in February 1913 he sent for his chauffeur, a Londoner called Stephen Bullock, and, spreading out a large map on the table, asked him if he would undertake a difficult and dangerous job. He then outlined a plan for purchasing arms in Birmingham and bringing them to Donegal, in his little steamer the S.S. *Ganiamore*. Bullock at once agreed to play his part in it.

Every week the *Ganiamore* made a round trip from Glasgow to Portrush, Derry and Mulroy Bay in Donegal. Bullock's task was to transport the arms from Birmingham to some port on the west coast of Britain. He took the train to Belfast, where he purchased a four-ton Dennis lorry, and two days later he drove it into a factory in Birmingham. To his surprise he found waiting for him the manager of a well-known Donegal hotel. The first consignment was ready, and next day he drove it north to Workington in Cumberland. But the scarcity of lorries there made him conspicuous, and a former employee of Lord Leitrim's recognized him and told the police.

Bullock changed to Glasgow, renting a timber yard at Renfrew to store the rifles. Once a week he and his colleague David McElhenny completed the round trip of 600 miles, a marathon for the automobiles of 1913. At Renfrew a staff of sympathetic Scots repacked the load for shipping. Then one night a weary driver misjudged the ramp outside the depot, a crate broke open, and a neighbour awakened by the noise was horrified to see rifles poking through his railings. As a good citizen he informed the police, and an obliging constable dropped by with a warning that the depot would be raided the next night.

This time Bullock moved on to an engineering works in Clydebank from which he continued to smuggle rifles and ·303 ammunition by a variety of ingenious methods. The rifles went to Derry in furniture crates and steel cylinders innocuously labelled 'filters'; the ammunition in barrels of pitch, petrol tins, and drums of carbide. During the summer of 1913 the consumption of carbide, which was used for lamps, trebled in Mulroy and surrounding districts. It was largely on account of Bullock's efforts that the Donegal regiment was by then the best equipped with arms.[7]

Meanwhile, in the late spring, Crawford had been testing the possibilities of the British League for the Support of Ulster, of which he formed a very poor opinion. They told him that while they would send men over to Ulster in great numbers to fight they could not send arms or ammunition, and he told them that they should change their plans or dissolve their society, since Ulster had enough unarmed men already. It was Crawford's impression that the older men had damped down the enthusiasm of their younger colleagues. Colonel Hickman took his part, however, and was able to help him considerably later in the year.

A short time after this Crawford was introduced to Sir William Bull, the Conservative M.P. for Hammersmith. Sir William, a stout red-faced man who looked remarkably like the John Bull of the cartoons, was a staunch supporter of Ulster, and through him Crawford was able to secure the yard and stables of an old inn in King Street, Hammersmith, as a safe London depot. The premises were taken by Bull's brother-in-law, Captain Budden, trading under the name of 'John Ferguson and Co.' in second-hand scientific instruments, and antique furniture, armour, and weapons, merchandise which arrived and departed in heavy wooden cases. Crawford accumulated several thousand Italian Vetterli-Vitali rifles in the stables, and arranged to transport them by short stages from one depot to another until they reached Ulster.

Then without warning came disaster. On 3 June the Customs in Belfast seized and opened eight large cases labelled 'high class electrical plant' which had arrived from Manchester that afternoon. They contained rifles and bayonets, and it was obvious that the consignment was expected, since the principal Customs Officer and the City Commissioner were present.[8] The papers reported that the authorities in London had uncovered 'an elaborate plan for the supply of firearms to the Ulster loyalists'. On 6 June the *Evening Standard* told its readers that a large quantity of rifles, bayonets and ammunition had been found 'in a suburb of London' and that detectives of the special branch at Scotland Yard had begun inquiries. The same day a furniture van addressed for forwarding to Lord Farnham in Co. Cavan was seized at the North Wall, in Dublin, and found to contain several hundred Italian rifles. They also came from 'John Ferguson & Co.' of London.[9]

The Metropolitan police raided the Hammersmith store on 10 June at 7 o'clock in the morning. No one was present and no arrests were made, but a police guard was placed on the rifles and bayonets found there.[10] Crawford hurried to London and consulted a firm of solicitors. They were informed by the Home Secretary that under an Act of 1868 every gun-barrel in England must bear the proof-mark of the London and Birmingham Gun Makers' Guild. The penalty for infringement was a fine of £2 per barrel, which meant that Crawford would be liable to a fine of several thousands of pounds if he claimed the rifles, and he would also have to come into the open.

The loss of the rifles was a serious setback, the more so since Crawford could not find out how the police had received their information. After the war he suspected that Captain Budden himself might have informed the police. Later in the month there were more seizures. Since the beginning of the year about 400 Vetterli rifles from the consignments sent by Spiro to West Hartlepool had been held up in Newcastle under constant observation by the Customs. On 14 June they were sent openly by rail to Glasgow, Manchester, Liverpool, and Fleetwood. The police watched their removal but could not interfere without a Home Office order.[11]

Most of these rifles were eventually seized on arrival at Belfast. One case, sent from Glasgow by Lord Leitrim's little steamer, was ingeniously saved. The Customs watched it until it went on to the ship at the beginning of July; then, just before she sailed, two Customs officers went on board to follow it to its destination. The night was unexpectedly rough; the officers were very sea-sick, and while they took shelter with the captain in the chartroom, the case was quietly dropped into the sea off Ballycastle, with a float attached. When the *Ganiamore* reached Portrush there was no sign of the case, nor did it appear in the manifest. In vain the ship was searched. When questioned, Captain Morrison said he knew nothing more than the manifest disclosed, but the officers only gave up the chase when they reached Milford in Donegal.[12] The rifles were recovered from the sea by the U.V.F. on the day after their immersion.

After the Hammersmith seizure Crawford reported to the committee that he could do no more to import Continental rifles, and that he had come to the conclusion that the only way to get the proper quantity was to bring in a shipload in one organized *coup*. In June he crossed over to Glasgow to put his idea before Carson and Craig, who were addressing Unionist meetings there. 'Whether you are prepared to risk this or not is a matter for you to decide,' he told them, 'I feel beaten and prefer to step aside.'

On his return Craig discussed the matter with the committee. Crawford reported all that he had done, and the result of his efforts, which on the whole he thought disappointing, and stated that, unless they wished him to bring in a cargo, he could not see his way to get any more in from the Continent. No one else had a plan, and Crawford had nothing to suggest 'except the big run', so in the end it was decided to ask another member of the committee, George Clark, to take over the task of organizing the gun-running.

Clark, a Scotsman who had worked for many years in Belfast, was one of the partners in the shipbuilding firm of Workman & Clark. The shipyard provided excellent cover for the importation of arms, but Clark had no illusions about the difficulties involved, and he pointed out that his business responsibilities would not allow him to do what Crawford was doing. The committee urged him to employ whomever he liked so long as he supervised the activity, and, reluctantly, Clark consented. For the rest of the year he and his collaborators worked at the task, but Crawford had, in his own words, 'closed every seaport so effectively' that they were unable to bring in more than a few hundred rifles altogether.

For a brief period the committee decided to suspend gun-running, until the excitement of the discoveries had simmered down, but, as might be expected, Crawford's restless mind was already occupied with a new scheme 'to vary the programme', for it was at this juncture that he proposed the purchase of the Maxim guns. He pointed out that a machine-gun mounted on an armoured lorry could do the work of 500 soldiers and clear a road in next to no time. He even made a model and showed it to the committee, but once again there were voices of dissent, and one perceptive member called the Maxims 'engines of death'. Crawford felt like Hotspur when the courtier protested that

> *but for these vile guns*
> *He would himself have been a soldier*

In the end, however, he got his way and was authorized to buy from Vickers six guns of the latest pattern.

After his successful dispatch of the first one from London, he went to Hamburg, where Spiro tried to interest him in a German machine-gun that was £50 cheaper. He obligingly arranged for Crawford to test it on the ranges of the Army Corps of Hamburg district. As he drove him to the practice ground he warned Crawford on no account to speak any English; a law had recently been passed which required all foreign officers to report to the police, and Crawford, who held the rank of major in the Militia, had not done so. He was in any case travelling under the name of Hugh Matthews, so that he would certainly have been treated as a spy if he had been discovered.

When they arrived at the camp, a genial N.C.O. assured Spiro that no officers were about. The gun was assembled and Crawford tested it on the 300-metre range, declaring after each burst, *Ja, das ist gut*, the only words of German which he knew. He was just about to try it over the 600-metre range, when a soldier dashed up, his face streaming with perspiration, and spoke to the N.C.O., who became very agitated. Spiro called out to Crawford to run, and all three made for the main gate, where the N.C.O. disappeared. Spiro pushed Crawford into the car and drove off at high speed. Later he explained that the commandant had not gone into town with the other officers, and on hearing the machine-gun, he had wanted to know what was going on, since no practice was scheduled for that afternoon. The N.C.O. had kept the gun to show that he was testing it for the next day's practice.

On his return to London Crawford made his plans for getting the five remaining Maxims to Ulster. He had arranged to take a lorry to the Vickers works very early in the morning, collect the guns, and bring them to a garage in Hammersmith, where four trusted U.V.F. members would be waiting with five cars. On the appointed day he set off at 5.30 a.m. The outward run and the loading up of the lorry went according to plan, but on the way back they were held up in a traffic jam and it seemed to Crawford that 'from Vickers to London was one long street in which everything that moved got into our way and blocked us wilfully'. But at last he reached Hammersmith safely; the guns were transferred to the cars, and ultimately put on board trains for Liverpool, Fleetwood, Heysham, Stranraer and Greenore.

Four of the guns went to Belfast, and were hidden in Crawford's business premises. The Greenore gun was taken over by Captain Frank Hall and kept at Narrow-water for the 2nd Battalion of the South Down Regiment. He and his brother Roger Hall were very keen to see whether it would work, so they set it up at once on the tennis court and fired a belt. The bullets ricocheted off the bank, up into the estate a thousand yards away, and one of the estate men came down to complain that bullets were coming down all around them.[13]

From September 1913 the arms committee, with Clark as its chairman, was a department of the Ulster Provisional Government, operating under the innocuous title of 'the business committee'.* By now it had recruited into its organization some of the Belfast gun-smiths, with whom the gun trade was much more willing to do business. Two of these men in particular played an active part in later gun-running — William Hunter, whose shop was in Royal Avenue, and Robert Adgey, who was in business as a pawnbroker at Peter's Hill.

According to Adgey (who many years later published a little account of his exploits) it was Spiro who mentioned his name to Crawford when they were discussing the losses of June 1913. 'There is your man', said Spiro. 'He can do the job for you. He is in the trade and knows how.' As a consequence Crawford called at Adgey's shop in Belfast, and, after some preliminary fencing, explained his mission. 'In those days', writes Adgey, 'you were suspicious of most people.'[14]

The result of this meeting was the setting up of a small, but highly efficient, gun-running organization in Great Britain, under the control of the arms committee. The financial end of the business was conducted through an old-established firm of Belfast stockbrokers, Josias Cunningham & Co. James Cunningham, the head of the firm, was a member of the arms

* Not to be confused with the Finance and Business Committee which had a different membership, and was what it claimed to be. (See p. 77.)

committee, and Richard Cowzer, his office manager, supplied the necessary funds to the gun-runners and also saw to the storage of the arms on their arrival in Ulster. He had valuable contacts in the offices of the steamship companies and, through them, with the stevedores at the docks. Cunningham told Adgey, 'Any money you require, I will see that you get it. Don't be afraid to get plenty of stuff. Ulstermen mean business this time. We will not let you down'.[15]

Adgey went first to Birmingham, where within a month he located 50,000 rifles, 100 Maxim guns, 1,500 Webley revolvers and two batteries of field artillery, all in the market for sale. The problem was to find the means of transporting these desirable goods to Ulster, without drawing official attention to them. A meeting was held in Cunningham's office, at which Captain Andrew Agnew of the Antrim Iron Ore Steamship Co. was present, and plans were drawn up for smuggling rifles and ammunition by road and sea.

Adgey and his colleague William Hunter went to England with six assistants and two five-ton lorries and their drivers. They began to set up a network of disguised depots for the packing, storage and distribution of arms in Liverpool, Manchester, Glasgow, London, West Hartlepool, Bedford, Rugby and Darlington. Each depot operated behind the front of a reputable business owned by a sympathizer with the Ulster cause, and eventually about forty men were employed in the work. Adgey and Hunter came to spend nearly all their time in Birmingham and London, or in travelling about England from store to store, devising plans for the shipment of hundreds of tons of 'goods' into Belfast and Derry.

A battle of wits began with the police and Customs. 'The police did not count for so much,' writes Adgey, 'but the Customs officers had their heads screwed on, they required watching.'[16] The game provided a spice of adventure to many a young Ulsterman who felt stifled in the dreary routine of an office. One such was W. P. Johnston, whose father sent him to Manchester in August 1913 to manage the branch of the family textile-printing business. As this necessitated his travelling to Belfast about once a month, it occurred to him that he might be able to help in a small way in the gun-running.

He got in touch with Crawford, and was called to an interview with the arms committee in the Old Town Hall. He was asked to estimate the quantity of arms he could handle, and replied, with a certain amount of youthful bravado, that he supposed nothing less than a few hundred rifles and several thousand rounds of ammunition per month would interest them. Crawford nodded approvingly. How much money would he need? He suggested £200 as a beginning, and was instructed to call for it at 5 o'clock that afternoon at Cunningham's office. There Cowzer handed him a brown paper parcel containing banknotes, for which no receipt was demanded, and after that whenever he needed money he simply wrote a figure on a postcard and addressed it to Cowzer. A day or two later someone whom he had never seen before would call at his office in Manchester and deliver the notes.

With the actual purchase of arms he was in no way concerned, as this was arranged by Crawford. He was provided with three lorries, and each morning from Monday to Friday one of them would set off from Manchester at 5 a.m. and return at 5 p.m. laden with three tons of ammunition in tin-lined wooden boxes. It was then carefully packed into large barrels capable of holding up to fifty rifles or 8,000 rounds of ammunition. Ostensibly, the barrels contained bleaching powder, which was forwarded to various bleach-works in Ulster. The hollow spaces between the ammunition boxes and the sides of the barrel were filled with farina, a finely ground starch, so that, when the barrels were rolled on the quayside, some of the powder ran out at the seams in a most convincing way. Real bleaching powder could not be used because it was deliquescent, and likely to ruin the ammunition.

Other consignments went to chemical merchants as 'blank fix' and as 'black jointing' to Workman and Clark's shipyard. At the outset Johnston employed a staff of six, including a skilled cooper who saw to it that no faulty workmanship endangered the supply line. Ultimately fifteen men were employed, and the wages, £4 or £5 a week, were exceptionally high for the period to ensure their discretion. From August 1913 until September 1914 some 3,000,000 rounds of ·303 ammunition and 500 rifles were shipped to Ulster from Manchester, and about £3,000 spent in wages and handling.[17]

Another very useful agent was Major F. T. Tristram of Darlington, an officer of the Territorials who was a cement manufacturer and owned works in several towns in the North of

England. He undertook to help in the gun-running, and in the early months of 1914 his business provided excellent cover for the activity. A disused cement works which he owned in West Hartlepool was taken over for the manufacture of patent cement; it comprised several buildings and about five acres of ground with a huge pond at the centre.

In the manufacture of cement small pieces of metal are introduced into the revolving cylinders in order to break up the lime and other materials into a fine dust. These were made for Tristram at Rugby, and were sent in boxes similar to ammunition boxes, a circumstance which proved very convenient. Adgey had a very good friend in Bedford, a gunsmith who possessed a large store and a traction engine and who was an active sympathizer. The traction engine and two trailer wagons were used to bring large quantities of ·303 rifle and machine-gun ammunition from London to Bedford. In the store the words EXPLOSIVE and AMMUNITION were erased from the boxes and CEMENT MANUFACTURE substituted; then the boxes went on to West Hartlepool via Rugby without arousing suspicion.

At the cement works 500 cartridges were packed into each bag of cement, and shipped to Belfast from the small privately-owned harbour of Haverton Hill. Crawford even bought for the purpose a small schooner which altogether transported more than a million rounds of ·303 ammunition to Ulster before the operation was dramatically uncovered at the end of June 1914.

The foreman stevedore at Haverton Hill was, from the gun-runners' point of view, a reliable man and in the secret. Many of the dock-labourers, however, were Roman Catholic Irish. Their routine loading instructions required them to look out for bags in which cement had become hard or lumpy, and if they found any, to open the bags and remove the lumps. One man who did so found that the lumps were cartridges, and immediately reported his discovery to the foreman. Realizing that the ammunition was intended for the U.V.F., the men became very indignant and stopped work. The foreman acted with great shrewdness and presence of mind. Affecting to share their sense of outrage, he went to telephone the police; then he ordered every bag of the thirty tons already on board to be taken off, and replaced with a cargo of ordinary cement, thus saving the ship from possible confiscation.

Adgey, who had chosen this moment to pay a long-postponed visit to Belfast, was immediately recalled to Newcastle by a telegram from Major Tristram. As it turned out, the Customs were very slow in getting to work, and did not arrive on the scene until the following day. Adgey ordered two of the five-ton lorries from Manchester up to Middlesbrough, and during the night Hunter and he loaded up about half of the bags from the harbour and hid them under tarpaulin sheets in the field of a friendly farmer outside Darlington. They managed to make another run before the Customs officers arrived, and the ammunition was then transported to Manchester. They left three or four fully-loaded railway wagons, judging it best, as Adgey says, to let the Customs have 'something for their trouble'.[18]

That evening he went on to West Hartlepool and ordered all the cartridges waiting there to be unpacked and put into barrels for shipping as 'bleaching powder' from Manchester. Instructions were left that if the police or Customs arrived to ask questions, the undisposed of ammunition was to be dumped into the pond. In the event, it took the authorities a week to trace the source; by that time the birds had flown, and the premises were deserted.

The ship had meanwhile sailed from Haverton Hill to Belfast, where she was stopped at the Hailing House and thoroughly searched. The Customs officers who went on board were in full uniform, to forestall any quibble about their authority, and the very genuine cement made a sad transformation in their smart appearance, before they were satisfied and allowed the ship to discharge her innocent cargo.

The discovery at Haverton Hill occurred only a month before the outbreak of the War, and the story of the activities of the arms committee in Britain has taken us far beyond the events of the autumn of 1913. The truth was that up to that time, despite all the ingenuity and enthusiasm displayed, the number of rifles brought into Ulster was relatively small, and it was rifles that counted. What was worse, the U.V.F. was being armed piecemeal with weapons of varying calibre and obsolete design; for the most part they were Martini Enfield carbines, Lee Metfords, Italian Vetterli-Vitalis, and B.S.A. ·22 miniature rifles. If this was allowed to go on, the Force would be equipped with weapons requiring many different kinds of ammunition, a situation which could only lead to indescribable confusion and disaster in action.

Crawford had preached this gospel all along, and this was why he so strongly advocated the large-scale arms *coup*. Always a military realist, he refused, for example, to purchase rifles without bayonets, knowing that if Ulster were blockaded, supplies of ammunition would very quickly run short. The raising and drilling of the volunteers had produced a stupendous effect on British public opinion, but purely as a military force the U.V.F. did not impress the professional soldiers. Despite the unhappy memories of the South African war they did not seriously expect it to put up much of a show in the field, against an Army equipped with artillery and modern weapons.

Nevertheless, the fervour of the volunteers was boundless. For months they had waited patiently, accepting the promises of the leaders that when, and if, the time came for resistance, they would be armed and equipped. They were growing weary of the drills. Musketry practice was rationed, because of the shortage of rifles; often there were only a score or less for a battalion. As the autumn advanced, and the Home Rule Bill went on its inexorable way through Parliament, dissatisfaction increased.

Various schemes were being thought out to increase the importation of rifles. On 17 October Colonel McCammon wrote to Lord Leitrim, Lord Farnham, and Captain Ricardo: 'Captain James Craig will be responsible for the payment of £1 towards the cost of each serviceable rifle or carbine taking the ·303 ammunition, on the conditions that the same are purchased by responsible persons, and stored in safe-keeping, in your county, and not issued until directed.'[19] Another paper, dated 31 October and initialled by Lord Leitrim, says: 'I agree to be responsible for the payment of £2.10.0 per rifle up to 1,500 rifles or carbines imported into Ireland, on the understanding that Headquarters have the right of distribution.' It is endorsed: 'All right. James Craig. 1.xi.'13.'[20]

On 20 October McCammon informed the regimental commanders that since foreign rifles could not be issued for the time being, arrangements had been made to purchase Martini-Metford ·303 rifles and carbines for instructional purposes, including musketry practice. These would be issued at the rate of two per section to each battalion, and requisitions signed by the responsible officers were to be forwarded to Headquarters, which would pass them on 'to the department concerned'. It was made clear that Headquarters would not issue the rifles; they would merely inform the person named in the requisition where and when he was to take delivery, and the intention was probably to allow the demands to be dealt with directly by the arms committee.[21]

But since the ports were now so closely watched, the further importation of rifles was becoming very difficult, and meanwhile the requisitions and complaints from battalion commanders began to pile up on McCammon's desk. 'If you could let the East Belfast Regiment have at once three rifles per battalion, say twenty-one in all, to teach the men sighting, they would be of great help.' . . . 'As it is considered that there should be at least one rifle at each place where drill instruction is given, we would like to know if you could supply us with two or three dozen in addition to the fifty we have already received.' . . . 'Kindly note that I shall require at least forty and will take delivery of them myself.' . . .[22]

Following a special meeting on 10 November, the instructions were changed; it was decided that in order to avoid confusion only one man in each county should be deputed to ask for arms, and that the issue of rifles should be rationed to sixty-four for each battalion, approximately eight to a company and two to a section. This allocation fell far short of the number required for training, let alone arming, the volunteers.[23]

9

COUNCILS OF WAR

The turning point came in December. All in all, 1913 had not been a good year for the Government; it was still reeling from the Marconi scandal; its Radical supporters wanted a reduction in the Navy estimates; there was a rising ferment of Labour troubles; the Suffragettes had launched a campaign of arson and violence throughout the country. Above all there was Ulster, growing every day more menacing and defiant. Carson and his citizen army were rapidly taking the Home Rule question out of the control of Parliament, but Asquith still held the initiative — only just, for now there were urgent warnings that even he must, at last, take some action.

In the last months of the year the Irish scene had suddenly grown darker. Until then attention had been focused on the north, and the rest of Ireland had been unnaturally quiet, but now there came news of disturbing events in the south. The trouble began with violent labour disputes in Dublin in August, centred upon James Larkin, a Liverpool man who had first made headlines in 1907 by organizing the dock labourers in Belfast. Now the champion of the ill-paid Dublin workers, he was engaged in a bitter conflict with the privately-owned Dublin Tramway Company. When he and four other trade union leaders were arrested on 28 August, violent street fighting took place in the city, the police were showered with stones and broken bottles, and troops had to be called out to put down the riot. Larkin was charged with seditious libel and conspiracy on account of his inflammatory speeches, in which he had said, among other things, that if Carson had advised the Ulstermen to arm, he did not see why the Dublin workers should not do so as well. His chief supporter, Captain J. R. White, even undertook to raise among the strikers a citizen army on the pattern of the U.V.F.

White, in association with another Ulster Protestant, Sir Roger Casement, and Alice Stopford Green (the widow of the historian J. R. Green) had been for some time campaigning against Carson in the north. Yet another group of young Nationalists, holding extreme Republican views and again, by curious coincidence, hailing mostly from Ulster, met in Dublin in August to discuss the possibility of forming an Irish Volunteer Force. With so much excitement going on in the north it would indeed have been strange if the youth of Ireland had waited passively upon events.[1]

Earnestly believing that politics were far too serious a matter to be left to the politicians, these men longed to follow the Ulster example. Far from condemning the U.V.F., they regarded it with an approving and comradely eye, and Padraic Pearse, a young Gaelic League schoolmaster, declared that he found the Orangeman with a rifle a much less ridiculous figure than the Nationalist without one.[2] Behind this movement shadowy forces were at work, the most important being the secret, oath-bound, Irish Republican Brotherhood, which drew its strength mainly from the United States of America.

In October the Republicans persuaded Professor Eoin MacNeill, the Celtic archaeologist who as a young man had been a pioneer in the revival of the Irish language, to become their chairman. MacNeill, a Catholic from the Glens of Antrim, felt a paradoxical admiration for the U.V.F. and thought that it pointed the way for the Nationalists.[3] A manifesto was issued, advocating the formation of Irish Volunteers; then in November a huge public meeting was held in the Rotunda in Dublin, and before it ended, some 4,000 men had been enrolled.

Thus, spontaneously, the Irish Volunteers sprang up and were organized on the pattern of the U.V.F. Drilling began, halls were engaged, reservists from Irish regiments in the British Army acted as instructors, and Colonel Maurice Moore, who had commanded the Connaught Rangers, was appointed Commander-in-Chief.[4]

To Redmond these events were like a nightmare. If he deplored the militancy of the north, its spread to the rest of Ireland filled him with despair. At Westminster he had to insist more than ever on the Bill, the whole Bill, and nothing but the Bill, while in Ireland he had somehow to gain control of a popular movement with which he had little sympathy. He might have echoed the words of a French political leader in 1848: '*Je suis leur chef, il faut que je les suive.*'

The Cabinet, brooding over these events with no less alarm, decided upon an action which did nothing at all to strengthen Redmond's position. On 5 December two royal proclamations were published banning the importation of arms and ammunition into Ireland, and their coastwise transport.[5] The timing of the proclamations was bitterly resented by the Irish Volunteers, for they pointed out that for a year the U.V.F. had been arming without serious legal restraint, and that the Unionists were openly boasting that they had now enough arms to resist Home Rule.

The real facts were not, of course, known to the public at the time. It has been shown that the U.V.F. were very far from being effectively armed, and the proclamations were aimed as much at the northern movement as at the southern. In any case the Government could not reasonably be accused of assisting Carson; whatever unfair advantages he possessed were the result of circumstances outside their control. In public speeches Carson and his friends made light of the proclamations, but the evidence of the U.V.F. records shows that they were regarded as a serious setback by the Headquarters Staff and that they were the cause of some friction between the political and military leaders. They also led to a complete reappraisal of the arms policy.

Meanwhile in secret the last attempts were made to find the solution which Asquith, Redmond and Carson, each in his own way, hoped would avoid the appeal to the sword. Asquith held the last of his unavailing conversations with Bonar Law on 10 December, and found him even more pessimistic than at the outset. On the very same day he invited Carson to have 'a little talk' with him in conditions of strict confidence. They met twice, at 24 Queen Anne's Gate, and continued the negotiations in correspondence over Christmas and into the New Year, but on 22 January Asquith reported to the Cabinet that Sir Edward Carson had flatly refused 'anything short of the exclusion of Ulster'.[6]

Certain unpleasant facts had now to be faced. On 16 December, the day of Asquith's first meeting with Carson, Colonel John Seely, the Secretary of State for War summoned the Commanding Officers in Chief in England, Scotland, and Ireland to meet him at the War Office. Unlike most War Ministers Seely (later Lord Mottistone) was a soldier, and a very dashing and gallant one at that. He had entered the House of Commons as a Conservative, after distinguished service in the South African war, but his dissatisfaction with Balfour's policies induced him to join the Liberals. Seely was a twentieth century D'Artagnan; his bravery was well-known, and would have commanded even wider admiration if he had not been so addicted to discussing it with his friends. F. E. Smith liked to tell the story of how Seely, after rescuing a man with great difficulty from a raging sea, had remarked, 'That was the most troublesome man whose life I have ever saved'. He then discovered that he had rescued a swimming champion who had been giving an exhibition of life-saving.[7]

Seely's engaging qualities were offset by his tendency to assume on occasion an unwarranted arrogance and hauteur which his fellow officers found simply irritating, and this was particularly unfortunate at a time when relations between the Government and the Army were about to be subjected to tremendous strain. Haldane, his predecessor at the War Office, had not found it easy to establish himself with the soldiers; when asked by the generals what kind of army he had in mind, he had replied, 'A Hegelian army'. He recorded that 'the conversation then fell off'.[8] But despite this unpromising beginning, Haldane soon won the respect of the generals, and his energetic reforms made him the most successful Secretary of State for War since Cardwell. Had he remained at the War Office instead of becoming Lord Chancellor, it is probable that the Army crisis of March 1914 would have been averted.

On the whole the Army officers of the pre-war period were not profoundly interested in politics, and they tended to distrust politicians. Most of them came from families with a military tradition, and regarded their career as a vocation with the highest possible standards of honour and loyalty. By virtue of their commissions, they were the King's men, committed without reservation to his service, and acting on the assumption that he would only command them to do whatever was in the best interest of the country. They had never had any reason until now to concern themselves with the constitutional subtleties of the Sovereign's position.

The Ulster crisis, however, affected the Army in a peculiarly intimate way. In the first place many officers were themselves Irishmen, and belonged to Anglo-Irish families which felt they had everything to lose by the ending of the Union. Moreover, when officers said that they had no politics, they meant in fact that they were instinctively Conservative; any move to disturb the status quo aroused their dislike and mistrust, and they were bound to share the Opposition's view that Home Rule and the coercion of Ulster were threats to the unity of the British Empire. Their sympathies lay naturally with the Ulster Protestants, who also claimed to be 'the King's men'; they knew from first-hand experience that the British flag and the British uniform were exposed to insult in southern Ireland, whereas in Ulster they were welcomed. Could they, pledged as they were to fight the King's enemies, be expected in all fairness to take up arms against the most loyal of his subjects? Already many officers who were retired, or on the Reserve, had gone to Ulster to serve with the U.V.F., while others were actively assisting the British League for the Support of Ulster, and these men were in close touch with serving officers.

Nevertheless the soldier's first duty was to obey such lawful commands as were given to him, and most officers felt that the more they avoided the topic of Ulster, the less risk they ran of being compromised. But there were others, and some of high rank, who made no secret of their political attitudes. An outstanding example was the Director of Military Operations, Sir Henry Wilson. Wilson, who was gazetted Major-General in November 1913, having risen from the rank of Captain in twelve years, was an Irishman whose family had been given land in Antrim by King William III. He had not made a brilliant start to his military career, for he had failed twice to get into Woolwich and three times to get into Sandhurst, but like Sir John French, the Chief of the Imperial General Staff, he had entered the Army by way of the Militia. Membership of a crack regiment, considerable Irish charm, and a marked ability for making friends and influencing people, soon made up for this uncertain beginning. Before many years had elapsed he was in the Intelligence Department of the War Office, and shortly afterwards he was commandant of the Staff College, where his fluent and scintillating lectures, spiced with humour and calculated indiscretions, were much enjoyed. In 1910 he was appointed Director of Military Operations.

Wilson remains an enigmatic figure. Since the posthumous publication of his diaries in 1927, his reputation as a soldier has suffered from much hostile criticism, and may well be due for restoration. Certainly his influence was out of all proportion to his actions, a consequence no doubt of his mysterious ability to impress people who wielded power; he was, moreover, an inveterate gossip who loved intrigue and had no qualms whatever about meddling in politics.

Wilson's views on the Irish question were forthrightly partisan, and early in November 1913 he recorded in his diary that he had had 'a long talk about Ulster' with Sir John French.

'He is evidently nervous that we are coming to civil war, and his attitude appears to be that he will obey the King's orders. He wanted to know what I would do. I told him that I could not fire on the north at the dictation of Redmond, and that is what the whole thing means . . . I *cannot* bring myself to believe that Asquith will be so mad as to employ force. It will split the Army and the Colonies, as well as the country and the Empire.'[9]

A few days later he advised French to state in writing that he could not be responsible for the whole of the Army. 'This Ulster business is getting serious.'

Wilson did not stop at giving advice to his colleagues; he gossiped freely with the Conservative politicians, and kept Bonar Law informed of the state of opinion in the Army. 'I told him', Wilson wrote, 'that there was much talk in the Army, and that if we were ordered to coerce Ulster there would be wholesale defections. It had been suggested to him that 40 per cent of officers and men would leave the Army. Personally I put the per cent much lower, but still very serious. I then told him of Cecil's idea that Carson should pledge the Ulster troops to fight for England if she was at war. I pointed out that a move like this would render the employment of troops against Ulster more impossible than ever. He was much pleased with the suggestion, and at once tried to get Carson on the telephone.'[10]

A few days later Wilson lunched with Edward Sclater, and heard from him an account of the progress of the U.V.F., which he found 'most interesting'. He warned him that the Volunteers must avoid such pitfalls as seizing arms depots, or any action hostile to the Army, which was becoming most sympathetic to the Ulster movement. It would look well if the readiness of the

Ulstermen to come over and help England in time of trouble were stressed.[11]

It was against this background of threatened resignations in the Army that Seely held his conference with the generals on December 16, and his purpose was to explain to them what attitude soldiers ought to take in the crisis. In his statement, which was subsequently published, he made the following points:

'The law clearly lays down that a soldier is entitled to obey an order to shoot only if that order is reasonable under the circumstances. No one, from general officer to private, is entitled to use more force than is required to maintain order and the safety of life and property. No soldier can shelter himself from the civil law behind an order given by a superior if that order is, in fact, unreasonable and outrageous.

'If, therefore, officers and men in the Army are led to believe that there was a possibility that they might be called upon to take some outrageous action, for instance, to massacre a demonstration of Orangemen who were causing no danger to the lives of their neighbours, bad as might be the effects on discipline in the Army, nevertheless, it is true that they are, in fact and in law, justified in contemplating refusal to obey.

'But there never has been, and is not now, any intention of giving outrageous and illegal orders to the troops. The law will be respected and must be obeyed. What has now to be faced is the possibility of action being required by His Majesty's troops in supporting the civil power, in protecting life and property if the police are unable to hold their own.

'Attempts have been made to dissuade troops from obeying lawful orders given them when acting in support of the Civil Power. This amounts to a claim that officers and men can pick and choose between lawful and reasonable orders, saying that they will obey in one case and not in another.

'The Army has been quite steady. During the past year there has not been brought to the notice of the authorities one single case of lack of discipline in this respect. At the same time, in view of the statements in the Press and elsewhere, it is well to make the position clear.'[12]

This ambiguous statement did nothing to alleviate the generals' anxiety, and probably served to increase it, since it left as obscure as ever that most embarrassing of military problems, of how to distinguish between reasonable and unreasonable orders. Nevertheless, whether they understood it or not, the generals were to 'make the position thus outlined perfectly clear to all concerned'. The Minister told them that he would hold each of them 'individually responsible to see that there was no conduct in their commands subversive to discipline'. If there were, it would immediately be dealt with under the King's Regulations, and if an officer sent in his resignation because he contemplated refusing to obey a lawful order, he would at once be dismissed from the service.[13]

While Seely was outlining the situation for the generals, the potential enemy were holding two important conferences of their own, at which the officers outlined the situation for the politicians. The first took place in London on 17 December. Recognizing that their plans for military resistance must depend upon, and be secondary to, the leaders' political moves, the U.V.F. Staff desired illumination on several important points. The questions they asked, and the answers they received, are recorded on four large sheets among the Unionist Council archives, and are worth quoting in some detail. The first section dealt with possible moves by the Government.

'What early developments should the military leaders be prepared to meet, especially in regard to the following contingencies:

    (a) Seizure of arms on a large scale?
        Resistance, organized if possible. No shooting.
    (b) Seizure of arms from individuals on a small scale, and with no provocation on the part of the individuals?
        See (a).
    (c) If action is taken against the leaders in England?
        Not probable. Bonar Law come to Ulster.
    (d) If action is taken against the leaders in Ulster?
        Leader (Carson) come to Ulster at once.
    (e) If the Belfast population show grave signs of getting restive and riots appear likely?
        Every effort should be used to stop.
    (f) If the Imperial Government begin to draft into Ulster (or the borders of Ulster) large numbers of extra troops or police?
        Must hear of beforehand. Action then considered.'

The second section dealt specifically with the arms problem.

'(a) Is it intended that no steps shall be taken at present in regard to continuing the importation of arms into Ulster? *Officially, yes.*

(b) If the importation is to be discontinued, should plans be made for their future importation on a large scale in view of possible emergencies? *Yes.*'[14]

The slightly reproachful tone of these questions sharpened into criticism when the military members turned to the matter of the Arms Proclamations. On 4 December Carson's colleague J. H. Campbell, K.C., had said in a speech at Manchester that a ban on the importation of arms would be proclaimed 'within a day or two', and it was now pointed out that if the military authorities had only been given this information confidentially four days earlier, they would have been able to bring in extra quantities of arms in time. 'Much dissatisfaction has been expressed among the rank and file that this notice was not given them by Headquarters of the U.V.F., and serious monetary loss has been entailed as a consequence by private people.' In future it was hoped that the military disadvantages of such public announcements would be carefully weighed against their political advantages.[15]

Two days later the arms situation was discussed again, this time at Craigavon, where two questions were put to Clark, the chairman of the arms committee. First, was he prepared to bring in arms and ammunition under the existing circumstances, and if so at what rate? Unless an average of one hundred a week could be maintained it was not worth while carrying on. Secondly, was he ready to bring in 20,000 rifles and two million rounds of ammunition quickly if the emergency arose? If so would he make all the necessary arrangements at once, and state what notice was required to carry them into effect. Presumably forcible measures would be required when the time came, and it was suggested 'that the G.O.C. be told confidentially what to prepare for so that his staff may begin to think out the arrangements'.[16]

There is no record of Clark's reply, but almost certainly he gave his opinion that only Crawford could arrange the running in of 20,000 rifles in one consignment. At any rate General

Richardson's notes indicate that the first subjects discussed were the purchase and storage of rifles, and what resistance might have to be met in bringing them in, and he wrote after them 'approved. G.R.'. But clearly some members of the Standing Committee, including the G.O.C. himself, had misgivings about giving Crawford a free hand, for at the bottom of the page he scribbled 'Crawford — the orders he has received. He has been instructed to proceed — perhaps he had better be stopped'.[17]

10

NEW YEAR RESOLUTIONS

When it was still only a few hours old the Archbishop of York declared that 1914, which was entering upon the scene of history surrounded by dark and threatening clouds, might prove to be a very fateful year. With regard to Ireland all thoughtful men were bound to admit the danger of civil war, and he urged the politicians to seek every means to avert such a catastrophe. Most of the New Year messages were in similar terms, and full of the metaphor of storm and lowering skies; an undertone of disquiet ran through the seasonal celebrations. Mr. Asquith alone was determined to whistle at the churchyard gate. 'It is eight years since we came into power', he told his supporters, 'and never within my experience has the Liberal Party been in better health and spirits.'[1] In Belfast the mood was grave but uncompromising. The crowd which gathered round the Albert Clock to welcome the New Year waved thousands of Union Jacks and solemnly sang the National Anthem before dispersing. The sombre thoughts in many minds were reflected in the verses printed in a local newspaper:

> *O Britons while your bells ring forth*
> *To welcome in the new born year,*
> *Remember there is sorrow here*
> *For clouds hang heavy o'er the North.*

But sorrow or not, there was no hint of concession or surrender, for, as the writer continued, '*Our race is stern, 'twas sternly nursed*'.[2]

And yet, as far as the world at large was concerned, mankind seemed unnaturally at peace on that first day of 1914, and the newspaper headlines were more cheerful than they had been for some time past. Shackleton was planning a new expedition to the Antarctic; England had just beaten South Africa in the test match; in New York the latest rage was a dance called the tango. Mr. Lloyd George declared that Anglo-German relations were far more friendly than they had been for years, and that there was no need to strengthen the Navy.

Apart from Ulster, the world's only trouble spot was Mexico, where the revolutionary dictator General Huerta was defending his régime against a rival favoured by President Wilson of the United States. In February Huerta was to find an unexpected ally in the German Emperor, who offered him military aid against the rebels, if he would agree to deprive the British Navy of oil in case of war.[3] Already in the free port of Hamburg, the centre of the international arms trade, the agents of the various Mexican factions were at work, and their activities were to mingle curiously with those of their solitary Ulster competitor.

The U.V.F. was at least as worried about arms as General Huerta, and one important county division made a New Year resolution to do something about it. At a meeting of Co. Antrim U.V.F. Committee on 6 January very great dissatisfaction was expressed at the inadequate supply of arms, even for instructional purposes. Only 150 rifles and carbines of ·303 calibre and 50 Vetterlis had been issued for a force of 10,000 men, and no ammunition had been allowed for the latter rifle. It was decided that a deputation should ask to be granted an interview with Captain Craig, in order to express the Committee's feelings. During the next fortnight Headquarters assigned another 150 Vetterlis to the Antrim Division, and these, together with some newly-acquired private rifles brought their total up to 377, approximately one rifle to every thirty men, although because there was ammunition for only about 180 of these rifles, the proportion was nearer one to every sixty men. The battalion commanders all reported that the men were 'manifesting considerable disappointment at the present condition of affairs' and were tiring of elementary drill.

Inevitably a strong suspicion arose that other divisions had received more favourable treatment. 'It is believed that other counties have been given a larger proportion of arms, for which ammunition is forthcoming. The County Antrim Committee would be glad to receive some information on this point, and, if the report is true, some explanation seems due.' They believed that some counties had withheld part of their contribution to the Carson Fund to buy their own rifles. 'The Committee therefore asks for a grant of money with which to arm itself.' On 20 January the deputation, consisting of Sir William Adair, the tall, bleak, retired General of the Royal Marines who commanded the Antrim Division, and his three regimental commanders, met Carson and Craig and no doubt put their views to them in equally strong terms.[4]

Carson had arrived in Belfast on the 17 January, immediately after the ending of his negotiations with Asquith. That afternoon, although the shipyards were working overtime, the six battalions of the East Belfast U.V.F. mustered at Ormiston, the residence of their commanding officer, Colonel Spencer Chichester, with their full complement of officers, chaplains, doctors, ambulance and transport — they had everything except arms. 'The nearer we approach the day of crisis', Carson told them, 'the more grow your courage and my courage, your determination and mine.'

Next day the Ulster Unionist Council met to hear the annual report, and in the evening there was a public assembly in the Ulster Hall, at which Carson made a direct appeal to the King to rescue Ulster from what now appeared to be her inevitable subjection to an Irish Parliament. 'We will go to the end,' he declared, 'first using every peaceful means. We will prostrate ourselves before the throne and ask the King to save us.' This appeal, however rhetorical, could scarcely have failed to make the King's position more uncomfortable.

On the day of Carson's arrival, Colonel Hacket Pain had written to Crawford: 'General Sir George Richardson is asking Sir Edward Carson to call a conference on the arms question at the Old Town Hall at 10.45 a.m. on 20 January 1914, when your attendance is especially requested. In order that we may know exactly how we stand, I shall be grateful if you will prepare a written statement showing exact details (1) of the number of arms imported *by you* already, with their description, and of the number of bayonets and rounds of ammunition (2) of the present distribution of these arms . . . (3) of any movements of these arms, etc., which have been authorized but not yet carried out.' At this meeting Carson was to be asked to define the future policy with regard to the importation of arms. 'As this may depend to a great extent', the letter continued, 'on the information given to him regarding the arrangements which should now be made if importation on a larger scale is determined, I shall be greatly obliged if you will bring with you a separate written statement showing (*a*) whether you would be willing to undertake the full arrangements for this importation if the leader authorizes it; (*b*) *if so* whether you will give an estimate of the time required by you for putting it into execution, the funds that you will want for the purpose, and the help that you will require from the U.V.F. military authorities to enable you to land and distribute the arms and ammunition.'[5]

In a long, detailed reply Crawford said he would prefer, for business and family reasons, to have nothing to do with further gun-running, but if he did agree to organize a large-scale *coup*, it would be on the conditions that at least 20,000 rifles and 2,000,000 rounds of ammunition were brought in at one time, and that his instructions were given to him in writing. 'My duty', he went on, 'would be to get all alongside the quay, but someone must be nominated to work with me, responsible for their distribution. I have a plan, but think it better not to put it on paper.'

He stipulated also that no one should be allowed to compete with him in buying arms at the same source, or to run in arms on a small scale until the operation had been completed, 'as it would probably draw down on our coasts a patrol of torpedo or other war craft and frustrate our more important work'.

As for the arms held up in Birmingham (because of the proclamations), he suggested that they should be sold to the British League at cost price. If this offer was not accepted, the League should help to lift the arms and place them at convenient places on the coasts, a manoeuvre which would have the advantage of distracting the authorities from their real plans.

The chance that these plans would be uncovered was, he considered, very slight until the ship was actually at her destination, but to be more definite he would have to study charts of home and neutral waters. To this scheme he attached an estimate of cost, necessarily rough since prices varied from week to week, and a war breaking out anywhere could double the price.[6]

The plan which Crawford had earlier outlined to the arms committee was basically simple. He would negotiate for the rifles in Hamburg, purchase a suitable steamer in a foreign port, and after loading either bring her direct to Ulster or transfer the cargo to a local steamer in some estuary on the Scottish coast.

All this was carefully considered at the Old Town Hall on the 20th in conditions of the greatest secrecy. Clearly some members of the arms committee felt from the outset that the risk involved in a gun-running was too great, and that Crawford was hot-headed and likely to bring the Provisional Government to ridicule or disaster. But both Craig and Carson were convinced of the logic of his arguments. Once Craig had made his mind up, it was simply a question of when and how it could be done; for Carson the decision was much more difficult. If he gave his assent, it was his nature to accept the full responsibility. He was a lawyer, and they were planning an act of breath-taking illegality, one which, he saw, might well have international repercussions. It was staking everything upon a single throw; the Ulster cause just might survive its failure, but he would not — his enemies would see to that.

Several factors contributed to his decision. The military leaders were pointing out that, since Asquith showed no sign of weakening in his resolve, the U.V.F. might very soon be put to the test. If the Government did decide to use force against them, they would act suddenly, hoping by the use of surprise and overwhelming numbers to avoid bloodshed and seize effective control of the province before the U.V.F. was mobilized. As early as July 1913 the U.V.F. Staff had been advised to this effect, for among the Unionist Council papers is an unsigned assessment of the military situation which begins: '*You say that you intend to sit tight until the Bill becomes law, and then act if it is enforced.* If the Government dares not face real fighting of course this will do all right, but they would be forever discredited and ridiculous, and fear of ridicule is the thing that drives men to fight. If they fight at all, they will surely fight to win, and to get it over as soon as possible.

'The British Army will hate it, but as a whole I believe they'll fight against you. Anyhow is it not safer to assume that they will fight?

'They, the Government, will probably wait as long as they dare in the hope of things quieting down, and at the last suddenly move 20,000 to 30,000 men into Ulster — secure railways, bridges, etc., and reinforce weak police posts.

'If they are allowed to do this (and with the help of the Navy they could certainly do it in two days) I do not see how you can hope to get your men out, and concentrate them in suitable positions.

'*Must you give up the enormous advantage of the first move?*

'I assume you have, say, 30,000 serviceable rifles, and enough ammunition for a big fight (say 2,500,000 rounds).

'To impress the English you must not only put up a fight, you must put up a good fight, and I cannot see how you can put up a good fight unless you seize the first move.

'Your speeches saying you will wait, etc., are all so much to the good; the art of war, including civil war, is to deceive your enemy and try to hit him hard before he is ready.'

This document is interesting, if for no other reason, because it predicted so accurately the move made by the Government in the following spring; and its mention of the number of rifles and rounds of ammunition thought to be necessary for effective resistance, may also have had a bearing on the planning of the arms *coup*. The writer believed that neither the U.V.F. nor the country was suited to guerilla warfare or 'Boer tactics'; everything must be staked on 'a stubborn stand up fight', and even if the volunteers were beaten, they would probably achieve their object. 'I don't advocate moving in a hurry,' he concluded, 'I advocate moving before the Government move. They have very able ambitious men on the Army Council — and if they move at all, they'll pounce.'[7]

If the volunteers were surprised before they had enough arms, it would look as if the political leaders had let them down. Almost certainly this was the gist of what the Antrim Division delegates told Carson on 20 January. They were told nothing of what was in the wind, but given assurances that immediate steps would be taken to improve the arms situation. Either on that day, or shortly afterwards, Carson gave his blessing to Crawford's plan, leaving its detailed execution to Craig. Not more than a dozen people knew the secret, and it was well-kept during the next three nerve-racking months.

While Crawford's plan was being considered, Spender decided, after some hesitation, to attend the annual dinner in London of officers who had passed through the Staff College, knowing that the C.I.G.S. and other senior officers would be there. He discovered that most of the officers present were warm supporters of Ulster, and many took the opportunity to tell him that if it came to trouble 'they would be across the water'. After the dinner General Reed, V.C., invited him round to the Army and Navy Club for a chat, and they were soon joined by some of Spender's Staff College friends who offered him the following advice.

First, if disorders occurred in Ulster which could be classified as rioting, the Army would have to support the R.I.C. in restoring order. Secondly, it would be the wish of the Government to put this complexion on any resistance that might be offered. Thirdly, the Army would not take part in warlike operations if it was clear that the reason for the resistance of the people of Ulster was to prevent their being thrown out of the United Kingdom and placed under a Dublin parliament. It must be made plain to the British people that any attempt to do this would mean civil war.[8]

On his return Spender gave the gist of these conversations to Richardson and Craig, and forcibly expressed the view that unless drastic steps were taken promptly Carson's pledge to his followers that they would be armed could not be honoured. He was then told that Crawford had put forward a plan for obtaining rifles abroad,* but that some of Richardson's advisers held the opinion that, even if Crawford could get them through, 'the risks of their importation, and still more, of their distribution when landed, were too great'. However, Spender was asked to submit a scheme, and he at once began to work on it.[9]

The choice of a suitable harbour required much careful thought. Belfast Lough was well-guarded, and in Belfast itself swift action by the military and police could make unloading impossible. Bangor and Donaghadee in County Down had good harbours, but they were both situated on the Ards Peninsula, which could easily be cut off from the rest of Ulster. But the harbour at Larne was excellent, and, even if the volunteers were surprised, they would be able to hold the town and the Belfast Road long enough for the cargo to be dispersed through the Antrim hills.

Larne possessed another advantage because the harbour was privately owned, and William Chaine, the chairman of the

---

* Since it is inconceivable that Spender was not aware of the plan until this stage, he must mean that he had not seen Crawford's letter, quoted above, until his return from London.

harbour board, was an enthusiastic volunteer and commander of the 2nd Battalion of the Central Antrim Regiment. With his help, Spender was able to form an estimate of 'how long it would take to unload a vessel after dark and other details'. He also found a collaborator in the manager of the Great Northern Railway, who was able to work out details with the Midland Northern Counties Railway staff without involving the Midland authorities in London.

Spender's original proposal was that Carson should hold a grand review at Larne of U.V.F. contingents from the nine counties who would come by special trains. After Carson's departure in the Larne–Stranraer steamer that evening, Crawford was to bring his ship alongside, and the volunteers who had come unarmed would return with rifles and ammunition. This plan was to undergo several modifications during the next three months.[10]

Meanwhile the U.V.F. resolved to get on to a war footing with the minimum of delay. One of the problems was that many officers, however enthusiastic, were businessmen who could not devote their full time to Staff work. To get round this difficulty, half-pay and reserve officers were recruited from England, with the help of the British League for the Support of Ulster, to take command of the Belfast U.V.F. Colonel G. H. H. Couchman, D.S.O., who had once commanded the Somerset Light Infantry, took over the Belfast Division, and set up his own Staff within the organization at the Old Town Hall, with Captain J. D. Scriven as his Chief Staff Officer. Other English officers took command of three of the Belfast Regiments: Colonel J. H. Patterson was assigned to West Belfast, Major Tempest Stone to South, and Captain Malone to North.*

These officers bent their energies to giving the U.V.F. all the requirements of a self-respecting army — transport, communications, intelligence, armouries, a medical corps, maps, plans, and mobilization timetables. In at least one of these aspects the U.V.F. was ahead of contemporary military thought. By the end of 1913 the U.V.F. transport and com-

---

* Col. Patterson was the author of a very popular book, *Maneaters of Tsavo*, about lions in Kenya which held up the construction of a railway until Patterson shot them. This may have suggested the code-name for the Larne operation. (See Chapter XVI.) Major Tempest Stone had been in the Younghusband expedition to Tibet in 1904.

munications section had been brought by Spender to a high degree of efficiency. His committee had registers of all available farm wagons, steam and petrol lorries, and motor cars in each divisional area, and by February 1914, had drawn up plans for the swift mobilization of transport in an emergency.[11]

For some time to come the military mind still thought of transport in terms of horses, but Spender had impressed upon the G.O.C. and his Staff the tremendous potentiality of the motor car. In this he was greatly helped by the enthusiasm of the motorists themselves.

The number of motor cars in the north of Ireland was then relatively small, and motoring was still regarded as the hobby of the well-to-do.* Most of the people who owned cars employed chauffeurs. In 1914, however, there was a boom in the popularity of motoring, and many younger men preferred to drive and maintain their own cars.

Before the turn of the year the G.O.C. had announced to a meeting of motor-car owners in the Old Town Hall that a U.V.F. Motor Car Corps would be formed, and he invited them to register their vehicles on forms which had been printed for the purpose. On 20 December, which was a Saturday, twenty-four cars assembled at Stranmillis in Belfast, and forming up in six squads of four cars each, proceeded to a rendezvous in County Down, where they spent the afternoon performing various manoeuvres to the satisfaction of all concerned.[12]

The Corps grew rapidly in the New Year, and put on a special display in January when it escorted Carson on his way from Mount Stewart to Belfast. By that time between three and four hundred cars had been registered at the Old Town Hall, and F. H. Rogers of Belfast had been appointed commanding officer of the Corps, which the Press described as a unique body because, although the Army was already using motor cars for the conveyance of staff officers, no one had planned to use them for the transportation of troops or refugees in considerable numbers.[13]

In February Spender was able to issue details of the organization. A motor car squad consisted of four vehicles, one of which was driven by the squad leader. A section consisted of nine cars,

* Official returns for 1913 showed that 9,351 motor-cars were registered in Ireland, 999 in Belfast, against 201,469 in England and Wales and 17,087 in Scotland. (BNL. *Motoring Supplement*, 7 March 1914.)

that is, two squads and an extra car for the section officer. Twenty-eight cars, the commander's car and three complete sections, formed a squadron 'suitable for the conveyance of one company of the U.V.F. or one hundred refugees'.[14]

Another scheme to which the professional soldiers gave their support advocated the formation of a small, highly-trained, striking force capable of holding a sudden attack while the rest of the U.V.F. was mobilized. The idea was first discussed at the meetings held in December, when Carson and the political leaders gave it their approval, stipulating only that it should attract as little publicity as possible. Since the force was most likely to be needed in Belfast, for instance in the event of the Army being ordered to seize public buildings or the Old Town Hall, it was proposed to recruit it there.[15]

A memorandum on the subject stated that as the enrolments in the Belfast Division stood at about 25,000, and would probably increase to 30,000, it was apparent that it would be quite useless to arm them all, and in fact might be 'very inadvisable to do so'. Therefore it was proposed to raise a Special Service Force of 3,000 volunteers. Each of the twenty Belfast battalions would be asked to raise a Special Service company of 150 men, most of whom were to be ex-regulars, special reservists, and militia. They were to be attested regularly on attestation papers closely resembling those used in the British Army. They were required to serve anywhere, and when called out they would be paid £1 per week. Rations, arms, and equipment were to be provided, although at first they were expected to find their own boots and clothing. Later this decision was changed.[16]

This plan, somewhat modified in practice, was put into operation in the first two months of 1914, and by March there was a Special Service Section attached to each of the four regiments. Spender had worked out the cost of equipment, and eventually up to £20,000 was earmarked for the Force. It was also decided to provide the men with uniforms. At first Spender proposed a 'serviceable dungaree material, like modern battle-dress', but there were such violent protests that Army khaki was substituted instead. The men also objected to the soft-peaked caps issued, because they were not like the regular Army cap, but here, too, the U.V.F. was in advance of its time.[17]

The section which was later to attract most attention was attached to the smallest regiment, West Belfast. It was raised and commanded by Captain F. P. Crozier, a tough but not unimaginative soldier who was to inscribe his name in the pages of later Irish troubles. Crozier's background was typical of many Army officers of his time. Of Anglo-Irish stock, he spent his childhood at Castleknock in Co. Dublin, while his parents were in India, and received his education in England, first at a small private school and then at Wellington. Among the boys who were his contemporaries at the private school were three who appear elsewhere in this narrative — F. E. Smith, Leo Amery, and Winston Churchill.

Crozier had resigned his commission in 1909 and taken up farming in Canada, subsequently submitting himself to the physical hardship of trapping expeditions and telephone construction work, and winning a complete victory over the drinking which had threatened to ruin his career. In 1912 he returned to England, and in the following year joined the British League for the Support of Ulster and the Union.[18] A few days after he had signed the membership form, he received by carrier a mysterious brown paper parcel which, when opened, was found to contain a ·303 carbine. Some time later, at a luncheon in the Hotel Cecil he met Carson and Craig, and accepted an invitation to come to Ulster and serve with the U.V.F.[19]

He was posted to the West Belfast Regiment and 'given the congenial duty of commanding, raising, and training' the 300 men of the Special Service Section. 'I was given a room in an office', he recalled, 'but declined to mix myself up with red tape and paper transactions, as I had been told my men were required for active work, and might be called upon to *do* things. . . . I was my own clerk, sergeant-major, adjutant, quartermaster, and commanding officer all rolled into one.'[20] Crozier was not by temperament a 'staff' officer, and from the start he saw his task as the creation of an active force to deal with any sudden emergency in the field.

Most of Crozier's recruits came from the fervently Orange and loyal Shankill district of Belfast, and though they were not renowned either for docility or for awe of strangers, they held him in great esteem, and he formed the highest opinion of their soldierly qualities. Under his leadership they came in time to regard themselves as the cream of the Belfast U.V.F., and their smartness and discipline were widely admired. Crozier's only hold over them was the threat of dismissal. Rather than face the disgrace of having his rifle and uniform taken from him, and having the women and children call after him in the streets, a special volunteer would make any sacrifice, even to giving up drink.[21]

Along with all these preparations went the drawing up of plans of action which were never revealed at the time. In order to perfect a defence scheme to come into operation when the Ulster Provisional Government was established, the county divisions were asked to supply information and statistics on certain specific points. What number of men would be required to maintain order in the county area, and what number would be immediately available for service elsewhere? Assuming that enrolment was closed on 1 March what number would be ready to bear arms on 1 May? Could arms be distributed to them before an emergency arose, and would they be responsible for looking after them?

In addition to answering such questions, the commanding officers were asked to prepare suggestions for the best methods of communication between Headquarters and the regimental commanders, and so on down to the company and section leaders, to work out arrangements for the concentration of their men at railway stations, and to estimate the time required and the number of men to be entrained. On the basis of this information mobilization timetables were later prepared.

Each county division was also to have plans ready 'should it be necessary to relieve the Constabulary of their duties', and to ensure that the Government was compelled to draft the maximum number of troops or police into its area, if such a policy was required by the leaders. The system of road and railway communications through the county was to be considered carefully, so that they could be disorganized in the event of emergency, and suitable positions chosen which might be occupied to prevent troops from passing along the roads.[22]

From this intelligence there emerged a plan of action to be followed if the U.V.F. was called upon to assume the military control of Ulster. Among the U.V.F. records are copies of a three-page typed document headed 'The No. 1 Scheme'. From internal evidence it would appear to have been drafted early in 1914, since the first two pages are concerned with the organization of 'a special flying column of 5,000 men' in Belfast.

It states that the members of this corps should be detailed for the exact duties required of them well in advance, 'so that at the time of action no confusion can occur, i.e., certain units are required for police work, and the safety of the town against any rioting or destruction or incendiarism from the Nationalist inhabitants, or from the irresponsible youths and unenlisted men of the Orange side,' while other units are to be detailed to guard the entrances to the city, and take up positions 'so that access to and egress from the city can be denied to the enemy'. Each unit should be familiar with the position it is expected to hold, and where possible each man should know 'which stone, ditch, wall, or building, etc., he has got to be behind and fire from, and as far as possible the range of all objects in front of him'.

The third page, which is headed 'The Coup' may be quoted in full:

'I recommend a sudden, complete and paralysing blow should be struck at the right moment, i.e., simultaneously

1. All railway communications should be severed whereby forces of police and soldiers can be sent to ULSTER.

2. All telegraph, telephone, and cable lines to be cut.

3. All depots of arms, ammunition, and military equipment should be captured.

4. All avenues of approach by road for troops or police into ULSTER should be closed by isolated detachments of men occupying defensive positions commanding such roads.

5. Wherever possible the guns of any Field Artillery should be captured either by direct attack or else by previous arrangement with the gunners concerned.

6. All depots of supply for troops or police should be captured.

'To carry out the above, most careful inquiries should be made as to the present position of all depots referred to, and the troops guarding each one. Where possible secret arrangements should be come to for the handing over of same without fighting, but in case of fighting . . . the force for attack should be overwhelmingly superior to the defending force.

'Most careful investigations should be made as to the points for cutting the railways which will render the isolation of ULSTER most complete, with the least amount of damage to railway property, i.e., where the blowing up of one bridge (say DROGHEDA) cuts 3 or 4 lines of railway approach, it is preferable to blowing up 3 or 4 bridges on respective lines.

'Telegraph wires should be cut in several places, and poles and wire carried away or destroyed.

'In every district men should be detailed for this work, and properly instructed, so that they can continue the cutting at night, whenever the wires are repaired, and carry on their usual occupations by day, so as to give no clue to their identity.

'Each man forming a part of a body to attack a depot should be made to study beforehand the work required, so that at the moment of action there should be no doubt in his mind as to his particular job.'[23]

As we shall presently see, the existence of this military plan may explain some curious features of the crisis which was to take place in March.

When enrolment for the U.V.F. closed on the last day of February the numbers had reached approximately 90,000, excluding the Motor Car Corps and the U.S.D.R.C. In addition there were the three squadrons of the Enniskillen Horse, and at least one other semi-official mounted force, the Ballymena Horse, raised and commanded by Captain the Hon. Arthur O'Neill in mid-Antrim.[24] Altogether the numbers were not far short of the 100,000 originally stipulated. The four regiments of the Belfast Division, which had now increased their strength to twenty battalions, accounted for 30,000 men, nearly a third of the Force. Next in order of size came Antrim and Down with over 11,000 each, followed by Tyrone, Armagh, Londonderry, Fermanagh, Derry City, Donegal, Monaghan and Cavan. The last two each mustered a regiment of just over 2,000 volunteers. The armament of the Force consisted of several thousand rifles and six machine-guns. It possessed no artillery, and no aeroplanes.[25]

As the spring advanced, with very changeable weather, sunshine and blue skies giving way suddenly to showers of sleet and snow, the paradox of the Ulster rebellion became more apparent. Officers stationed in Ulster sometimes found themselves involved in Gilbertian situations, and they had to consider carefully the implications of dining at rebel tables, or fraternizing with old friends now on the rebel staff. Fortunately General Gleichen was a broad-minded and cultivated soldier with a keen sense of humour, and he was shrewd enough not to allow niceties of etiquette to prevent him finding out whatever he could about the plans of the other side.

Countess Gleichen's position was a little difficult, for most of the ladies of her acquaintance were enthusiastically involved in support of the volunteer movement. She solved this social problem in the simplest possible way; when she paid her afternoon calls she joined her friends in their first aid classes, though on account of her husband's position she did not actually enrol as a U.V.F. nurse.[26]

Some Belfast homes came to be accepted as 'neutral ground' where the Army and the U.V.F. could meet without embarrassment. In March Countess Gleichen and Mrs. Spender were both guests at a musical evening in the home of Dr. Grierson, the Dean of Belfast, when Mr. Broadwood, 'the musical subaltern from the Norfolks' apologized for not bringing a certain captain with him, as he had been sent off suddenly with sixteen men to guard the arms and ammunition stores at Carrickfergus. 'He said it quite naturally,' Mrs. Spender recorded, 'and not at all as if he remembered that we (so to speak) were the people against whom (or for fear of whom) the move was directed!' Though no one present realized it, the order which had deprived the captain of his evening's entertainment marked the beginning of a new and critical phase of the Ulster crisis.[27]

3

11

LORD MILNER INTERVENES

The extent to which the Ulster question obsessed British politics in 1914 is widely recognized. What is not so well known is that the supporters of Ulster in Britain and throughout the Empire took practical measures to ensure that if she were attacked she would not fight alone, and that there were influential figures who were prepared to go to any lengths to stop the Home Rule Bill from becoming law, or at least to force the Government to hold a general election first.

Foremost among them was Lord Milner, the former High Commissioner for South Africa, and the great 'proconsul' of the Empire. Ever since 1906, when what was virtually a vote of censure was passed on him by the House of Commons over the 'Chinese slavery' affair, Milner had kept disdainfully aloof from party politics, although, by means of his young disciples of the Round Table group, he exercised considerable influence on political thought. In December 1913 he suddenly descended from Olympus and threw himself heart and soul into the Ulster struggle. His participation began with this remarkable letter to Carson.

Very Confidential   *47, Duke Street, S.W.*
December 9, 1913

'My dear Carson,

'It seems an awful thing to suggest, to a man who must be so overwhelmed as you are, but I should immensely value 10 minutes quite straight and confidential talk with you.

'Let me quite briefly explain my position. For all ordinary purposes, I have done with politics. But the business we have been brought face to face with goes far deeper than ordinary party struggles.

'*I am completely in accord with you about Ulster*, and what I want to know is whether there is not something which men like myself, who disbelieve in mere talk at this juncture, can do to help you.

'I don't think the Government are serious in their advances. I think they are just passing the time. If they are not serious, there must very soon, certainly in less than a year, be what would be technically a "rebellion" in Ulster. It would be a disaster of the first magnitude if that "rebellion", which would really be the uprising of unshakeable principle and devoted patriotism — of loyalty to the Empire and the Flag — were to fail! But it must fail unless we can *paralyse the arm* which might be raised to strike you. How are we to do it? That requires forethought and organization *over here*. You may say "Why can't you make a plan for yourselves? I have surely hay enough on my fork". Quite quite true. And I don't want to waste your time or add to your burdens in any way. Indeed I think people over here had better act, in appearance at any rate, independently of you. But I, for one, can't even make a plan without knowing a little more than I do of the probable course of affairs on your side. And volumes of correspondence, for which you have no time, would not enlighten me as much as a single interview.

'Please realize (1) that I am speaking entirely for myself (2) that this thing *goes very deep with me*. I can honestly say there is nothing I personally desire except *retirement*. I am getting old, I am not very well, and I am dead sick of party politics. But if I can see my way to being of any real use in this matter, no personal consideration shall be allowed to count.'[1]

Carson suggested that Milner should come to Belfast, but Milner declined on the first day of the New Year, saying 'for the moment I think I am of more use here. I have got a little bit of a move on, and I don't want to go away from London more than I absolutely must, till I see that this thing has some momentum of its own'.[2] When the two men met, Milner offered to take Carson's place if the latter should be arrested, which now seemed very probable. Great secrecy was observed about the choice of Milner as leader, for it was vital that Whitehall should not know the name of Carson's substitute.[3]

On 8 January Milner told Leo Amery, his friend and principal lieutenant, 'we have no time to lose in thinking how we are to implement our promise to "support" Ulster in the last resort. We must be getting ready for that detestable contingency, and it must be by doing something over here.' Evidently the something which Milner had in mind was of a revolutionary nature.[4] The actual initiative probably came from Amery, who was then Conservative M.P. for South Birmingham. Amery felt strongly that Bonar Law's reiterated declaration that the Conservatives would go to any lengths to support Ulster meant little, unless there was something more behind it than mere political demonstrations.[5]

He had discovered the existence of the British League for the Support of Ulster and the Union, and had got in touch with it. By the beginning of 1914 the League had enrolled 10,000 members, 'mostly for the purpose of going over to Ulster to join the volunteers if it came to actual fighting,' but Amery believed this was not likely to have any influence on the result, and in any case, it would only emphasize the purely local aspect of the struggle. 'What was wanted was an organization which would be effective in paralysing the Government's action before it reached Ulster, and which would, above all, be concerned with the defence of the Union, and with Ulster only in so far as coercion of Ulster precipitated that issue.' What Amery proposed was to adapt the Ulster model to British circumstances. A British Covenant widely signed could provide the starting point for an organization which was prepared to go beyond mere political talk. How far would depend on circumstances.[6]

On 10 January he put these ideas, both in a long letter and in conversation, to Milner, who took them up warmly. On the 11th Milner spent the morning in his rooms 'thinking out plans for the support of Ulster' before lunching with Lady Londonderry,[7] and next day he and Amery met the League's committee and persuaded them 'of the necessity of expanding their organization on our lines'. Bonar Law was then consulted and ound to be very sympathetic; he said that he would back the movement, provided that it was kept quite separate from the Conservative Party.[8]

Apart from its open political activity, the British League for the Support of Ulster had from its foundation assisted the U.V.F. by activities of a quasi-military nature. The part played by Colonel Hickman in finding a suitable G.O.C. has already been mentioned. Hickman was also deeply involved in gun-running and in recruiting English officers for the Force. On 29 November 1913 he imprudently announced in public that he was buying rifles for Ulster, and that he had the same day interviewed in London twenty-six officers who wanted to go to Ulster at their own expense and serve without pay. This statement created such a furore that he had later to explain that he meant 'retired officers'.[9]

The kind of support which was offered to the association is well illustrated by a letter which Hickman received as a consequence of this speech, and which he passed on to the Unionist Council in Belfast. It was written on December 4, the day before the publication of the Arms Proclamations, and part of it runs as follows: 'The object of this letter is to suggest to you a means by which the surveillance of the Home Office may be avoided, and of eluding the Customs altogether, in the very probable case of further supplies of arms being interdicted by the Home Office.

'We are the owners of a small salvage steamer . . . and our business is the purchase and salving of wrecks. If you could give us a contract for gun-running we would buy a small wreck on the Ulster coast and another on the English coast. We would be able to hoodwink the authorities who, if any suspicion were aroused, would suppose us to be employed on the wreck or moving from one to the other.

'Arms and ammunition could be ferried to us by night whilst lying at anchor by our English wreck, and ferried again by night to the Ulster coast whilst we were lying at the Ulster wreck.

'This letter you will understand is written in *strict confidence* to you as a man of honour, but in case the matter needs discussion with any of your colleagues, please show it to the department concerned.'[10]

Hickman's volunteers fully intended to go over to Ulster to fight if the worst should come to the worst, and there were some who feared they might fight in England as well. T. M. Healy wrote in January 1914 that the nephew of an English peer had told him 'there would be civil war in England as well as in Ireland, and that Willoughby de Broke and his men would ride up to London and attack Asquith, and that the soldiers would not resist'.[11]

Among the other exponents of direct action was Lord

Winterton, in later times a very popular and much respected Father of the House of Commons, who advertised in the newspapers for a small group of men 'of courage and determination', prepared to 'undertake a desperate task'. From men who had experience of war in South Africa or revolution in South America he formed a commando ready to fight in Ireland if certain circumstances were to arise.[12] No doubt there were similar schemes which have never been disclosed.

What Milner required for his purpose, however, was a larger organization, capable of making a wider appeal to British opinion. Since time was short, he could not afford to spend weeks in setting up an administrative headquarters — he had to act at once. Therefore he turned to the Union Defence League, which had been in existence since 1907 to keep resistance to Home Rule alive. This body, of which Walter Long was President, was ideally suited to Milner's need, for it had years of experience of propaganda work in the constituencies. On 19 February Milner addressed the Council of the Union Defence League, and as a result the staff was placed at his disposal and a special sub-committee was appointed to assist him in his campaign.[13]

Meanwhile Amery had been active. He had spent a weekend at Englemere discussing the proposed Covenant with Lord Roberts and Wilson, and had found the veteran field-marshal eager to support, but, above all, concerned to prevent the coercion of Ulster 'before the Army was dragged in and wrecked in the process'.[14] Next Amery went over to Ulster to consult the leaders there and co-ordinate plans with them.

All was now ready for the launching of the project. Milner's objective was to obtain for the British Covenant a list of impressive names, not closely connected with politics. He began by seeking the support of his friends in the City; then he wrote to the editors of *The Times*, the *Observer*, the *Spectator* and the *Morning Post*, asking them to give the Covenant as much publicity as possible. Amery, a Fellow of All Souls, was sent to Oxford to engage the support of the academic figures. At this stage in the agitation, Milner's only fear was that the politicians might get cold feet. 'It will be a bore', he told Amery, 'if Bonar Law tries to turn the thing down. *But I mean to go on with it.*'[15]

On 3 March the British Covenant appeal appeared in the Press. 'The time is fast approaching', it declared, 'when the

evident intention of the Government to pass the Home Rule Bill
into law, without giving the nation, either by means of a general
election, or a referendum, an opportunity of pronouncing
judgment upon it, would plunge this kingdom into civil turmoil
without parallel in living memory.' The Government having
failed utterly to appreciate the intensity of feeling which their
contemplated action excited among vast numbers of people in
Great Britain, just as they had underestimated the resistance in
Ulster, it was now proposed to test that feeling by inviting
signatures to the following Declaration:

'I . . . of . . . earnestly convinced that the claim of the
Government to carry the Home Rule Bill into law without
submitting it to the judgment of the Nation is contrary to the
spirit of our Constitution, do hereby solemnly declare that if
that Bill is passed I shall hold myself justified in taking or supporting any action that may be effective to prevent it being put
into operation, and more particularly to prevent the armed
forces of the Crown being used to deprive the people of Ulster
of their rights as citizens of the United Kingdom.'

The first signatories included besides Milner, Lord Roberts,
Lord Balfour of Burleigh, the Duke of Portland, Viscount
Halifax, Admiral of the Fleet Sir E. Seymour, Rudyard Kipling,
Sir Edward Elgar, Professors A. V. Dicey and H. Goudy, and
Dr Herbert Warren, the President of Magdalen College,
Oxford.[16]

Encouraged by the public response Milner and his friends
took offices in Victoria Street, and appointed an energetic
secretary, Philip Cambray. Later in the year a magazine called
the *Covenanter* was published to which Milner, Kipling, Amery
and Carson contributed; its motto was 'Put your trust in God
and keep your powder dry'. The work of collecting signatures
throughout the country was undertaken by the Union Defence
League, which estimated that nearly two million people signed
the British Covenant by the end of July 1914, when the lists
had to be closed.[17]

Milner's efforts to support Ulster were not confined, however,
to the launching of a vast agitation. When he wrote to Carson
that their object must be to 'paralyse the arm' raised against
Ulster he was not indulging in a mere flight of metaphor, and
he had secretly taken a number of practical steps to this end.
The first was the creation of a vast fund of money contributed

by his wealthy friends to support the resistance. Documents marked 'very secret' among his papers indicate that Waldorf Astor (the son of an American millionaire) had subscribed his name for £30,000 'subject to certain conditions', and Lord Rothschild, Lord Iveagh, and the Duke of Bedford for £10,000 each.[18] Rudyard Kipling sent Milner £30,000 at the end of March.[19] As we shall see, it is virtually certain that some of this money was used to purchase Crawford's rifles in Hamburg.

The Army was the key to the Ulster situation, and Milner was, in the words of one historian, 'particularly well equipped to interfere with the military arrangements of the country', since he had devoted a good deal of his time to the National Service League and was on friendly terms with many officers including Roberts and Wilson.[20] When all the efforts to force a general election upon the Government had failed, the Unionist leaders turned to consider, as a last desperate measure, the possibility of amending the annual Army Act in the House of Lords so as to ensure that the Army could not be used to coerce Ulster. It was a very dangerous scheme, particularly in view of the increasing menace abroad, and Bonar Law approached it with caution and reluctance.

The Army Act is one of the peculiar safeguards of the British system of government, whereby the whole organization and discipline of the Army depend on the annual approval of Parliament. Its purpose is to prevent the Executive from ever using the Army to deprive the subject of his rights, and since 1689 it has been passed as a matter of form. To interfere with it would be to pull out one of the very cornerstones of the constitution.

Nevertheless in January Bonar Law came to the conclusion that the step would have to be taken, since, serious as it was, it was preferable to civil war. But though Lansdowne and Carson agreed with him, they were anxious to postpone a decision on it for as long as possible, and at a meeting of the Shadow Cabinet on 4 February the matter was delegated to a committee for further consideration. The truth was that Conservative opinion was sharply divided on the question, and most of the back-benchers were opposed to amendment. The editor of *The Times* was surprised to find that Ian Malcolm, the secretary of the Union Defence League, reacted to any mention of it with 'unusual ferocity'. Such considerations explain why Bonar Law eventually dropped the plan in March.[21]

Milner had no misgivings whatsoever about the idea. Having perceived in it the ideal way to 'paralyse the arm', he used all his endeavours to win support for it. On 18 March when he dined with Carson, Dr. Jameson (of the Raid), Wilson, and Sir Charles Hunter, they all agreed that 'the Lords must amend the Army Annual Act'.[22]

On the same day Carson sent Milner a letter from one R. King Stephens, a lawyer familiar with insurance schemes, suggesting that the British Covenanters should establish a guarantee fund for 'officers in the Army who decide to resign rather than violate their consciences'. The value of such a scheme obviously depended on the officers *knowing* that they would be provided for if they resigned over Ulster, and the correspondence implies that Carson was prepared to agree to officers being told this in confidence. Milner and Wilson could be relied upon to see that the word was put around.[23]

Milner had already attempted to influence the attitude of officers in the reserves, and Ian Malcolm had been collecting signatures to the British Covenant from the Territorial Army. Malcolm found that many officers who were sympathetic refused to sign, and he suggested that Lord Roberts should be consulted in order to discover a way of overcoming their objections.[24] Roberts had already drafted a letter for the newspapers, with the approval of Bonar Law and Carson, giving his opinion as to the course all officers should take if the Government ordered them to march on Ulster. 'It is a soldier's duty to obey,' he wrote, 'but if and when Civil War breaks out no ordinary rules will apply. In that case a soldier will reflect that by joining the Army he has not ceased to be a citizen, and if he fights in such a quarrel he will fight on the side he believes to be right.' In the event this letter was never published.[25]

By this time Hickman's volunteers had held a parade in Chelsea, at which there was talk of drilling and arming in the Ulster style. However, the essential difference between British and Ulster Unionism was illustrated by the fact that many of those on parade were Roman Catholics.[26] A few days earlier a meeting was held in London of the Ulster Aid Ambulance Corps. In the previous October, an Ulsterwoman, Miss Constance Bloomfield, had written to the U.V.F. medical board that she proposed to raise an ambulance corps in London, and extending to the provinces if necessary, 'with the intention of coming to the assistance of the sick and wounded in Ulster should there be civil war in Ireland.'[27] The corps now consisted of four companies, each complete in itself with a surgeon in command. At the meeting Lady Londonderry said that there was hardly a Unionist woman in Ulster who was not connected with a base hospital, clearance hospital or volunteer aid detachment.[28]

Nor were such practical expressions of support confined to Britain itself. An Ulster influence was particularly strong in Canada, where there was a long tradition of immigration from the north of Ireland, going back to the eighteenth century. Much of the Scots-Irish population was concentrated in the Province of Ontario, and a series of mass meetings protesting against Home Rule took place in Toronto throughout the spring and summer of 1914. But Orangeism was widespread throughout Canada, and as early as October 1913 the Orange Association of Manitoba was making plans to send a regiment of volunteers to Ulster if hostilities should occur.[29] For some reason Winnipeg was an especially strong centre of Ulster support, and there were scenes of great enthusiasm at anti-Home Rule meetings there.[30] Similar demonstrations were held in Saskatchewan and Alberta, and in Vancouver, British Columbia, 'the extreme of his Majesty's dominion', a crowded assembly organized by the local branch of the Unionist Clubs of Ireland declared: 'we will to the utmost limit support our brother loyalists in their resistance.'[31]

These activities had repercussions in the Canadian Parliament, where the Conservative administration of Sir Robert Borden was accused of taking sides with the Ulster rebels. Was it not true, one member asked, that the Minister of Railways and Canals had attended the presentation of a sword to Carson in London on March 13?[32] And had not the representative for Centre York, a captain in the Canadian militia, cabled to Belfast: 'We are ready, if necessary, to help you with men and money to the last ditch'?[33]

On 20 March the *Montreal Daily Star*, a journal which was believed to be in the Government's confidence, reported that the Minister of Militia and Defence, the colourful Sam Hughes, had informed the Orange organizations that the Canadian Government proposed to take no action to prevent the departure of the first contingent of one thousand picked Orangemen for Belfast in May. Colonel Hughes was obliged to state in the House that he had not sent any cable dealing with the affairs of the Ulstermen, or in relation to anyone leaving Canada for Ireland, but he rather spoiled the effect by adding, 'If any men were leaving Canada for Ireland, they would not see the hedge fence artists that are discussing this question going ....' at which point he was interrupted by shouts of 'order, order'.[34]

In Australia, where the Irish immigrant population was predominantly Catholic, it was assumed that public opinion was generally in favour of Home Rule. The very strength of Nationalist support, however, stimulated the Australian Orangemen into action. The Ulster community included in its ranks one of Australia's wealthiest citizens, Sir Samuel McCaughey, who had emigrated as a youth from Ballymena in Co. Antrim, and was now a millionaire and the owner of vast sheep stations in New South Wales. Sir Samuel was a member of the state legislative council, and in October 1913 reference was made in the federal Parliament to a 'seditious and disloyal message' he had sent to 'Sir Edward Carson and other anarchists in Belfast'.[35] His name appeared on Milner's secret list and now, at the beginning of March 1914, he sent a contribution of £25,000 to the Carson Defence Fund, and thus became one of the principal backers of the gun-running.[36]

In April a huge meeting at Melbourne Town Hall was told that over 100,000 signatures had been obtained for a petition against Home Rule for Ireland and that a list of those prepared to go and fight for Ulster included the names of many men holding rank in the Australian Army and Navy.[37] Less than six months before, the member for Melbourne Ports, evidently no friend of Ulster, had been ruled out of order by the Speaker for asking the Minister of Defence 'if he will give me the use of some of the drill halls in my electorate, and a couple of worn-out generals, so that I may raise a band of loyalists'.[38]

It was the same story, on a smaller scale, in the other Dominions; from Auckland came news that thousands of New Zealanders were rallying to the loyalists' support; in Johannesburg an Ulster committee was formed and plans made for raising volunteers.[39] More surprising, perhaps, was the degree of support in the United States, where thousands of demonstrators flocked to Orange meetings in Chicago, Pittsburg, and Philadelphia. Even in New York, where Irish Catholic opinion was so influential and so bitterly hostile to Britain, plans were made for training a contingent of Ulster volunteers.[40]

While all these reports were comforting to the Unionists, it is difficult to say how much they meant in practical terms. The expatriates' most valuable contribution was probably their financial aid, which was considerable,[41] but the impression was being created of a worldwide campaign on Ulster's behalf, exactly the kind of agitation which Milner had in mind. The juggernaut had begun to roll, and its momentum was increasing.

Before Milner could perfect his plans, however, the Government took the initiative. On the evening of Friday 20 March, while he was dining with Bonar Law and F. E. Smith at Mrs. Bischoffsheim's, Milner heard news so astounding that he could hardly believe it. Almost all the officers of a cavalry brigade in Ireland had resigned. 'We could talk of nothing else the whole evening,' he recorded, 'and made various attempts to elicit further information but without success.'[42]

12

ENTER CONSPIRATORS

When the discussions which Asquith held with Bonar Law and
Carson ended in January, they were followed by new negotiations with Redmond. In these talks the ministers were represented by Birrell and Lloyd George, who now suggested a way
of breaking the deadlock. His plan was that the Government
should propose an amendment to the Home Rule Bill, giving a
separate option to each of the Ulster counties to remain outside
Home Rule for six years, at the end of which time they would
automatically be included unless Parliament should have
decided otherwise in the meantime.

In a memorandum to the Cabinet, a copy of which was given
to Redmond, Lloyd George frankly admitted that the purpose
of this scheme was tactical. Such a proposal, he argued, must
(a) be an offer the rejection of which would put the other side
in the wrong as far as the British public was concerned, and
(b) not involve any alteration in the essential nature of the Bill.
If the Unionists rejected the offer, as they almost certainly
would, it would not be possible for them to justify armed
resistance in the counties, at least for the present. The plan was
very ingenious, but Redmond disliked it, and consented to it
only with reluctance. He also insisted that it should be the last
concession made by the Government.[1]

On 9 March Asquith introduced these proposals in the House,
on the second reading of the Home Rule Bill. Carson rejected
them outright; Ulster, he declared, wanted the question settled
now and forever. 'We do not want sentence of death with a stay
of execution for six years.'[2] While the debate was going on, the
Prime Minister, apparently because of alarming intelligence
from Ulster, appointed a special Cabinet committee to consider the situation and report to him without delay. The

committee consisted of Lord Crewe, a veteran Home Ruler who was now Secretary of State for India, Birrell, Churchill, Seely and Sir John Simon the Attorney General. Crewe, a former Lord Lieutenant of Ireland, was to take the chair, and, as an elder statesman, to exercise a moderating influence on his younger colleagues.

Carson's abrupt rejection of the Government's proposals angered the Cabinet, and especially Churchill and Seely. Both these men, by temperament, would have been happier on the other side, and now that negotiation had failed, they were eager to accept Carson's challenge, and perhaps call his bluff. Lloyd George, who knew considerably less about Ulster than either, clearly believed that a show of force was all that was needed. He may also have thought that it would provoke the U.V.F. into some violent countermove which would cause it to lose sympathy in Britain, and allow the Government to place Ulster under military law before the Home Rule Bill was passed. On 11 March he breakfasted with the Nationalist leaders, Redmond, Dillon, and Devlin. Birrell was also present. We do not know what was discussed; there is, however, no evidence available to connect Lloyd George directly with the decisions now taken by Churchill and Seely.

On 12 March, after a dinner at the Savoy at which he was the guest of honour, Lord Crewe was suddenly taken ill. The illness was temporary, but its timing was important, for it left Churchill and Seely a free hand at the beginning of the committee's deliberations. On the following Saturday, 14 March, Churchill made a very belligerent speech at Bradford, which created a Press sensation. Declaring that there were 'worse things than bloodshed even on an extended scale', he described the Ulster Provisional Government as a 'self-elected body, composed of persons who, to put it plainly, are engaged in a treasonable conspiracy'. Great Britain must not be reduced to the condition of Mexico. If her civil and parliamentary systems were to be brought to the crude challenge of force, he could only say: 'Let us go forward together and put these grave matters to the proof.'

On the same Saturday Lieutenant-General Sir Arthur Paget, Commander-in-Chief of the Forces in Ireland, received a letter from the War Office, warning him that according to reports reaching the Government, attempts might be made in various parts of Ireland 'by evil-disposed persons' to raid government stores of arms and ammunition. He was instructed 'to take special precautions for safeguarding depôts and other places where arms or stores are kept'. From information received, the letter added, Armagh, Omagh, Carrickfergus and Enniskillen were 'insufficiently guarded, being specially liable to attack'.[3]

On Monday 16th Seely himself telegraphed Paget, asking him to report by wire what steps he had taken to carry out his instructions, and summoning him to the War Office at 10.45 a.m. on Wednesday with his 'full plans in detail'.[4] Paget replied: 'Have issued general instructions and taken all available steps. Will send details to-morrow by post.'[5]

But the next day he revealed that he was far from happy about his orders. Some months earlier Brigadier-General Count Gleichen, who commanded the infantry brigade stationed in Ulster, had advised his chief that no more troops should be sent into Ulster, 'for the main object of the Unionist leaders was to preserve order, and the local Ulster Volunteers were not only quite willing but quite capable of putting down every disturbance.'[6] Sir Arthur trusted Gleichen's judgement, and very sensibly he did not want to provoke disorder. Therefore he sent a second telegram to the War Office, stating that for the present he was not moving troops north to protect the four places named in his orders although reinforcements were being kept in readiness.[7]

In the promised letter he was more explicit. Carrickfergus and Enniskillen were being guarded, and steps were being taken to remove reserve arms from Armagh and Omagh. In the present state of the country, however, he thought that the movement of troops 'would create intense excitement in Ulster, and possibly precipitate a crisis. For these reasons', he continued, 'I do not consider myself justified in moving troops at the present time, although I am keeping a sufficient number in readiness to move at short notice in case the situation should develop into a more dangerous state.

'I would, however, point out that there is no intelligence service in this Command, and that all the reliable political information is received by me at second-hand, so that I am placed at a considerable disadvantage in attempting to judge the urgency of the situation and to foresee possible dangers in time to act.[8]

Then, on the evening of that wet, cold St. Patrick's Day, Paget crossed to London. What occurred at the conferences he attended at the War Office on 18 and 19 March can only be deduced from the accounts given later by those present, accounts which must be used with care since the chief object of the writers was to exculpate themselves. On Wednesday morning the Prime Minister presided over a meeting of the Ulster sub-committee, the principal members of the Army Council and Paget. Among 'other officers' present was Major-General Sir Nevil Macready, the son of the famous Irish actor. Macready was Director of Personal Services at the War Office, and his responsibilities included the use of troops in aid of the civil power.[9]

As Macready well knew, the suppression of civil disorder was 'one of the most trying and disagreeable duties a soldier can be called upon to perform'. A general faced with such a situation could be sure of only one thing; whatever he did, he was sure to regret it.[10] Macready had acted with great firmness and tact when he had quelled a disturbance among striking miners at Tonypandy in 1910, but it was an uncomfortable reputation for a soldier to acquire. In the spring of 1914, no one could be in any doubt as to where such special talents might be employed.

The Cabinet committee decided to appoint Macready as General Officer Commanding the Belfast district, superseding Gleichen, and to give him authority over the Belfast police. This was, in effect, to make him a military governor. It also decided to move troops into Ulster. Field-Marshal Sir John French, the C.I.G.S., and Lieutenant-General Sir Spencer Ewart, the Adjutant General, both advised against this, and agreed with Paget who 'took a very serious view' of the consequences. But the ministers argued that the risk of disturbance was not great so long as the U.V.F. were not attacked.[11]

Later the Government was to claim that the decisions of 18 March merely implemented the orders Paget had already received, but this was clearly not so. On Wednesday evening Paget telegraphed to Friend, his Major-General in charge of administration, instructions which went far beyond the protection of the arms depots:

'Bedfords to move to places which have been decided. Battalion of 14th Brigade to go to Newry and Dundalk. Battalion, Victoria Barracks, to go to Holywood with all ammunition and bolts of rifles if unable to move rifles themselves. These movements to be simultaneous if possible and to be complete by dawn Saturday, 21st, with all secrecy.'[12]

As it happened, Gleichen had been inspecting the Bedfordshire Regiment in Mullingar that very morning, and while so engaged had been astonished to receive a warning message that the Carrickfergus garrison was to be strengthened, the gates of all barracks in his command shut, and their guards doubled.[13] At 5 p.m. on Thursday, Major-General Sir Charles Fergusson, who commanded the 5th Division at the Curragh, received these orders in more detail from General Friend. The 1st Battalion of the Bedfordshire Regiment was to travel by rail to Ulster next day: of its four companies one was to go to Omagh, one to Armagh, and two to Enniskillen. This was not in itself inconsistent with the motive of reinforcing the depots, but Fergusson was also ordered to select a battalion of the 14th Infantry Brigade, and send it to Newry and Dundalk, two companies being assigned to each place. In addition the 1st Battalion, Dorset Regiment, was to vacate Victoria Barracks in Belfast and go by road to Holywood. A note added to these orders stated that 'in consequence of later instructions' a company from one of the Dublin battalions, probably the King's Own Yorkshire Light Infantry, would proceed to Carrickfergus from Kingstown.[14]

The barracks at Newry had not been occupied for eight years, and had no army stores; but the town commanded an important railway junction and was the gateway into Ulster. Dundalk was the headquarters of the XXVIII Brigade, R.F.A., and while the Ulster Volunteers had no field guns of their own, it seemed unlikely that they would attack an artillery brigade in order to obtain some. Both towns, besides, lay in Nationalist areas. The withdrawal of a battalion of the Dorset Regiment from Victoria Barracks in Belfast and its transfer to Holywood seemed even more significant. The Victoria Barracks was peculiarly situated, its main entrance being in a short street which was a *cul-de-sac*, and the U.V.F. had seen that in an emergency the exit of troops might be delayed for a time by blocking the street with barbed wire entanglements. Crozier reconnoitred the Barracks one Sunday while the troops were at church, measuring the width of the gates and approaches and selecting suitable positions for machine-guns to cover the exits, but he did his work so thoroughly that he aroused the suspicion of the guard.[15]

This incident may well have alerted Gleichen, who foresaw that if there was trouble in Belfast, the U.V.F. 'could paralyse the action of my troops by blockading the exits from the barracks and streets leading thereto with a silent and solid mass of armed men'. Such a situation would place the military in an intolerable dilemma; either to acquiesce passively or to shoot their way out and so precipitate civil war.[16]

The decision to evacuate Victoria Barracks has been treated with scorn by some writers, who point out that the Dorsets were far more vulnerable as they marched through an intensely Orange sector of Belfast with some thirty tons of stores and ammunition than they could ever have been in the Barracks. The order to take only the bolts of the rifles with them has been seen as evidence of a ludicrous panic on the part of the authorities, but, as Sir James Fergusson has clearly established in his book on the Curragh incident, it did not refer to the troops' *own* rifles but to the reserve rifles, for the orders which his father received were quite explicit on this point: the Dorsets were to move by road to Holywood taking with them all small arms ammunition and all reserve rifles. 'If impossible to do this, the bolts of the reserve rifles and all S.A.A. will be taken.'[17] It was therefore a perfectly proper military precaution.

Plainly some kind of trouble was anticipated in Belfast, and the battalion was being stationed outside the city and close to Craigavon, at a place where it was in easy communication with naval vessels in the Lough and with Carrickfergus on the opposite shore.

We must now return to the discussions in London, which continued throughout Thursday morning and afternoon. It was probably on Thursday that Paget had outlined for him the situations with which he might have to deal. They were all formidable, but the most serious was the possibility of 'an organised warlike movement of Ulster Volunteers under their responsible leaders'.[18] Such a movement would have to be met by concentrated force, and he was promised large reinforcements from England if they were needed.

Sir Arthur was far from being reassured. Three points in particular worried him. First, as we have already seen, he

believed that the movement of troops would provoke a disturbance in Ulster. On this he was over-ruled by Seely who
promised him as many troops as he needed 'even to the last
man'. Secondly, he was afraid that the employees of the Great
Northern Railway might refuse to transport his troops northward. Though it seemed exaggerated at the time, this fear was
not without grounds, for the U.V.F. had already drawn up
detailed plans for the disruption of road and railway communications in the event of an emergency, and the manager of the
Great Northern Railway, a Mr. Bagwell, was working in close
liaison with Spender, who had charge of the U.V.F. transport
and communications.[19] To meet this difficulty Churchill
immediately undertook to provide naval vessels to carry troops
to Carrickfergus and Dundalk if necessary.

Paget's third point was the most serious. What if some of his
officers, whose sympathies, like his own, lay with Ulster, should
object to taking part in active operations against the U.V.F.?
He finally elicited from Seely two principles on which to act.
First, that officers ordered to act in support of the civil power
should not be permitted to resign their commissions; if they
refused to obey orders they must be dismissed from the Army.
Secondly, that indulgence might be shown, if specifically
requested, to officers whose homes were in Ulster.[20]

While Seely was thus defining the situation for Paget,
Churchill, with characteristic energy, was already carrying out
his part of the bargain. From just before two o'clock that afternoon a spate of orders had been going out from the Admiralty.
H.M.S. *Attentive* and H.M.S. *Pathfinder*, two light cruisers lying
in Bantry Bay, were to proceed to Kingston, to arrive by noon
on the 20th. The instructions to the captain of the *Attentive*
showed that the ships were not only to act as transports, but to
support the troops if necessary. He was to embark one company
of the Bedfords* (*sic*), one half in each ship, and proceed to
Belfast Lough so as to arrive off Carrickfergus at daybreak on
Saturday, 21 March. 'The troops are to be landed at once,' his
orders continued, 'you should then take *Attentive* to Bangor,
County Down, land yourself in plain clothes, and proceed to
Holywood Barracks and interview General Sir Nevil Macready
as to co-operation with the military in certain eventualities.' He

* This was a particularly confusing error, as in fact it was a company of
the King's Own Yorkshire Light Infantry which was to be embarked.

was to comply with requests made 'so far as practicable without landing men'.

Meanwhile, the captain of *Pathfinder* was to arrange with the senior military officer in Carrickfergus Castle for guarding the ammunition and stores there. The Castle was to be defended against attack by every means, and if the co-operation of the Navy was necessary, 'by guns and searchlights from the ship'.[21]

At Portsmouth the captain of H.M.S. *Gibraltar* was ordered to sail to Kingstown, with H.M.S. *Royal Arthur*, and be prepared to embark 275 infantry in each ship, and convey them to Dundalk.[22]

So much for the transport of troops, but this was not all. The Admiralty, like the War Office, had a wider plan afoot. On Thursday afternoon the Third Battle Squadron, consisting of eight battleships, was lying in Arosa Bay in north-western Spain, when its commander, Vice-Admiral Sir Lewis Bayly, received the following orders:

'Send *Britannia* to Gibraltar and proceed at once with remainder of squadron at ordinary speed to Lamlash. After clearing Ushant, you are yourself to proceed in your flagship to Plymouth, handing over command of squadron temporarily to the Rear-Admiral. From Plymouth you are to come to London and report yourself at the Admiralty, subsequently rejoining the squadron overland at Lamlash, whither your flagship is to proceed in the interval . . . .'[23]

At the same time the Commander-in-Chief of the Home Fleet at Plymouth was ordered to send eight destroyers to join the squadron at Lamlash on Monday, 23 March.[24] These destroyers did not leave Southampton Water until 7.30 p.m. on Saturday. He was also to dispatch yet another destroyer, the *Firedrake*, 'for the purpose of embarking the General Officer Commanding-in-Chief, if necessary.' She was to arrive at Kingstown on Friday evening and her captain was to report himself at the Royal Hospital (Paget's headquarters) in plain clothes.[25]

These preparations suggested an operation far more ambitious than the mere safe-guarding of the depots against the U.V.F. or other 'evil-disposed persons'. At least two battalions of infantry were to be moved to Ulster, the garrisons of Enniskillen, Omagh, Armagh, and Newry, encircling the main area of U.V.F. activity, were to be reinforced, and the strongholds of

Carrickfergus and Holywood, on either side of Belfast Lough, were to be made secure. A squadron of warships was being assembled at Lamlash in the Firth of Clyde, sixty miles from the Antrim coast, and the Navy had been ordered to support the Army, if necessary, 'with guns and searchlights'. General Macready, an officer who was known to be unsympathetic to the Ulster movement, had been appointed Military Governor of Belfast in all but name. Zero hour for the operation, whatever form it might take, was to be daybreak on Saturday 21st.

The prospects conjured up by these sinister orders gained so great a hold upon the mind of Sir Arthur Paget that they caused him during the next two days to lose his grasp of the real situation. He had after all (and this is the most astonishing feature of the whole affair) received *no written orders of any kind*. On Thursday he believed that he understood his instructions perfectly, but when he came to explain them to his officers next day he was not so sure.

Unfortunately Paget was the last person to be relied upon for discretion if anything did go wrong. A grandson of the famous Marquess of Anglesey who, as Lord Uxbridge, had lost a leg at the Battle of Waterloo, he had been a Page of Honour to Queen Victoria and a close friend of Edward VII, but his military career had been chequered, for he devoted more time to racing, hunting, golf, and botany than he did to soldiering, and an incident during the South African war had already shown that, despite his debonair manner, he was liable to lose his head in a situation which called for tact and self-control. Whatever his faults, however, two things ought to be said in his defence: that he took the blame for subsequent events entirely on his own shoulders, and that his original advice (i.e. that it would be unwise to order troops to Ulster) was not proved wrong, though this was conveniently overlooked.

The storm which burst over the United Kingdom that week-end had its still centre, appropriately, at Belfast. This steadiness was partly explained by the excellence of U.V.F. discipline, but even more by the strange fact that the Headquarters Staff were the only people outside the War Office who knew exactly what was going on. The source of their information was Wilson.

After lunch on Wednesday French had confided to Wilson all the decisions taken that morning, with the grumble that the politicians intended 'scattering troops all over Ulster as though

it was a Pontypool coal strike'. He had tried to convince them
that this was opposed to all true strategy, but they had replied
that the political situation demanded dispersion; as far as he
could judge, the Government was determined to see the thing
through. Wilson thought the whole business a 'nightmare'.
That evening he dined with Lord Milner, Dr. Jameson, and
Carson, and presumably told them all he knew of the Government's plans.[26]

There can be little doubt that what was said at the dinner
table determined the content of Carson's speech in the Commons next day, when Bonar Law moved the vote of censure,
warning the ministers that 'soldiers are citizens like the rest of
us'. Asquith replied, in his usual careful and moderate way, and
then the Speaker called on Carson. He had not been well, and
when he rose to speak his face was pale and his manner subdued.
But any relief felt on the Front Bench was short-lived, for this
was a familiar prelude to Carson's best courtroom manner. He
began by observing that, after listening to the Prime Minister,
he felt that he ought not to be in the House but in Belfast.
Someone shouted: 'With your sword drawn?'* His fist came
down on the brass-bound boxes before him. 'If this is to be the
last word of the Government, what more have we to do here?'
he asked. 'Let the Government come and try conclusions with
us in Ulster. Ulster is on the best of terms with the Army. It is
the only part of Ireland of which that can be said.'

His accusing finger raked the Front Bench. 'Having been all
this time a Government of cowards, they are going to entrench
themselves behind his Majesty's troops. They have been
discussing over at the War Office in the last two days how many
men they require and where they should mobilize.' One can
only guess what the ministers still in the House were thinking;
Seely had already gone back to the War Office conference.
'They have all this time been manoeuvring for position',
Carson continued, 'the First Lord said on Saturday that he
would manoeuvre, if it came to an outbreak, for a good political
position, and that they would rather have a soldier shot than a
poor Protestant working man. This has always been the policy
of the Government — if they could only get an outbreak, if
they could only get an attack made, so that they could have a

* This was an allusion to the presentation of a sword and an illuminated
book to Carson on 13 March by the British Covenanters. (Colvin, ii, 305.)

good pretext for putting them down. I should like to say this to them — Gamble in whatever else you like — but don't. . . .' The rest of the sentence was drowned in Opposition cheers.

When Carson had finished Devlin taunted him as 'a young lawyer who deserted Home Rule and Liberalism when he saw a chance of bettering his fortunes'. 'The observation of the hon. member is an infamous lie,' Carson retorted, 'and he knows it.' Immediately there was uproar in the House, and the Speaker said that he would see that however strong his feelings, he had used an expression that was unparliamentary. Carson withdrew 'infamous lie' and substituted 'wilful falsehood'. Then he left the House by the door behind the Speaker's chair, to deafening Opposition cheers. As he reached the chair he paused, raised his hand in acknowledgement, and, in a moment of expectant silence, muttered 'I am off to Belfast'. The time was 5.15 p.m. At 5.55 he boarded the boat train at Euston, telling the *Daily Express* reporter: 'I go to my people.'[27]

The rumours which had been circulating in London all week now seemed to gather substance. It was widely believed that McKenna, the Home Secretary, wanted warrants prepared for the arrest of the Ulster leaders, but that Asquith, supported by Crewe and Grey, was opposed to the step. No proof that such warrants existed has ever come to light, but there is a good deal of circumstantial evidence relating to them.

According to one account, an Ulster lady who was the wife of a high official called at 5 Eaton Place and informed Carson and Craig that large-scale arrests, in which they were to be included, would be made in Ulster. Craig thereupon decided to go to Belfast at once. Carson wanted to come with him but was persuaded by Bonar Law to remain for the vote of censure.[28] Whether this is correct or not, it is clear that Craig suddenly decided on Wednesday to return to Belfast, that he had reliable information which caused him to believe that the arrests were imminent, and that he had warned the U.V.F. Headquarters to this effect.

Newspaper reports estimated the number of arrests contemplated at from 28 to 200. On 19 March, for example, the *Observer* claimed information that the Government were determined to issue about 200 warrants for the arrest of the leaders in Ulster, but that the warrants were not to be executed by the police until the receipt of a codeword, which was to be changed every Sunday. This rather improbable story receives some confirmation in a reminiscence of Spender, who says that he was woken up one morning by a U.V.F. dispatch rider bringing a copy of a code message that was being delivered to the Belfast City Commissioner. His wife and he decoded it; it said that a messenger was being sent over by Holyhead, and that he was to be met by the R.I.C. at Balmoral station, where the train would be stopped, and that the R.I.C. was to be ready for instant action. 'We were fairly certain that this messenger was bringing an order for the arrest of the leaders, which from another source was confirmed with the actual number — 210 I think — who were to be taken.'[29]

On Wednesday Headquarters issued the following directive to all U.V.F. commanders:

'Information has been received that the early arrest of the leaders is probable. As this may affect yourself, please take *immediate* steps to warn your second in command, adjutant, or other officer, whom you desire should act for you in such an unfortunate event, to hold himself in readiness to do so, and you must arrange means whereby communications from Headquarters delivered at your address are at once taken to him.'[30]

On his arrival on Thursday morning Craig went straight to the Old Town Hall. Clearly two tasks were uppermost in his mind; to prepare for the arrests, making it as embarrassing as possible for the authorities to carry them out, and to ensure that the U.V.F. had absolute control of the Protestant population, especially in the city. First a stand-by order went out to the Volunteers: 'The position being now extremely grave, be prepared to MOBILIZE at a moment's notice. Orders will be sent to you in detail if the necessity arises.'[31] At the same time Craig wrote a letter to the Press to urge calm and restraint on the populace 'despite the grave crisis and the outrageous insult to Sir Edward Carson in the House of Commons yesterday, which one and all of us bitterly resent'. The letter ended reassuringly: 'He will be with us to-day.'[32]

Next Craig arranged for the entire Headquarters Staff to move from the Old Town Hall to his residence at Craigavon, where they remained until 4 April. Richardson and Hacket Pain who were attending inspections elsewhere in the Province were warned not to return to the city that night. (Nevertheless they apparently did return.)[33]

During the afternoon Spender telephoned his wife to come at once to the Old Town Hall. When she arrived he told her that 'things were as serious as they could be, that arrests were quite probable and that he had orders not to sleep at home at night'. They decided to seek temporary refuge with friends at Glengormley, on the other side of the city. Mrs. Spender hurried home to pack a few clothes and tell the maids that they were going away for the night; then, half-afraid that she might be stopped and interrogated, she set out for Glengormley. Spender arrived at 7.45 p.m. 'having taken a devious route, and doubled several times in case he was being followed'.[34]

Late that evening Crozier was warned by Colonel Couchman to spend the night at a commercial hotel, where he was to register under the name of Percy. He was also told to muster his Special Service Section, 'as strong as possible' and fully armed at 6 a.m. next morning in order to meet Carson as he came off the Liverpool boat. The warning of three hundred men by word of mouth was not, he recalled, an easy task, and it kept him busy for the rest of the night.[35]

Other units of the Belfast U.V.F. were mobilized in the evening and told off for duty throughout the night. Equipped with bandoliers, haversacks, waterbottles and belts, they were stationed at points in and around the city. The Signalling and Dispatch Rider Corps was kept busy providing rapid communication with every part of Ulster, and despite the treacherous March weather, with rain and sleet, there was an almost total response to the mobilization orders.

As the *Belfast Telegraph* reported next day, extensive preparations had been made 'for certain eventualities', but happily for the peace of the city 'there was no attempt on the part of the authorities to execute warrants if they have them or to make raids for arms and ammunition', and when day broke it was felt that the tension had been somewhat relaxed. 'Only those who are connected with the Volunteer Force', it concluded, 'are aware of the deadly struggle which any hostile move on the part of the authorities would have precipitated last night'.[36]

At first light Spender made his way to the docks on a borrowed bicycle, to find Craig with Richardson and his Staff, two companies of the West Belfast Special Service Force, and an impressive escort of motor-cycle dispatch riders drawn up on the quayside. There was also a considerable force of police standing by, and many men on their way to work had stopped out of curiosity.[37]

Crozier took his orders very seriously; they were, he says, quite clear and definite and he would have carried them out to the letter. If the arrest of Carson had been attempted that morning, he would have 'wiped out the R.I.C.', and the match would have been set to civil war. Couchman had made him responsible for Carson's safety, and his last whispered injunction was: 'Stick to him through thick and thin and damn the consequences.' Fortunately, as Carson came down the gangway, accompanied by Frank Hall the U.V.F. Military Secretary, Crozier received a broad wink from 'a burly police sergeant from Derry' which told him that all was well, and the tension relaxed.[38]

Carson waved to the crowd and climbed into Craig's car; the motor cycles started up and the whole convoy moved off slowly through the streets. When they reached the outskirts of the city Craig signed to Crozier to mount the running board and told him that he was going to dash on to Craigavon unguarded, leaving the escort to follow.

When Crozier and his men arrived they found the house and grounds in possession of 'a motley crowd of volunteers in civilian clothes with bandoliers and rifles', who had been on guard throughout the night. Crozier is quite specific about the source of Craig's 'reliable information' — the news about the warrants for arrest was received 'owing to the breach of trust of an official of Dublin Castle'.[39] Elsewhere he states that Lady Aberdeen, the wife of the Lord Lieutenant of Ireland at that time, told him years later that a warrant for Carson's arrest was actually issued, but that the Government vetoed its execution, largely on the advice of Redmond.[40]

The weary volunteers departed, and the West Belfast men took over. Crozier received orders to place Craigavon in a state of defence, to guard the gates and see that nobody entered the grounds without a pass, and be prepared to stay there while the crisis lasted.

At about the same time General Sir Arthur Paget, in an excited mood, and without having had much sleep, was arriving in Dublin. At 9.30 a.m. he assembled seven of his senior officers and explained matters to them. He began by saying that what followed might seem theatrical, but the situation was very serious. Certain measures were to be taken, and it was conceivable that trouble might result. In his opinion the whole place would be ablaze by next day. He outlined the precautionary moves already made, adding that if trouble did occur such enormous force would be displayed that Ulster would be convinced of the impossibility of resistance.

He then said that the Government buildings in Belfast were to be occupied at daybreak on Saturday 21st. The Government were determined that no aggressive act on their part should begin the conflict; if anyone started fighting it should be the Ulstermen. Should they occupy the buildings first, the Government would have to turn them out and bloodshed would result.

Thus Paget described the measures as an operation of war, saying nothing about the duty of the Army to maintain law and order. He went on to make a blunder of such magnitude that it altered the course of British history. He explained to the six generals and one colonel that he had 'only at a late hour', and with the help of Sir John French, obtained the following concessions from Colonel Seely.

Firstly: Officers actually domiciled in Ulster would be exempted from taking part in any operations that might take place. They would be permitted to 'disappear' (that being the exact phrase used by the War Office), and when all was over would be allowed to resume their places without their career or position being affected.

Secondly: Officers who stated that they were unwilling to serve might tender their resignations, but these could not be accepted. And officers doing so would be forthwith dismissed from the Service.

Any officer present who was not prepared to take his part must come to a decision, and stay away from the second meeting to be held that afternoon. Brigadiers were to put the alternatives before their officers, who must decide before that evening. Turning to Brigadier-General Hubert Gough, who commanded the 3rd Cavalry Brigade, he said that a squadron of cavalry was to be held in readiness to march north next morning if necessary.[41]

When the Commander-in-Chief had finished he asked if anyone had any remarks to make. Only Gough spoke. He was

not a resident of Ulster, but on account of birth and up-
bringing, and many friendships, he did not see how he could
bear arms against the Ulster loyalists, and that if he did take up
arms against them he could never face his friends again. Paget
replied that the domicile condition was to be strictly interpreted, and he warned Gough sternly that he need expect no
mercy from his old friend in the War Office, meaning Sir John
French. 'The only effect of this menace', Gough recorded later,
'was to put all my hackles up at once. Why should I be picked
out to be threatened?'[42]

When he left Paget's office Gough had already made up his
mind that he 'would not go', but he set off at once to carry out
the order he had been given, that is, to put the alternatives
before his officers and obtain their decisions. At that point the
'Curragh Incident' began.

At 2 o'clock in the afternoon Paget held his second meeting,
from which Gough was conspicuously absent, and revealed
more of the plans. Once again he allowed no notes to be taken,
and there is some difference of opinion as to what he did say.
The account written seven days later by General Fergusson,
though obviously toned down, is most likely to be accurate on
essentials, and is here followed.

Fergusson gathered that if there was any disturbance in the
north, the 5th Division supplemented by the 11th Brigade from
Colchester would move to the line of the Boyne. It would be
reinforced by the 1st Division from Aldershot. The 6th Division,
less garrisons necessary for the south, would move to Dublin;
reinforced by the 18th Infantry Brigade from England. Three
infantry battalions from Scotland would land in the north and
would garrison certain points forming a ring round Belfast, i.e.,
Larne — Ballymena — some point west of Belfast — Lisburn
— Holywood — Bangor. Bangor was to be the naval base, and
a naval brigade was to be landed there.

The Commander-in-Chief explained at length that there was
to be no act of aggression. It was hoped that a big demonstration would be sufficient, and all detachments were to be given
orders that there must on no account be conflict with the
opposing side.

The impression left on Fergusson's mind was that the
measures planned were primarily precautionary. His account
continues: 'The occupation of the Government Buildings in

Belfast did not seem to be in any way intended as a provocative measure; the reason explained to us seemed perfectly natural and reasonable. It was conceivable however that some of the Ulster adherents might get out of hand and attack the police, and thus initiate an outbreak, which would entail the adoption of the preliminary measures already decided on, and further movement of troops in support.' Sir Arthur Paget had said more than once: 'They wanted to use the soldiers as bait (i.e., in occupying the Government Buildings in Belfast), but I would not have that, and told them it was a matter for the Civil Power, not for soldiers.'[43]

Meanwhile on Friday the troop movements were going forward as planned. During the afternoon the 1st Battalion of the Duke of Cornwall's Light Infantry was travelling northward by rail. Two companies detrained at Dundalk, the rest went on to Newry. At both places they were given a friendly and even enthusiastic welcome.

The battalion of the Dorset Regiment duly marched out of Victoria Barracks on its way to Holywood, headed by a band and accompanied by guns and supply wagons. The progress of the column was closely watched by U.V.F. scouts, and when it entered the Old Holywood Road at Gelston's Corner, a cyclist pedalled furiously ahead to Craigavon, where the U.V.F. guard turned out and presented arms as the troops came by. Their C.O. was, as it happened, distantly related to Spender, who was full of curiosity to see how he would react. He was immensely pleased when the officer called the battalion to attention and himself saluted the guard. Each company commander saluted and gave 'eyes right' as he passed.[44]

In Belfast an atmosphere of tension persisted throughout the day. The movement of the Dorsets caused a great deal of speculation and the wildest rumours were flying about, the most popular being that the troops in Victoria Barracks had mutinied. From Craigavon, Carson wrote to Bonar Law. 'I found Belfast and surroundings very excited. The Government have been moving troops and police all day through the province and from the south. I imagine that it is a scare on their part and that they were under the impression our people were going to take action — or it may be they desire to provoke an outbreak. . . . This place is an armed camp.'[45]

By this time Crozier had made certain that the arrest of the leaders would require a full-scale military operation, and for the next few days Craigavon was virtually in a state of siege. Each entrance gate was guarded by volunteers who could communicate with the house by field-telephone, and who allowed no one to enter unless he could prove his identity and give the password, which was changed every twenty four hours. Armed pickets patrolled the grounds night and day.

Press reporters, photographers and cinematographers were warned that they would not be admitted to the grounds without a special pass from the Military Secretary who remained on duty at the Old Town Hall.[46] Nevertheless Carson gave a great many interviews during the week which followed and countless photographs were taken. These appeared not only in the London illustrated papers, but throughout the Dominions and America, and were also reproduced widely in Europe. In Paris, Berlin and Vienna the newspapers printed graphic descriptions of Craigavon and its defenders. A few days later two Russian newspapers were asking Carson to explain the Ulster situation for the benefit of their readers; for once, it seemed, the Czar of Russia had his eye on the *Skibbereen Eagle*, or at least its northern counterpart.[47] In Norway, too, the events in Ulster had reached the papers, and in Bergen an elderly master mariner read them out with disapproval to one of the two foreign gentlemen who proposed to purchase his ship, for a purpose they had not thought fit to reveal to him.[48]

Mrs. Spender, who visited Craigavon during the 'siege', wrote a description of it in her diary. 'There was a tent by each gate, with a number of men on guard, in plain clothes except for putties, bandoliers, and military greatcoats; in a field by the house was a large tent with a small hospital tent beside it. On the big lawn opposite the house was a flagstaff and huge Union Jack, and grouped all over the drive were cameras, waiting to pounce on Sir Edward as soon as he should appear.'

'We went in to tea with Captain and Mrs. Craig, Colonel Hacket Pain, Captain Crozier, Mr. Young and one or two others, and then Sir Edward came in. . . . We talked a little, but he was coughing and looked tired so I wouldn't bother him.'

'The whole house is of course turned upside down. The drawing-room is full of typewriters and women clerks and every other room teems with men in uniform.'[49]

The drawing-room had in fact become the Staff Room, 'with

an enormous map of Ulster showing every unit of the U.V.F.'
The study was occupied by records and more typists, while the
billiard-room was used for the conferences of the leaders. The
permanent house party included Carson, Richardson, Hacket
Pain, Spender, Crozier, and McCammon, but the other leaders
were constantly coming and going throughout the next fortnight. The Craigs' three children with their nurses were sent to
Crawfordsburn, the home of Colonel Sharman Crawford, and
Spender, Crozier and McCammon had to share the empty
nursery. The men slept in the lofts and stables, their messing
being arranged by a firm of caterers who put up the tents in the
grounds.[50]

To this embattled stronghold dispatch riders brought
astounding news early on Friday evening. Strange as it may
seem, the first intimation of events at the Curragh reached
Craigavon before it reached the War Office in London. In her
diary Mrs. Spender recorded that her husband telephoned her
several times during the day 'and in the evening told me of the
resignation of practically all the officers of the cavalry regiments
at the Curragh, which appeared in the papers the next day'.[51]
Crozier reveals that they received this intelligence from the
Curragh by motor-cyclists, 'who carried news emanating from
reliable sources, gathered and collated at the Sandes Soldiers'
Home.'[52]

Despite this cheering report the nerves of the U.V.F. leaders
were on the stretch as night fell. The evidence suggests they
were not aware until afterwards that zero hour had been fixed
for daybreak on Saturday, but they knew that the police had
received special instructions by telegram from Dublin and
assumed that an attempt would be made to effect the arrests
that night. Once again there was partial mobilization of the
volunteers in Belfast, carried out with more than usual secrecy,
and strong U.V.F. pickets patrolled the road leading to
Craigavon. The police were out in force in the same area, which
was far from reassuring. In country districts also there was
widespread U.V.F. activity, and light sleepers were disturbed
by dispatch riders going and coming throughout the night. In
the west the whole of Tyrone Regiment was mobilized, involving
a total of 7,500 men.

The phlegmatic Craig retired to bed about midnight, only
to be wakened at 2 a.m. by his butler knocking on the bedroom

door. 'I expect', he told his wife, 'that is to say that the police are trying to get in with warrants for our arrest.'[53] It turned out, however, not to be the police at the gates, but Colonel Chichester, who was in command of the East Belfast U.V.F. patrolling near the house. He had come to report that some time after midnight, when the police and volunteer patrols were keeping a wary eye on each other, he had chanced to meet Mr. Smith, the City Commissioner, who was inspecting his posts.

'Don't you think', said the policeman, 'that we might all go to bed?'

'No,' Colonel Chichester replied, 'I don't think we can, because we happen to know that you have a certain telegram — and it is upon that information that we are out.'

Whereupon the commissioner laughed and took the decoded telegram out of his pocket. 'Here it is,' he said, 'read it for yourself. There's nothing in it.' Chichester took the piece of paper and read: 'Expect important document tomorrow morning.'[54] This was apparently the only instruction which the police had received, and Chichester hurried at once to Craigavon with this valuable piece of intelligence.*

The night wore on, with the police and U.V.F. pickets, like the rival armies at Agincourt, receiving the secret whispers of each other's watch. From time to time shadowy movements were executed, as if to prepare for some positive action which never developed. 'To-night,' wrote the *Daily Express* reporter on the spot, 'there is a watching Covenanter in every church tower in Ulster, ready to sound the tocsin that will . . . bring the citizen army into being. When two rocket bombs are fired over the Old Town Hall . . . it will be too late to talk of compromise, for at the signal Ulster will go to arms.'[55]

The tocsin did not sound, and as the hours passed the tension relaxed. Then just at dawn there was a sudden thrill of alarm as the watching eyes picked out two warships coming up fast at the entrance to Belfast Lough.

---

* Several writers state that this encounter enabled the U.V.F. for the first time to break the Government cipher, since they had copies of every official telegram supplied by their agents in the Post Office, and that Smith blundered in allowing Chichester to see the message *en clair*. But Lady Spender remembers deciphering police messages for long before this 'behind locked doors in the Old Town Hall', both in simple substitution codes and in more complicated ciphers.

13

PLOT AND COUNTERPLOT

The two cruisers, *Attentive* and *Pathfinder*, were making for Carrickfergus, where according to plan they disembarked a company of the Yorkshire Light Infantry at the very foot of the castle walls. The *Attentive* left at once and crossed the Lough to Bangor. Her commander went ashore in plain clothes and reported to the Admiralty that all was going well.

To the First Lord, if he ever saw it, this message must have savoured of irony, for by that time 'daybreak on March 21' had already taken its place among the non-events of Irish history. At some time between Friday evening and first light on Saturday the plan to coerce Ulster by military force had simply ceased to be on the cards.

The decision of the cavalry officers was in itself enough to bring the whole operation crashing to a halt. The first ominous news from the Curragh had reached the War Office at seven o'clock on Friday evening in a telegram from Paget: 'Officer commanding 5th Lancers states that all officers except two, and one doubtful, are resigning their commissions today. I much fear same conditions in the 16th Lancers. Fear men will refuse to move.'[1]

About the same time the first *frisson* of trouble reached the sensitive antennae of Fleet Street. An Exchange Telegraph message reported that the Curragh had received an intimation that any officers not prepared to serve against Ulster must immediately send in their resignations, and it was thought that about a hundred officers had sent in their papers. The story was not at first believed, but it strengthened in the later editions. Dublin correspondents, pressed for hard news, telephoned in every scrap of information they could lay hands on, noting the doubling of sentries, the issue of ammunition and movement of naval vessels.

At the War Office Colonel Seely was working late, one of his tasks being to draft a statement to quiet public fears about the troop movements. It was not until 11.00 p.m. that he sent Paget's message on to the Prime Minister, and he was still working on the reply to it when Paget's second telegram arrived. It said: 'Regret to report Brigadier and 57 officers, 3rd Cavalry Brigade, prefer to accept dismissal if ordered north.'[2]

In other ways, too, the scheme had gone slowly but surely awry. French and Wilson had conveniently decided that active operations against Ulster must be regarded as 'home defence', and therefore technically the responsibility of Major-General Sir William Robertson, the Director of Military Training. 'Wully' Robertson was not a man to shirk responsibility, but his mind was of a very practical turn, and he immediately asked a series of obvious but devastating questions. 'Are we supposed to be going to war with Ulster; that is, will the troops be on "active service"? If we are not going to war what are we going to do, as the case is obviously not one of suppressing civil disorder, because there is no disorder at present? If we are going to war, is mobilization to be ordered, and what ammunition, supplies, and transport are the troops to take? What instructions are to be given to the general in command regarding the nature and object of his mission?'[3]

Robertson had no doubt whatsoever that the Government intended to use troops to coerce Ulster, but that they had given no consideration at all to 'its practical side'. He consoled himself with the thought that an operation which had not been planned was in little danger of being executed. His questions remained unanswered when the news from the Curragh arrived.

For the second time illness became a factor in the crisis. On Friday Sir Nevil Macready, the secretly-appointed Military Governor of Belfast, was indisposed, and Paget was asked to arrange for some other officer to represent him in the meantime, since Birrell had already told the Belfast police to take instructions from the officer appointed G.O.C. there. Paget was placed in a difficulty. Gleichen was a Brigadier-General and could scarcely have a junior officer put over his head, so Paget had to nominate Major-General Friend, his own second-in-command. He could ill afford to be without him in this crisis: moreover as he had not been told exactly what Macready was supposed to do, his instructions to Friend were necessarily somewhat vague.

Gough had called on Friend in the course of that eventful afternoon, and told him of his decision to resign. Friend was very distressed and asked him if he could not consider the operation as one designed to maintain law and order. Gough said 'No'. They then discussed Gough's position and Friend's only hope was that if there were enough resignations, the government might be forced to change its policy. 'I have not got a very pleasant job either,' he added, 'I have to go to Belfast to-night as Military Governor.'[4]

He left Amiens Street Station at 6.00 p.m. and was met in Belfast at 9.00 p.m. by Gleichen, who was desperately curious to know what was going on. Friend told him about the troop movements already undertaken, and also that the Government intended to send the 1st Division, the 18th and 11th Brigades and three battalions from Scotland to Larne. There would be a big movement on next day and the whole country would be ablaze.[5]

Finally, about midnight on Friday, Asquith suddenly realised that his ministers were going beyond the measures he had sanctioned. Because of pressure of work he had been present only at the opening of the War Office discussions on 18 and 19 March. Seely now had to break to him the news of the grave situation at the Curragh. In the early hours of Saturday the Prime Minister also had a short, and no doubt sharp, discussion with the First Lord. Learning for the first time of the dispatch of the 3rd Battle Squadron to Lamlash, he immediately ordered its cancellation. The warships, which were then off the Scillies, were ordered to join the Channel Fleet. At the same time Churchill signalled the eight destroyers to return at once to Southampton. Apparently he omitted to tell the Prime Minister about *them* for Asquith later said in the House, with patent surprise, 'I know nothing about eight destroyers'.[6]

Belfast, unconscious of the fate it had so narrowly missed, awoke and went to work. As if to celebrate its deliverance the cold spring weather had given way to glorious sunshine. Mrs. Spender, going into town to shop, was disturbed to see the two warships lying in the Lough, 'a most strange sight'. But the city was calm, 'except that the streets were fuller than usual and there was a tendency among people to gather in knots, especially near the Ulster Club and the newspaper offices.'[7] The cavalry resignations made sensational headlines in the morning editions.

Gleichen inspected the troops at Carrickfergus; General Friend reported to the War Office, 'All quiet Belfast. Have arrived at Holywood Barracks'. Friend's position was a very difficult one. All the troops in the vicinity of Belfast, two warships and their personnel, and the Belfast police, had been placed at his disposal. But what orders was he supposed to give them? Against his force of 'about 1,000 soldiers, 100 sailors armed with rifles and twenty with cutlasses, and the police' the U.V.F. could mobilize (so Gleichen informed him) upwards of 23,000 men.

Only Macready, who was to have come direct from the War Office, knew the plan of action, if one existed. Friend therefore sent for the Commissioner of Police and asked him what orders he had received and if he intended to occupy the Post Office, Custom House and other Government buildings. Smith looked astounded and said that he had no instructions to take any such action.

Unlike his chief, Friend was a very sensible and level-headed soldier. He decided to make a show of activity, without taking any step which was irrevocable. He drew up the boundaries of the Belfast district and chose his headquarters. He nominated Gleichen O.C. Military Forces, the captain of the *Attentive* O.C. Naval Forces and the Commissioner as O.C. Police. Then, to quote his own words, he 'sat tight'.[8]

Meanwhile the soldiers and sailors were given a very cordial welcome by the local inhabitants. Parties of soldiers were seen out walking on the country roads, while the signallers of the warships engaged in friendly practice with the U.V.F. An English woman living in Carrickfergus wrote to the Captain of the *Pathfinder* 'I am asking you as a Christian not to fire on us who are only defending our rights'.[9]

The only people dissatisfied were the war correspondents from Britain and the Continent who, in the mysterious way of their calling, had assembled overnight in Belfast. Greatly disappointed by the turn of events, they spent their time taking taxi rides out to Carrickfergus and Craigavon. Four of them drove to Holywood to follow up a hopeful rumour that the Dorsets had mutinied and 'thrown in their lot with the army of rebellion'. They managed to interview Gleichen, who told them, 'You will be rendering the whole Army a great service if you will contradict this ridiculous rumour'. As a hotel porter remarked sourly to the *Daily News* man, 'There'll be no trouble unless you war correspondents start it'.[10]

The real story of the day, could they but have known it, was to be found at Craigavon, whither the U.V.F. regimental commanders and their adjutants had secretly been summoned at noon to hear Carson's views on the situation.[11] Crozier gives us a vignette of some of the figures grouped round the table in the billiard room, 'the efficient if verbose Captain Ricardo (later a brigadier in France), the child-like but polite Smylie, once a lancer and now a lost politician, Charles Craig, soldier-like although a civilian and practical though a member of Parliament, Bob Wallace of the Orangemen, a typical Harrovian of the jovial school'.[12]

It would seem that Carson emphasized the continuing gravity of the crisis. Although they could not but be pleased with the turn which events were taking, the real test still lay ahead with the passing of the Home Rule Bill, and he pointed out 'the possibility of greater military effort and sacrifice being required from Ulster in the near future'. Then he asked the officers for their opinions.

'A youthful-looking, clean-cut fellow with fair moustache and seductive manners', whom Crozier did not then recognize, was the first to speak. He was in fact Major Robert McCalmont, commander of the Central Antrim Regiment, who had succeeded his father as M.P. for East Antrim in 1913, and he took the chance 'to rub in certain hard indisputable military facts, which carried weight and conviction, owing to the uncompromising and logical manner in which they were presented. In effect he said the men of Ulster were being asked to give everything for the defence of their land and were being "let down", because, although the leaders were telling the world they were armed and would fight to the bitter end, as they undoubtedly would, still they were not supplying the rank and file with the necessary arms and ammunitions with which to fight'.

McCalmont's speech, which Crozier took to be a direct accusation of breach of faith on the part of those responsible for the direction of affairs in the U.V.F., burst like 'a bombshell in the midst of a mother's meeting'.[13] As we have already seen, the

Antrim regiments had been putting pressure on the political leaders to do something about the arms shortage ever since the beginning of the year, and the applause which greeted McCalmont's words showed that the other counties were equally resentful.

Unfortunately, Crozier does not tell us what Carson replied, or how he handled the situation. He could not tell them that in Hamburg the purchase of the guns had just been completed, nor that within a few days Crawford would be returning for his final instructions.

It is clear, however, that the crisis forced both the political and the military leaders to consider what action would have to be taken when the Provisional Government was declared. This was a problem which Carson had put off for as long as possible because he hoped that the contingency would not in fact arise. For all his determination in public to fight to the last ditch, Carson knew better than any of the others exactly what this would mean. He knew that, if it came to a collision between the Army and Ulster, the U.V.F. would quickly be overwhelmed, though there would be fearful bloodshed, for which he would be held responsible. He knew that if the Provisional Government were set up, Ulster could be reduced by blockade and economic sanctions. Finally he knew that the worst calamity of all would be civil war between the Unionist and Nationalist population, with the crown forces having to intervene to restore order.

Carson realized that the only worthwhile victories were political ones, and his acute intelligence was soon at work to make the best possible use of the Government's 'plot against Ulster' and the Curragh incident. The soldiers, however, did not see things in the same light; they wanted precise dates and definite orders, and so in the deliberations of that Saturday, and of the week that followed, the outlines emerged of the plan to seize control of Ulster as soon as Home Rule came into effect.

While he carried out the ordinary military routine at Craig-avon, Crozier discovered that his precise duty began 'to emerge from a sea of uncertainty', and conversations with the leaders and the county commanders helped to clarify it. In their heart of hearts the Ulster leaders accepted that Home Rule was inevitable, and that all they could hope for was some form of exclusion or local autonomy for Ulster.

If, and when, the Provisional Government was announced,

General Richardson would be responsible for the police and the maintenance of law and order. Crozier was to be the chief executive officer for this purpose in Belfast, and his West Belfast Special Force, which had shown such excellent discipline and attention to duty at Craigavon, was to ensure the safety of life and property in all parts of the city, including the Nationalist areas. 'Martial law seemed to be the answer', and Crozier was asked to prepare a plan for 'the performance of the police function and the defence of the capital of the State, without regard to creed or politics'. This plan would be put into force with the proclamation. Crozier was satisfied that the Army stationed in Belfast was, on the whole, sympathetically inclined to them, 'while the Protestant portion of the police could be relied upon to surrender their barracks and submit'. The whole question of arresting and disarming the R.I.C. was discussed at the meeting on 21 March.[14]

During these discussions Richardson and Hacket Pain may have felt that they were getting into deep and dangerous waters. Crozier, writing nearly twenty years later, makes a harsh judgement of them at this period, declaring that 'if the U.V.F. military hierarchy (at the very top) had had a little of the tenacity, courage and acumen of the two political leaders things might have been better'. He continues: 'As it was, saved by their chief "Q" man, Captain W. Spender . . . they lived in daily dread of arrest, forfeiture of pensions or assassination.'[15] But, while Richardson was certainly uneasy at the trend which events were taking, there is no other evidence to suggest he had 'cold feet', and it must be remembered that Crozier was writing at a time when he was very disillusioned with military leaders in general.*

Meanwhile the day on which Ulster was to have been in a blaze passed quietly amid rumour and speculation. For the moment the crisis had shifted to London, and it was expected that a few heads might roll in Whitehall. The province remained calm; the Nationalists made no move, and the Unionists, though their nerves were on the strain, 'showed the

---

* In 1920 Crozier raised and commanded the Auxiliary Division of the R.I.C., but in February 1921 he resigned over a disagreement with the military authorities in Ireland about the handling of cases of indiscipline among his men. He later became sympathetic to the Republicans, for which apostasy he was, needless to say, never forgiven in Ulster.

tranquillity of well-armed and well-conscienced men.'[16]

On Sunday Carson went to church, followed by the news-paper reporters, to hear a sermon on the text 'Fight the good fight'. The correspondent of the *Vossische Zeitung*, lured from Berlin by messages that 'a bloody conflict was imminent', listened in wonder and remarked afterwards that in Germany the preacher would have been stopped by a police officer in the congregation. When the service was over Carson spoke briefly to the journalists. 'The conclusion I drew from the action of the Government', he told them, 'is that in a fit of panic they have made up their minds to attempt two things — one to intimidate, the other to provoke. They will fail in both.'[17]

In London a very different atmosphere prevailed. During the afternoon the King, whose first intimation of the crisis had been the news in Saturday morning's papers, gave an audience to Asquith in the course of which he suggested that some communication should be made to the Press in order to calm public opinion. Asquith agreed to issue a statement to *The Times*.

Geoffrey Robinson,* the editor of *The Times*, was summoned to No. 10 and made an unobserved entrance by the garden door. He found the Prime Minister 'obviously in a state of considerable agitation — pacing the room in a tight green smoking jacket, and puffing out his cheeks after his manner, while delivering himself of a statement designed, he said, to clear away current misconceptions'. In the evening Robinson returned with the draft for final approval, by which time Asquith was calmer, 'more expansive, and dressed for dinner'.

The statement, which appeared next day, declared first that the movements of troops in Ireland were purely of a pre-cautionary nature; secondly, that the arrest of the Ulster leaders was not contemplated; and thirdly, that no inquisition would be made into the intentions of officers in the event of their being asked to take up arms against Ulster 'if only for the reason that the employment of troops against Ulster is a contingency which the Government hope may never arise'.[18]

There is no need here to re-examine the 'Curragh incident', the facts of which are now well known,[19] but its sequel must briefly be recounted. On Monday at 11 o'clock Brigadier-

---

* He is better known by the name he adopted in 1917 — Geoffrey Dawson.

General Gough and the two cavalry colonels* were summoned to the War Office. Gough, who had breakfasted with Wilson, was resolved that they would not accept any offer of reinstatement without a written guarantee that they would not be called upon to undertake operations against Ulster.

Shortly after 11 a.m. he was shown into a room where he found Sir John French and Sir Spencer Ewart, the Adjutant-General. French said in a very friendly way that there had been a misunderstanding, and that he wanted the three officers to return to their commands. Gough stated his request for a written guarantee from the Army Council that their troops would not be asked to enforce Home Rule on Ulster, and French offered his own verbal assurance to that effect, which Gough, not without embarrassment, declined. French then endeavoured to reason with him, telling him that a written guarantee was out of the question. Without allowing himself to be drawn into argument, Gough politely insisted that he could not return to his command without it.

A long and painful silence followed, during which Gough sat staring at the toe of his boot. Many years afterwards he vividly remembered the strain, and the ticking of the big clock on the mantelpiece: however, the silence was working for him, and he had the coolness to keep his nerve.[20] At last French said to Ewart, 'Well, we can't do anything more for him. You will bear me out that I have done my best for him. He will never know how much I have done for him. Very well, there is nothing for it but to take him before the Secretary of State'.[21]

The three then went down the passage to Seely's room, while French made a final effort to make Gough change his mind. Taking his arm he said 'For God's sake, go back and don't make more difficulties, you don't know how serious all this is. If you don't go back, all the War Office will resign'.[22]

Seely, who was with Paget and another officer, asked them to sit down at the table, indicating which chairs they should occupy. 'As soon as we were seated', Gough recalled, 'Colonel Seely in a very truculent manner turned his eyes on me and attempted to browbeat me and stare me out of countenance. I was not going to allow this, and he eventually dropped his eyes. His manner then altered. From excessive truculence, he went to that of superior wisdom.'[23]

* Colonel Parker (5th Lancers) and Colonel MacEwen (16th Lancers).

The Secretary of State embarked on a long explanation of the relations between the military and the civil power which seemed to Gough to be taken verbatim from the *Manual of Military Law*. He listened carefully, and when Seely paused, made no reply. The interview then followed the same pattern as with French. Seely said that there had been a misunderstanding, and that the proposed movement of troops had been intended entirely to safeguard stores. He insisted that the Government's statement and the Army Council's verbal guarantee ought to be enough, and that Gough should now return to his command. Gough replied that he would gladly return, but that he must have a written assurance.

At this point French intervened to say that perhaps General Gough had not made it quite clear that he would not be able to regain the confidence of his officers unless he could show them the assurance of the Army Council in writing, since so much feeling had been aroused. Gough hastened to thank him, and Seely with obvious relief in his voice, turned to Paget and observed, 'O I see, I think it only a reasonable request,' to which Paget assented. Seely then said that there would be no difficulty in drawing up a satisfactory note, and Gough was told to return for it at 4 p.m. that afternoon.[24]

Ewart drafted the note and it was sent to the Cabinet for approval. Seely had to leave for an audience of the King, and did not see the document until his return, just as the Cabinet was breaking up. He saw at once that it would not satisfy Gough and his officers as it stood, and therefore, with the assistance of Morley, he added two further paragraphs.

'His Majesty's Government must retain their right to use all the forces of the Crown in Ireland, or elsewhere, to maintain law and order and to support the civil power in the ordinary execution of its duty.

But they have no intention whatever of taking advantage of this right to crush political opposition to the policy or principles of the Home Rule Bill.'[25]

When Gough was handed the document by French, he asked for fifteen minutes to consider it. Reluctantly French agreed; he was in a very anxious state and said that the King was waiting to learn if all had been settled. In the waiting-room Gough talked it over with his brother, Brigadier-General John Gough, the two colonels, and Wilson, who had appeared on the scene. Gough was determined to have a guarantee clear beyond any possibility of doubt, and feeling that the phrase 'crush political opposition' was ambiguous, he took a sheet of War Office paper and wrote on it the following words:

'I understand the reading of the last paragraph to be that the troops under our command will not be called upon to enforce the present Home Rule Bill on Ulster, and that we can so assure our officers. H. P. GOUGH.'[26]

Gough returned and read this to French, who said, 'That seems all right'. After a moment or two of reflection he took Gough's paper and wrote at the foot of it:

'This is how I read it. J.F. C.I.G.S.'[27] Gough then departed with his guarantee, French went to Buckingham Palace to tell the King that the Curragh crisis was over, and Wilson, openly boasting that the Army had done what the Opposition had failed to do, spread the news in the War Office.

Later that day, when Asquith received a typewritten copy of the document, he immediately took exception to the addition of the two paragraphs which had not been authorized by the Cabinet. He sent for Seely and asked him for an explanation, only to learn that Gough had already been handed the letter and had taken it back with him to Ireland.[28]

Already a storm had begun in the House of Commons which was to seethe for a month to come. In Unionist eyes Gough and his officers were heroes who had saved Ulster by defeating a sinister and secret conspiracy to overwhelm the U.V.F., and the Opposition now determined to extract the whole truth from the Government.

On Tuesday the Conservative Press was in an exultant mood. The *Pall Mall Gazette* declared that 'the plot engineered, it is generally believed, by Colonel Seely and Mr. Churchill has ended in a fiasco unparalleled in the history of this country'. *The Times* leading article, under the heading 'The Plot that Failed' concluded that there had been 'a deliberate conspiracy to provoke and intimidate Ulster at a moment when the peace of the province was neither broken nor threatened', though it acquitted the Prime Minister and his more responsible colleagues of any effective share in it.

Wednesday was a stormy day in the Commons. The debate was concerned partly with 'the plot that failed' and partly with 'the peccant paragraphs' (as Balfour had happily christened them). Churchill, livid with rage, repudiated the 'hellish insinuation' that the intention had been to provoke bloodshed; Seely gave a rather feeble explanation of the Curragh events, but he 'put on the white sheet' and offered to resign, and the Prime Minister told the House that his resignation would not be accepted. Asquith adroitly disposed of the affair as a 'very moderate and modest operation', stated his belief that there had been an 'honest misapprehension' of what Paget had said to the generals, and announced that the Government could not possibly endorse the guarantee.

Next day he was still determined to write to Gough and repudiate the two paragraphs, but in fact he never went beyond his public disavowal of them, and on reflection he thought it best to allow things to remain as they were. Nevertheless French and Ewart both felt obliged to resign because the Government had repudiated the paper they had signed, and on the following Monday Seely resigned also. This time his resignation was accepted. 'I am satisfied', Asquith wrote to Haldane, 'we could not possibly survive any recognition, express or implied, of the Gough treaty, and it is equally clear that French will not remain except upon that footing . . . I see no way out of the imbroglio but for Seely to go also.'[29] Asquith took over the War Office himself, a move which did have a steadying effect, since the soldiers trusted him.

As for the paper, Gough gave it to his solicitor in Dublin to be kept for his eldest daughter, 'her heirs and successors for ever'. This was a prudent move, for some unofficial attempts were made to induce him to give it up. No application was ever made to the trustee.[30]

The sacrifice of Seely, French, and Ewart, all to save Paget, caused Bonar Law to conclude that the Government had something to conceal. 'What they are concealing we do not know,' he said, 'but we do know they are ashamed of it.' The publication on 25 March of a White Paper containing eight of the relevant documents only served to strengthen this suspicion, and it took the Opposition a month to extract another and much fuller White Paper.

In Ulster there were no doubts about the existence of the 'pogrom plot', as it soon came to be known, and the Ulster Unionist Council initiated its own inquiry into the whole affair. In this task they were able to draw upon the help of the Union

Defence League. On 26 March Walter Long wrote to Carson: 'We are convinced here that (*a*) warrants were signed for the arrest of political people, such as you and me, and (*b*) that a deliberate plan was arrived at to attack Ulster on Saturday last with a considerable force. The news that I cabled you to this effect last week came from an absolutely reliable source and is, I know, trustworthy.'[31]

At the same time the Union Defence League was organizing public support for Ulster on the grand scale. On 3 April Milner reported that signatures to the British Covenant were coming in at the rate of 30,000 a day. Next day he and A. J. Balfour appeared in the unusual role of Hyde Park orators at a vast protest meeting. Fourteen platforms had been erected to form a huge circle between the Serpentine and the Bayswater Road, upon which processions converged from twenty-two separate rendezvous. One column consisted solely of representatives of the City, another of members of the London clubs, 'a sombre but dignified parade of silk hats and black coats'. Bands played patriotic tunes, flags appeared everywhere, and thousands of men, women and children in holiday spirit assembled wearing the little red, white and blue badges inscribed 'Support loyal Ulster'.

At Hyde Park the proceedings began with the singing of 'O God our help in ages past' and the National Anthem. Then the following resolution was put forward: 'We protest against the use of the Army and Navy to drive out by force of arms our fellow subjects in Ireland from their full heritage in the Parliament of the United Kingdom. And we demand that the Government shall immediately submit this grave issue to the people.' Carson, Walter Long, Lord Londonderry, and Austen Chamberlain were among the other speakers.[32]

In Ulster on the same day the Special Force guard was withdrawn from Craigavon, and the Headquarters Staff moved back to the Old Town Hall.[33] It had been a tense and exciting fortnight, and in the course of it Craigavon had received, openly or by stealth, some interesting visitors. The most remarkable was General Macready, who paid a formal call on March 24, arriving unheralded in his car at the front gates, attired in full uniform under the grey overcoat of a Major-General. The sergeant of the guard, an old soldier, therefore received him with ceremony — the gates were thrown back by the sentries, and the guard clattered out of the lodge and presented arms. Macready raised an embarrassed hand to the peak of his gold-edged cap.

When the news of his arrival was telephoned to the house, Carson and Craig were talking to editors and journalists, and Macready was received at the front door by Spender, who found himself in something of a difficulty. He did not want to take Macready into the Staff Room with its map showing the disposition of every U.V.F. unit, nor into the study which was full of typists and records, and in the end he had two chairs brought into the hall. It was an uncomfortable few minutes, for Spender was thinking of their last meeting at the War Office when Macready had given him the Secretary of State's decision about his resignation.[34] They discussed the peculiarities of the Ulster climate, and Spender innocently inquired what he thought of the Ulster roads.[35]

Macready, in his own slightly different account of the visit recalls that 'Mr Craig*... received me in a small ante-room and with much solemnity informed me that Sir Edward Carson would see me directly. I did my best to play up to the evident honour that was being done me; but, unfortunately, for no reason at all, I constantly thought of the Dalai Lama'.[36]

When Carson came in there ensued a brief and guarded conversation in very general terms and then Macready left. His memoirs throw no light on the reason for his visit; it may well be, as Colvin surmises, that its intention was to discover what force would be required to execute warrants of arrest at Craigavon. Certainly no one of lesser rank would have been able to make the reconnaissance.[37]

At last, on 17 April, the Ulster Unionist Council issued to the Press its statement on the events at the Curragh, 'giving the main additional facts which a sworn inquiry would have elicited'. It revealed that Paget had told his generals that some 25,000 troops were to be employed in Ulster, in conjunction with naval operations. The gravity of the plan was revealed by his use of the words 'battles' and 'the enemy'. The cavalry were told that they would only be required to prevent the infantry 'bumping into the enemy'. A military governor of Belfast was to be appointed, and the general purpose of the operations was to

* His memory was at fault, unless Craig joined them while they were waiting for Carson.

blockade Ulster by land and sea, and to provoke the Ulstermen to shed the first blood.[38]

The question of whether there really was a plot to provoke the U.V.F. cannot be answered in the present state of the evidence.[39] Whatever may be said about provocation, there can no longer be any doubt that an operation was planned for the coercion of Ulster, and that it was badly planned. As Gleichen wrote, 'the whole matter was mismanaged from start to finish, and the chaotic bungle that ensued recoiled in entangling folds on the heads of those responsible for it'.[40]

One aspect of the affair which has always puzzled its students is that the Government at no time published any evidence for its fear that 'evil disposed persons' were contemplating a seizure of arms in Ulster. If police reports to this effect existed, why did Asquith not make them public, along with the other relevant documents, when the Government was under severe attack?

We have already seen that U.V.F. plans for the seizure of Ulster by a military *coup* not only *did* exist, but specifically referred to the capture of 'all depots of arms, ammunition and military equipment' and to the capture of artillery by attack 'or else by previous arrangement with the gunners concerned'.* Against this background, U.V.F. reconnaissance of installations, Crozier's activity at the Victoria Barracks and similar incidents would assume an ominous significance.

Much of this reconnaissance was connected with plans for landing arms in one of the Ulster ports, rather than with plans for taking control of the province. There was no reason for Carson to set up his Provisional Government in March, yet the Government acted as if he were about to do so. What other reasons could there be for ordering the Army to seize the key buildings in Belfast? But in fact, as Crozier's account of events at Craigavon curiously demonstrates, the plans for the arms *coup*, described in the next chapter, were not unconnected with those for taking control of the province, and in any case, if there was a clash with the Crown forces, the first event might precipitate the second.

While the uproar in Parliament and in the Press over the Curragh crisis and 'the plot against Ulster' continued throughout April, the Ulster Unionists, with great secrecy and thoroughness, were preparing their own plot against Asquith.

* See p. 127 above.

14

DAYBREAK AT LANGELAND

As soon as Crawford's scheme had been approved in January he had plunged happily into his favourite cloak-and-dagger world of codes and aliases and *poste restante* addresses. For the first few days of February he was disposing of arms and ammunition in England with the help of Major Tristram of Darlington. On the 6th, before leaving for Hamburg, he sent birthday congratulations to Carson. 'I hope before your next birthday you will see Ulster freed from all anxiety for the future, as a result of your labour. I believe now is the time to strike the last great blow; the heavier that blow will be, the better chance of success. But you know my views.' Then he wrote to Richard Cowzer to tell him that his address for the next few days would be 'W. H. Matthews, c/o Benny Spiro, Adolphsbrücke 9–11, Hamburg'.[1]

In Hamburg Crawford found Spiro as always most co-operative. They talked the whole matter over for a few days, and then Spiro made him three offers: first, 20,000 Italian Vetterli rifles for which ammunition could be made to order; secondly, 30,000 Russian rifles and ammunition; thirdly, 15,000 new Austrian and 5,000 German Army rifles, both to take standard Männlicher cartridges.

The Vetterlis were cheap, but further supplies of ammunition could be obtained only from Italy, and Crawford was afraid that the Italian Government might stop selling it. The Russian rifles were single-loaders of obsolete design. Only the third offer appealed to him, for the Austrian guns were up-to-date clip-loaders, which had been standard equipment for the German Army until a short time previously.

Crawford put the three offers before the arms committee, emphasizing the psychological effect of equipping the volunteers with the most modern weapons, which were naturally the most expensive. Craig, however, appreciated the point about morale, and persuaded the committee that Crawford was right. Feeling that some of the members were lukewarm about the whole project, Crawford took the precaution of calling on Carson at Eaton Place to make his position quite clear, before the deal was closed. Once he crossed again to Hamburg there would be no turning back; he would carry out the attempt even if it meant losing his life, and he asked Carson if he was willing to support him to the finish.

Years later Crawford vividly recalled the scene. 'We were alone. Sir Edward was sitting opposite to me. When I had finished his face was stern and grim; and there was a glint in his eye. He rose to his full height, looking me in the eye; he advanced to where I was sitting and stared down at me, and shook his clenched fist in my face, and said in a steady, determined voice, which thrilled me and which I shall never forget: "Crawford, I'll see you through this business, if I should have to go to prison for it." I rose from my chair; I held out my hand and said, "Sir Edward, that is all I want. I leave tonight." '[2]

For the next few weeks Crawford travelled back and forth between Ireland and the Continent, frequently in disguise and always under an assumed name. Spiro would receive cryptic letters from John Washington Graham, or W. H. Matthews, or Robert Smith, about the price of the 'goods' or the reaction of his 'lady costumiers and buyers' to the 'spring fashions'.[3] Spiro's command of commercial English was almost perfect, and in any case much of the correspondence was carried on by Edith Kanzki his very capable and clever secretary, who spoke half a dozen languages. To cover his tracks even further, Crawford often sent his letters to her address at *Poseldorferweg 17*.[4]

Crawford was not an easy man to do business with because he insisted that everything should be done in his way, with precautions which often seemed over-elaborate. But the quiet, slightly-built Spiro was unfailingly courteous and patient, as Crawford was the first to admit, and the two became firm friends.

On 26 February Spiro agreed to sell J. W. Graham 20,000 rifles 'amongst which 11,000 new ones, Steyr make cal. 7·9', and two million rounds of ammunition, for the total sum of £45,640. He estimated that it would cost Crawford a further £5,000 to

buy a steamer and pay for packing and other expenses. The
terms were that Crawford should pay £9,000 down, £15,000
on arrival in England and the rest later.[5] Ultimately the 20,000
rifles were made up of 10,900 brand new Männlicher rifles,
model 1904 with short bayonets, and 9,100 Mauser rifles, model
88 with longer bayonets. Both guns were 7·9 calibre and used
the same ammunition.[6]

Crawford insisted that each rifle should be wrapped up with
one hundred rounds of ammunition, and that five rifles should
be packed together in one parcel, so that they would be easy to
unload, and ready for instant use. The wisdom of this decision
was later proved, but it caused a considerable delay and the
spending of a further £2,000. It also brought into the story a
shipping agent called F. E. Schneider, who was to play an
important part in the whole adventure.

Towards the end of February the packing, which was being
done in barges in the free port, was well under way. The new
rifles arrived in Hamburg from the Steyr works in Austria by a
special freight train of ten wagons, to Crawford's considerable
alarm, but there was no interference by the authorities,
although the police made inquiries whenever he went down to
supervise the packing, and he had to limit his visits to a few
minutes at a time. In addition to the 20,000 rifles and 2,000,000
rounds in clips of five, Crawford also had packed several
thousand Vetterli rifles which Spiro had been holding since the
seizures of 1913, and 1,000,000 rounds of Vetterli ammunition.

In answer to discreet advertisements in several Scandinavian
newspapers Crawford had learned of a suitable ship due in
Bergen on 16 March. Some time before, the Antrim Iron Ore
Steamship Company had released Captain Andrew Agnew and
his chief engineer to assist in the enterprise. Agnew was completely devoted to the Unionist cause and had proved his worth
in earlier gun-running during 1913. He now joined Crawford
in Hamburg and they set out for Bergen, where the S.S. *Fanny*
had just arrived from Newcastle with a cargo of coal. After a
close inspection Agnew and the engineer were satisfied that she
would serve the purpose, and Crawford offered to buy her on
the spot, stipulating only that a few repairs should be carried
out. When the owner hesitated, he was given five minutes to
decide, as there was a Russian ship for sale in Bergen at the
same time. 'We do things in a hurry in the States,' Crawford

told him (he had adopted his American alias), 'I want that boat right now, or I don't want her at all'. The repairs were carried out.

The *Fanny*'s master, Captain Falck,[7] had once owned the ship, but the bank had closed on him and he had been forced to sell her. Crawford liked him and asked him to remain with them and bring his crew, which he at once agreed to do. He also helped them to get round a difficulty. Crawford wanted to sail the *Fanny* under the Norwegian flag, but this could not legally be done unless the owner was Norwegian. So, with the help of his solicitors, Falck mortgaged the ship to Crawford for her full value and became her nominal owner.

Although Spiro and Schneider both strongly advised it, Crawford would not bring the *Fanny* to Hamburg. Instead he arranged that the rifles should be loaded into a sea-going lighter and towed through the Kiel Canal to rendezvous with the *Fanny* near the Island of Langeland in the Baltic, the landlocked and shallow waters of which Falck considered safer for the transfer of cargo. To take the lighter into the North Sea would have meant days of towing in the teeth of March gales if the weather turned bad.[8] Crawford marked the spot on a chart and, telling Agnew to meet him there on Monday 30 March, he returned to Belfast to arrange the final details for the landing.

Arriving in the middle of the crisis week, he went to Craigavon to consult with the leaders and the arms committee. In the circumstances it was not surprising that they were divided in their counsels. One group led by Richardson, Hacket Pain and Alexander McDowell wanted the whole project abandoned, or at the very least postponed indefinitely, but Craig and Carson, now that the guns had been purchased, felt that they ought to wait for at least a few days before making an irrevocable decision, in the hope that the situation would improve. There was disagreement also about the best place for landing the arms. Crawford and Spender had discussed this question for hours, and both maintained that Larne was the only possible harbour. Richardson, however, anticipating that intervention by the authorities was inevitable, preferred Belfast, where the U.V.F. were numerous enough to take temporary control of the port and fend off any action by the police or military. This view found strong support in the committee.

When Crawford left Belfast on 26 March the question was

still unsettled.[9] It was arranged that he should bring the *Fanny* to a rendezvous in one of the Scottish lochs on the west coast and transfer the rifles to one or more steamers which would be waiting for him. He was to take with him a chart, of which Headquarters had a copy, and in consultation with Agnew mark on it with a pin the spot selected; the chart was then to be posted to Belfast. James Cunningham authorized Crawford and Spender to use his London office, and with Cowzer's help they drew up a code in stockbroking phraseology which would enable Crawford to communicate his intentions to Belfast. It was also arranged that if there was a serious change in the situation Crawford was to delay sailing, and instructions to this effect would, if necessary, be cabled to Kiel, where he was to call on 31 March.

Two days later Crawford was in Hamburg. Everyone was now beginning to feel the strain of this clandestine activity. Schneider, who had been on the Bergen trip, was 'worn to a shadow', and for once even Spiro was showing signs of nervousness. Meeting Crawford at the station, he bundled him hastily into a motor car and drove rapidly for about a mile; then they got out, walked through a large office building, and continued the journey in a second car waiting on the other side. All the way Spiro kept looking back to see if they were being followed.

The lighter was already laden, and waiting for the tug. Crawford had intended to travel to Kiel by train next day, accompanied by Schneider, but that evening as the three men and Frau Kanzki were sitting in a restaurant, he had a sudden premonition, and although the lighter was due to sail in half an hour he insisted on going with it that night.[10]

In vain did the Germans try to reason with him. At last Schneider said that he would come too, and they all set off by taxi to Schneider's house to collect his belongings. There his wife, 'a big soft hysterical woman,' insisted on coming down to the docks with them, and when they got there she 'clung on to her thin husband and made a scene'. Frau Kanzki managed to calm her, and 'while they were arguing the question', writes Crawford, 'I got hold of Schneider's arm and took him as fast as we could and disappeared into a labyrinth of railings, old boats, mud banks and dingy buildings'. A last backward glance showed him the two women talking as hard as they were able and Spiro 'listening, apparently wondering'.[11]

After some searching Schneider located the tug, and a sailor guided them on board across a gangway of floating logs. The night was bitterly cold, and they spent it wrapped in overcoats in the tiny cabin of the tug, as she towed the lighter down the Elbe. Dawn found them at the Brunsbüttel Gates of the Canal, where Crawford was thrilled to see the great Hamburg-Amerika liners tying up to give them right of way.

They passed through the Canal without incident, but at Kiel an over-inquisitive official had to be bribed with a 100-mark note before he found their papers in order. At Kiel also some Mexicans came on board while Crawford was ashore and asked if the guns were for Mexico. During the night the lighter cleared the Kiel forts and crossed Kiel Bay; the Baltic was calm, and next morning they sighted the *Fanny* exactly on time and drew alongside her. Crawford instantly disliked the situation, as there were a good many small craft about, and he suggested moving out of territorial waters, but Falck insisted that the Danish authorities would not interfere, and the unloading of the lighter began.

Crawford remained uneasy, and his fears were confirmed when about 2 p.m. a motor launch was seen making straight for them with a uniformed official in the stern. When he came aboard he asked to see the ship's manifest, which described the cargo as 'general' and destined for Iceland.* He departed, obviously suspicious, and returned three hours later with the port officer of Svendborg. This man, who had 'a face like a ferret', went into the hold and fingered the bales in such a way that it was clear he knew what they contained. He said he must

* By the strangest of coincidences, Crawford had sailed into another Home Rule controversy, and one he was quite unaware of, at that time. Iceland's struggle for independence, though not so violent, had much in common with that of Ireland. A groundswell of nationalist feeling had built up in the nineteenth century, and the final phase of the agitation began in 1885 after the King of Denmark had declared that Iceland was inseparable from the Danish realm. In 1903 a limited independence was granted to the Althing (the Icelandic parliament), and the minister for Iceland established his permanent residence in Reykjavik, but the demand for complete autonomy became even more insistent, and in 1914 it was at its height. Iceland finally obtained Home Rule by treaty in 1918, although the connection with Denmark was not finally broken until 1943. It was little wonder that the Svendborg officials took so much interest in the *Fanny*'s cargo, although the innocence with which the destination was stated must have indicated to them that the guns were bound elsewhere.

have the papers of both vessels, but promised to return them at 8 a.m. next morning. Reluctantly Crawford handed them over.

To the end of his long life Crawford shrank from the memory of the hours which followed. He felt himself caught like a rat in a trap. If only the *Fanny* had been taken by a warship, or sunk while resisting capture, things would not have looked so bad, but this was more than he could bear. 'To be brought into a naval base and to lie there while the whole Ulster plot was being unravelled and made known to the world as a ghastly failure, the leaders the laughing stock of the world! The thought of it caused the sweat to pour off me in an agony of remorse and disappointment. I walked up and down the deck tormented by the thought of all those men waiting for me to bring them the weapons with which to fight for their religion, their liberty and all that was dear to them. They trusted me implicitly; they believed in my ability to carry this through. I went into my cabin and threw myself on my knees, and in simple language told God all about it: what this meant to Ulster, that there was nothing sordid in what we desired, that we wanted nothing selfishly. I pointed out all this to God, and thought of the old Psalm, "O God our help in ages past, our hope for years to come".'

He rose comforted, and stoutly believing that God helped only those who helped themselves, he determined not to give up the *Fanny* without a struggle. In the last resort they would put the foreign crew into the lifeboats and fight their way out. The deck hands, who had been following all these developments with interest, now decided that the moment was opportune to strike for more money. They were offered double wages if the work was completed and, with this incentive, they finished the job before midnight.

Schneider sportingly agreed to cut and run with the tug and lighter, on Crawford's promising to pay the fines. He left about 4 a.m., taking with him some letters for Ulster, and the chart on which Agnew had marked a remote loch in the north west of Scotland. Then Crawford turned in for a few hours well-earned sleep.

He awoke at daybreak to find his prayers answered. It was blowing half a gale and a low mist hung over the water. There was no chance of the launch coming out to them in such conditions, but he waited until the agreed hour to 'put the port officials in the wrong'. At 8 o'clock the *Fanny* weighed anchor and moved off into the mist. She was now a ship without papers, and Crawford was anxious to be clear of Danish waters as soon as possible. He was just beginning to feel cheerful again when he heard the engines being reversed and old Falck 'dancing and shouting like a monkey on a stick'. He looked over the side and saw one of the willow wands marking the shallows, and in a moment the night's black horror returned, for if the ship went aground their last state would be worse than their first. But somehow Falck managed to worm the *Fanny* out of the channel, with mud churning up all round her. She crept unseen past the naval base and was swallowed up in the fog of the Kattegat. It was the last day of March, and next morning her escape was to be a topic of conversation at half the breakfast tables of England.

15

THE CRUISE OF THE 'FANNY'

On 1 April *The Times* had the whole story by Press Association telegram from Copenhagen. 'Yesterday morning the German lighter *Karl Kiehn* laden with 300 tons of rifles anchored off Dagelycke. Shortly afterwards the Norwegian steamer *Fanny* arrived, and all day and night men were at work transferring the rifles to the steamer. The harbourmaster detained their papers, but both vessels left this morning in a northerly direction without them.' The Berlin correspondent filled in the details; there were 'two English-speaking persons' on board the steamer, and it was assumed that the rifles were destined for Ulster.

That evening the Hamburg firm of Karl Kiehn, which owned the lighter, published a statement admitting the main facts. It said that the rifles had been properly consigned at Hamburg, and transferred to the *Fanny* in neutral waters; they were going to South America 'like many other cargoes', but beyond chartering the lighter the firm had no concern in the matter.[1]

It may be imagined with what emotions this news was received at Craigavon — the arms plan was a secret so well guarded that there is no reference to the *Fanny*'s arrest in correspondence or official orders, but it was undoubtedly the subject of those earnest consultations which Carson and Craig held in the billiard-room with Richardson, Spender, and members of the arms committee. Now was the time for 'the croakers' (as Crawford described those who had reservations about his ventures) to chorus 'we told you so'.

With all this publicity, there was little hope of getting the guns across the North Sea, past the gunboats and destroyers which would certainly be sent to intercept them, for it was too much to hope that their Lordships of the Admiralty did not take

The Times, and every hour brought in more circumstantial reports. A customs official called Thomsen had watched the ship for two days as she waited for the lighter, and he estimated that there were 30,000 rifles on board. From Stavanger in Norway came word that on the previous Monday she had put ashore a sick steward, who said that she was bound for Ireland.[2] It seemed as though the eyes of the whole world were on the *Fanny*.

This was all the more galling because the leaders had reluctantly, and after much hesitation, taken the decision to order Crawford not to leave Hamburg with the rifles. The order never reached him because of his last minute change of plan which caused him to leave Kiel a day early. According to Spender 'news somehow reached the U.V.F. Headquarters that Crawford's intentions were known to the British Government, and the Ulster leaders decided that it was necessary to cancel, or at any rate postpone, any attempt to bring arms from the Continent'.

Spender was therefore instructed to dispatch a coded telegram to this effect to reach Crawford at Kiel. Fearing that any message from Ulster might reveal what was afoot, Spender decided to cable from the G.P.O. in Dublin, as that was the last place from which the authorities would expect such a message to be sent. To make sure that he was not being followed, he left the train at Portadown, took a walk in the country, and boarded a later train for Dublin.

As he left the Post Office, his task accomplished, he was suddenly horrified to see newspaper boys carrying placards with the headlines:

ULSTER'S MYSTERY ARMS-SHIP CAPTURED

Deeply depressed, he returned to Craigavon to find Craig, Carson, Richardson, and Hacket Pain conferring with the arms committee. 'See what your mad plans have brought us to,' one member said to him, but Craig, who always believed that in a crisis it was essential to keep up one's strength, steered him firmly to the dining-room. While he ate the dinner which his host had thoughtfully kept for him, Craig and Richardson sat down beside him and tried to cheer him up, saying that there was still time to try again, especially as the whole Province would now be eager to help. Later on Carson came in and said,

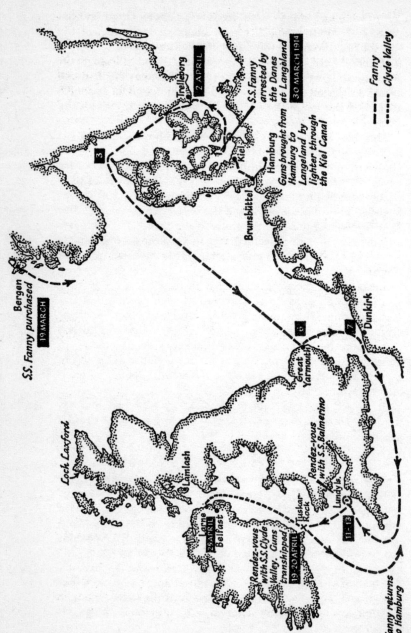

The route of the *Fanny* and the *Clydevalley*

'Now we must begin all over again, like a general after a defeat
— we must have a new plan!'[3]

Although they had now lost contact with Crawford, the
leaders determined to adhere to their decision to postpone the
attempt. A few days later there was a gleam of hope from an
unexpected quarter. A code wire from Cunningham's London
office said that someone had arrived from Germany and wanted
to see Spender at once. Could it be Crawford? Spender crossed
to England that night, and next day in London he met, not
Crawford, but Schneider. His news was that the *Fanny* had not
been captured, but was at large in the North Sea, and he produced the chart with the rendezvous marked at Loch Laxford
in Sutherland, in the far north of Scotland.[4] Agnew had chosen
the spot well, for it was as inaccessible as any place in Great
Britain could be.

Spender carried with him drastic orders for Crawford signed
by General Richardson and lated 6 April. They read as
follows:

'1. You are not under any circumstances to attempt to come
into British waters.

2. If you are shadowed, and escape is impossible, (*a*) throw
your cargo overboard, or (*b*) scuttle the ship; (*c*) act on (*a*) and
take the empty ship to any port and leave her there; (*d*) acting
on legal advice, run the ship into any port outside British waters
and try to sell contents.

3. If you are not shadowed, try to get back to Danish or
Norwegian waters, or act on legal advice.'[5]

Spender was now instructed to meet Crawford as arranged,
give him these orders, and if possible arrange with Schneider to
sell back the ship and her cargo even at a considerable loss.

He therefore asked Schneider if he would accompany him to
the rendezvous, to which the latter cheerfully agreed, apparently
without any idea of what he was letting himself in for, and the
two men set out on an adventure straight from the pages of *The
Thirty-Nine Steps*.[6] They were going to the Highlands ostensibly
for the salmon fishing, although they brought no rods, and
Schneider was wearing a black frock-coat, cashmere trousers,
and patent leather boots. He also had a 'very peculiar bowler
hat' which Spender thought made him look conspicuous in
London, let alone in the remoter parts of Sutherland.

It had been arranged that a motorship was to take them from Glasgow, and Spender was disappointed to find on their arrival that there was no sign of it. This was awkward, because study of a large-scale map showed that the nearest habitation to the rendezvous was an inn at Rhiconich, five miles from Loch Laxford and forty miles from the nearest railway station at Lairg. They discovered that they could get a train for Lairg very early next morning, so they put up at the Station Hotel, and Spender had just signed his name in the register as 'Mr. Bliss' when the hotel porter came up and said: 'Do you remember me, Captain? I was one of the Mess waiters when you were Mess Secretary two years ago.' Spender manoeuvred the man away from the book for a chat about old times, and then made his escape.

This was only the first of many shocks. As they got on the train next morning Schneider for some reason began to act and speak 'in a very mysterious kind of way', attracting the attention of a burly plain-clothes detective who was pacing up and down the platform. The detective came over and looked at them suspiciously, but to Spender's great relief, he seemed satisfied and went away again.

At Lairg new trials awaited them, for they were told that no car could get along the roads to Rhiconich at that time of year. However, a sporting chauffeur agreed to make the attempt, and succeeded in getting them near enough to complete the journey on foot before he had to turn back. Spender took the opportunity to reconnoitre, and they clambered over many miles of desolate moorland in hopes of finding the *Fanny* at anchor. At last Schneider gave up and took shelter under a rock while his companion went on to the next vantage point.

It was midnight before, wet, tired, and hungry they reached the inn, and as they approached it Spender saw something which made his heart sink. A vessel in Loch Inchard was signalling from her masthead to the shore, and he was convinced that this could only mean that the *Fanny* had been captured by a naval vessel which was communicating the news to the coastguard station. His fears seemed confirmed when he caught sight of a large white naval cutter drawn up on the beach. Since they could do nothing about it, however, they tapped boldly on the door of the inn, explained that their motor had broken down, and asked for rooms.

Neither of them slept well that night, and at breakfast next morning, Spender casually asked the innkeeper about the signalling and the naval boat. He replied that the steam trawlers always communicated with their homes in that way, and as for the cutter, it was an old boat which he had bought the previous year for his own use.

Schneider and Spender now calculated that the *Fanny* must arrive that evening, and anchor in Loch Laxford after dark, so they announced that they would take a stroll after supper. But still there was no sign of the ship, and they did not return until 2 o'clock in the morning, making the excuse that Schneider had sprained his ankle. This was near enough to the truth, for poor Schneider had undergone a severe trial in his patent leather boots. The climate did not suit him, either, and he had caught a bad cold. Luckily a doctor was coming to attend an inquest in the neighbourhood, so Spender arranged for him to take Schneider back with him so that he could return to London, which by now he was very anxious to do. Before he left, Spender drew up an agreement with him on a sheet of the hotel writing-paper for the re-sale of the *Fanny* and her cargo.

'Mr. Schneider agrees to buy back the goods purchased by Mr. Graham at half the price (less £2,500) given by Mr. Graham, and Captain Spender, acting on instructions, agrees to sell them at that figure.

The goods will be considered delivered to Mr. Schneider as soon as he takes them off the vessel in which they now are, and Mr. Schneider will make all arrangements for receiving them.

Mr. Schneider will make all arrangements to dispose of the steamer and will buy her from Mr. Graham on her arrival at the port named. The price will be fixed after she arrives but will not be less than half price, at which price he may sell her.'[7]

Spender passed another four miserable days and nights at the inn, discovering just what a tangled web the amateur secret agent is likely to weave for himself. Having introduced himself to the innkeeper as Mr. Bliss, he remembered that his real name was sewn into his pyjamas. Although the hotel had excellent fishing of salmon, seatrout and brown trout attached to it,[8] he was obliged to admit that he had no interest in fishing, and, worst of all, he dared not invent new reasons for his strange nocturnal excursions. Each night, therefore, after retiring to his bedroom, he had to let himself down from the window, and wander for miles in the dark over the eerie moorland, vainly searching for a light on the tumbling waters of Loch Laxford. On the fifth day, when he was convinced that the *Fanny* was lost, he was rescued by a telegram from Glasgow, though its terms did nothing to dispel the cloud of polite Highland suspicion which he now felt surrounded him. It said that if he wished to secure valuable fishing rights, he should return at once to meet the factor of the prospective vendor.

On his arrival in Glasgow he found that the whole situation had changed in his absence. For the *Fanny* had succeeded after all in crossing what Joseph Conrad called 'that dangerous and shallow puddle' of the North Sea, although she was nowhere near Loch Laxford.

As soon as he was clear of Langeland, Crawford had turned all hands to altering the ship's appearance. Her handsome yellow funnel, of which Captain Falck was so proud, was painted black, and on the bows and stern a new name appeared, that of Crawford's youngest daughter Bethia.

Unaware of any change of plans, since to go back to Kiel was now out of the question, they headed for the North Sea. But their luck obstinately refused to improve. During the afternoon the chief engineer reported that he had forgotten to get a supply of cylinder oil, and that there was only enough for forty hours. Crawford was furious, but he had to agree to standing off about eight miles from Trelleborg while the two captains went ashore and got the oil and some newspapers, from which they learned for the first time of their notoriety.

The weather was fine as they rounded the Skaw and set course for British waters, but next day it began to blow hard. The bunker coal was giving out, and though the ship carried a reserve of a hundred tons, to use it they had to open the hatch and coal along the deck, a difficult and dirty job which became impossible when the gale sprang up. Crawford had gone down with malaria, but he sent for the working plan of the ship and calculated that the coal could be reached directly if a particular plate was removed from the bulkhead. The engineer said that it could not be done, and had to be blackmailed by the threat of losing his bonus, before he proved himself wrong. The same gale smashed the starboard lamp, and the erratic manoeuvres of other shipping at night warned them that they must replace it at once.

Once again what seemed like bad luck turned out to be all for the best. At Trelleborg Crawford had already decided that the fleet at Lamlash might well be on the look-out for him off Scotland, and he proposed instead a rendezvous at Lundy Island in the Bristol Channel. Meanwhile, the nearest port was Great Yarmouth, and there they put in late one evening at considerable hazard, which was not lessened when they almost ran down a schooner in the channel. A new glass was obtained for the lamp, and Agnew dispatched to London to make contact with the committee.

Falck now set course for the English Channel, crossing over to the French coast to keep out of the way of British warships. On the second day Crawford's malaria returned and he could eat nothing. Falck came into his cabin and said 'Mr. Graham, you are very ill. I have sailed for over forty years, and I know a sick man when I see one. You have enteric fever and will die in two days if you are not put ashore. I am going to put you ashore'. Crawford ordered him to keep his course, and a brisk quarrel developed. 'I am taking you into Dunkirk,' Falck insisted, 'you will be dead soon. You have eaten nothing for a long time, and no man can live without eating.' 'Captain Falck, I am not a dead man by any means. Are you going to obey me or not?' 'No, I am taking you into Dunkirk.'

Crawford went to a drawer, took out a ·38 colt automatic pistol and put it to Falck's head, declaring, 'Captain Falck, I know I am alone amongst you and your foreign crew, but I am a match for all of you if you attempt to interfere with my orders. I will shoot you, or any of your crew who interferes, as dead as a herring. I ask you for the last time, will you obey my orders?'

The captain gave in, and they shook hands. Thereafter, says Crawford, they were the best of friends, and Falck even tried his hand at cooking to tempt the sick man to eat. 'He told me afterwards that in all his sea experience he had never sailed with two such men as Agnew and me, and I don't think he ever wanted to again.'

Delayed by gales the ship, which had now assumed the name of Crawford's second daughter Doreen, did not reach Lundy until Saturday 11 April. Coming up the Bristol Channel she was beset with pilot boats offering their services. In addition there were a number of trawlers, all equipped with wireless, whose crews seemed to take a great interest in her movements. Falck cruised up and down in the vicinity of Lundy, but there was no sign of a relief ship. All of Easter Sunday was spent in this way, and after dark Crawford from the top of the chart-house gave the pre-arranged signal every ten minutes with the aid of a bucket and a hurricane lamp. It was dreary work, and what was worse, it attracted too much attention.

At daybreak Crawford turned in to snatch some sleep, only to be wakened with the news that a steamer called the *Balmerino* was alongside, with Captain Agnew on board. There was a trawler with radio near by also, so they steamed on for ten miles to get clear of her, and then Agnew came on board the *Doreen* to report.

His few days in London had been rather trying, for the instructions coming in from Belfast were confusing and un-certain, although they all agreed on one point — the guns must not be brought to Ireland just now.[9] At last on Good Friday Dick Cowzer had arrived with firm orders. Agnew was to go to Holyhead, where the skipper of one of Lord Leitrim's ships, Captain Morrison, would meet him and inform him of the latest decisions. He got there on the 12th and the two men were picked up by the *Balmerino* at the breakwater.

The news had now to be broken to Crawford, and, in Agnew's words 'there never was a wilder man'. Morrison had handed him a letter which simply said; 'Owing to great changes since you left and altered circumstances, the committee think it would be unwise for you to bring the cargo here at present, and instruct you to proceed to the Baltic and cruise there for three months, keeping in touch with the committee during that time, or else take the cargo back to Hamburg and store the goods there until required.'

The words of this 'cowardly document' seemed to sear into Crawford's brain; he did not wonder that there were no signatures to it. If the British Government had thrown down the gage to Ulster, was it not all the more reason for Ulster to be armed? To Morrison he said: 'I do not know who gave you this document, but take it to the person or persons who gave it to you and had not the courage to put their names to it, and tell them to go to hell. . . .' He added that if he did not receive instructions for landing the cargo within the next six days, he would run the ship aground in Ballyholme Bay at high water, and rouse the County Down Volunteers to come and take her cargo off.

Agnew loyally stood by him and they put their heads together to concoct a new plan. Crawford proposed to ask his friend Sam Kelly, the well-known Belfast coal importer, to let them have a small coal-boat into which the guns could be transferred, since the *Doreen* with her foreign look would be too conspicuous. So he went ashore at Tenby and caught the Irish Mail. At Rosslare an efficient Customs man separated him from his faithful colt automatic, but he succeeded in reaching Dublin where he telephoned to Cowzer, making him swear to tell no one except Kelly of his return. However, when he met him at the station in Belfast, Cowzer insisted on driving him straight to Craigavon, on the grounds that Sir Edward had come over specially for the committee meeting. This was an appeal Crawford could not resist.

On that Easter Tuesday evening as Carson and the committee were again gathered round Craig's dinner-table, the host was called away by an urgent message. Outside the door he found a little man like an angry ghost, dishevelled and pale, with a baleful light in his blue eyes. Craig stretched out his hand, but, as Crawford writes, 'I did a cruel thing: I swept his hand aside and regretted it in the same moment. I said "I will shake hands with no member of the Committee until I know what they propose to do with the *Fanny*'s cargo".' Instead of being offended, Craig put his arm on his shoulder, and said: 'It's all right, Fred, the Chief is here.'[10]

When the others came in, Crawford's manner was distinctly cool, but Carson chose the right words to soothe his ruffled feelings: 'Well done, Crawford, I'm proud of you.' Hearing this, the gun-runner felt rewarded for all his efforts. 'We are gathered together', Carson continued, 'to hear what you have done and intend to do.' Crawford told them, in detail, and without mincing his words. 'Gentlemen, I want you to understand me: I will *not* take those guns back, and neither will Agnew, because he gave me his word. Agnew will keep his word, for he is a MAN.' Since the *Fanny* was to meet him off the Tuskar Light on Friday, he proposed to buy a collier and transfer the arms to it. General Richardson intervened to say it would be impossible to tranship in open water, and the others agreed with him.

Crawford insisted that he could do it, provided the weather was fine, and pointed out that he had carried out all his promises so far.

Carson, recognizing a kindred spirit, took his part. 'Crawford is right. We had better leave the details to him.' Sam Kelly then said that he knew of a ship which was just then for sale; she was the *Clydevalley*, which he had once owned, and she plied regularly between Glasgow and Belfast. Nothing could better suit their purpose than this nondescript coal-boat, so familiar in the Belfast Lough, and Crawford agreed to go to Glasgow at once and negotiate for her.

The problem of where the guns were to be landed was as yet unresolved. A majority of the Committee still thought that they could be brought into Belfast, and Crawford left on the understanding that he was to bring the *Clydevalley* into the Musgrave Channel, despite the obvious risks. He warned that any alteration of these plans would have to be signed by Carson himself.

In Glasgow he bought the *Clydevalley* for £4,500, signed on a new crew, and arranged that she should send a boat ashore for him at Llandudno next day. He arrived there early in the morning and began his vigil after breakfast. The day wore on; he had tea on the promenade overlooking the bay, and then, anxiously, he sent off a telegram, 'What has happened to Mary?' After a time he had an answer, 'Mary missed train, but will arrive late this evening'.

Darkness came, and he went down to the beach; a strong wind was blowing, and the sea was very choppy. When his patience was beginning to give way to apprehension, he suddenly saw the lights of the ship coming head on for the shore. As he watched she went about and, simultaneously, he heard a boat being lowered. He went down to the water's edge and began to signal with his flashlamp. 'The surf was high and the beach was covered with large boulders; the light was poor and there was no moon. Two or three attempts were made to come ashore but on each occasion the crew had to draw out to avoid being swamped or smashed on the boulders.' When the boat came fairly close he made a rush and tumbled into her stern with only a bad wetting. The *Clydevalley* hoisted them aboard and made off at full speed for Holyhead.

There he found the *Balmerino*, borrowed some of her crew,

and steered for the Tuskar Light, arriving at first light on Saturday. They steamed the four points of the compass, but there was no sign of the *Fanny*. Just when it seemed that Crawford's odyssey was nearing its end, he had to set off on a last wild-goose chase to — of all places — Great Yarmouth. There had been a misunderstanding between Agnew and Captain Luke, the *Balmerino*'s master, about the rendezvous, and the latter feared that Agnew might have gone there instead. Crawford left instructions that if the *Fanny* reappeared, they were to go ahead at once with transhipping the cargo. Agnew was to take over the *Clydevalley* and pick him up from the breakwater at Holyhead.

At Yarmouth there was no trace of the *Fanny*, but in the afternoon there was a telegram waiting for him at the post office. It read, 'All's well. Breakwater 5 p.m. Tuesday — Agnew.' He caught the night train for Holyhead, and went down to the breakwater next day, in warm spring sunshine, to scan the now familiar empty seascape. It was 7 o'clock before the *Clydevalley* came into sight round the headland, but Agnew had consoling news. The ships had been made fast together during the night of the 19th, and the cargo transferred while they steamed through the traffic with one set of lights. It was a considerable achievement, though it almost broke Captain Falck's heart to hear the *Fanny*'s top works grinding against the coal-boat as they came together.[11]

Having, at long last, time on his hands, Crawford indulged his favourite passion for changing the ship's name. He had, as it happened, a third daughter, but this time he thought it more appropriate to choose the name, celebrated in Ulster history, of the ship which broke the boom at the Siege of Derry. While he was engaged in painting *Mountjoy II* on three large strips of canvas, a warship steamed past on its way to Lamlash. Wednesday and Thursday were spent sailing, at a discreet distance, round the Isle of Man; then on Friday 24 April Agnew set course for Belfast Lough.

16

OPERATION LION

The master plan was now almost complete. Like all good plans it was essentially simple: on the night of the 24th a test mobilization would take place of the U.V.F. in every part of the province, under cover of which the Antrim Division would quietly take control of Larne and all roads leading to it, and be responsible for landing the rifles and getting them away.

The original scheme, whereby the volunteers were to have been reviewed by Carson at Larne, and the guns landed after his departure, had been altered. It was decided to avoid using the railways, and instead the counties were instructed to provide as much transport as possible to convey the arms to their own districts. Since it soon became apparent that the counties would not be able to take more than a proportion of their rifles in the time, the Motor Car Corps, which had increased so rapidly in size and efficiency during February and March, undertook to convey the remainder to secret dumps from which they could be removed later.[1]

The decision to make Larne the chief port for the landing was not easily arrived at. Right up until the last moment the exponents of Belfast seemed to have carried the day, and Crawford's instructions were to bring the *Clydevalley* into the Musgrave Channel on the evening of Friday 24th.[2] The arrangements for Carson's visit at Easter were presumably made some time ahead, and probably in accordance with the original plan, for he landed at Larne on April 13, went straight to Craigavon and returned to inspect the South Antrim U.V.F. on the same day. On the 14th he inspected the North Down Regiment in camp at Clandeboye, and on the 15th the Central Antrim Regiment in camp at Whiteabbey.[3] These were precisely the Volunteers who were to be employed in landing the guns.

On the surface, however, it would seem that the committee's decision to switch to Larne was made *after* Carson's return to London on Monday 20 April — for this reason: Crawford had made it quite clear on the preceding Tuesday that he would not accept any further orders unless they were signed by Sir Edward, and when the committee decided after Carson's departure to go for Larne after all they were faced with a difficulty. Richardson, in astonishment, observed 'But surely Crawford will obey orders?' He was assured by those who knew Crawford better that this was not the case, and Frank Hall had to cross to London to have the orders signed by Carson.[4]

This is very puzzling because in Antrim the secret summons to motor car owners to assemble at Larne went out on April 20, and a letter from Sir William Adair to Captain Arthur O'Neill shows that the plans for Larne were well advanced.[5] Could it be that Carson and Craig decided upon Larne in consultation with Adair, while allowing the committee to go on for a few days thinking in terms of Belfast? If this was what happened the ruse was a clever one — the plans made for Belfast were allowed to go forward, another ship was substituted for the *Clydevalley*, and a diversion created which proved very successful. To distract the authorities further it was planned to land some of the arms at the Co. Down ports of Bangor and Donaghadee.

U.V.F. security was uniformly excellent, but the gun-running was the best-kept secret of all. Apart from Crawford only twelve men knew of the whole plan, and even after fifty years it is not easy to trace their deliberations. Craig, Bates and Spender were most closely concerned with it, and the other members of the secret committee can be identified as Richardson, Hacket Pain, Frank Hall, Cunningham, Cowzer, Kelly, Clark and McDowell.[6]

No detail had been overlooked. A U.V.F. intelligence survey of Larne had been made, with the assistance of William Chaine, as early as 31 December 1913.[7] Since it was essential that information that the arms had been landed should be delayed as long as possible, Spender had been instructed in February to make arrangements for severing communications. He got in touch with the head of an engineering firm, 'and with some trepidation approached the subject of cutting all the telegraph and telephone lines so that Larne would be completely isolated'. With even greater diffidence he referred to 'the possibility of isolating northern Ireland from any contact with Great Britain, Southern Ireland, or indirectly through America'. He was assured that if he could supply a list of every line leaving the province, the job would be done.[8]

For the first time ever, careful and far-seeing plans were made for the assembly of several hundred motor cars at a given time and place for a military purpose, and for their subsequent dispersal. This was a brilliant piece of staff work, in which nothing was left to chance.

The secret summons which went out in Co. Antrim on 20 April began in this form:

'Sir,

In accordance with your kind agreement to place a motor car at the disposal of the Provisional Government in a case of necessity, it is absolutely necessary that your car should arrive at Larne in the night of Friday/Saturday 24/25th instant *at 1 a.m. punctually but not before that hour, for a very secret and important duty.*'

Detailed instructions followed: a reliable volunteer was to accompany the chauffeur; a supply of petrol was to be brought; on approaching Larne no car was to attempt to overtake another; the strictest obedience was to be paid to all instructions given by staff officers and marshals; towns and villages were to be avoided or passed through at a slow speed without horn-blowing. 'It is unfortunate', the summons added, 'that this unavoidable assembly must take place and Sir Edward is particularly desirous that no trouble should arise. Arms are therefore not to be carried; a determined attitude will probably overcome any possible show of interference by the police.' A card was enclosed which was to be produced on demand, and the recipient was to reply by Thursday evening's post at the latest, saying simply 'No. . . . will be there', or giving a good reason to the contrary.[9]

On the same day Adair and his brother met McCalmont, Chaine, and Lord Massereene in Larne and 'got through some details'; on Thursday morning they met again at Chaine's office in Belfast, and later made the final arrangements with Headquarters.[10] Terse mobilization orders for Friday night were drawn up. 'The men warned will assemble without arms at their various drill halls; they may be required to remain on duty most of the night. The men of the Belfast Division will assemble in their various drill halls and receive instructions. The police barracks should be watched to see what the police are engaged in and dispatch riders will be posted on the various roads towards Larne and Bangor and note any police movement. Dispatch riders will likewise be detailed to observe the military barracks at Holywood. Arrangements are necessary to tap telegraph and telephone wires in all directions.'

For the period of the mobilization Headquarters were to be at Maryville, the house at Malone, on the outskirts of Belfast, where General Richardson was living. The U.S.D.R.C. was to set up a system of signalling, using powerful lamps, between Larne, Bangor and some point in Belfast, from which the dispatch riders would bring the messages to Richardson and his staff.[11]

When, towards evening on Friday, the *Clydevalley* reached the Copeland Islands at the entrance to Belfast Lough, Agnew saw coming to meet her a tender from Workman and Clark's shipyard. On board were Dawson Bates and Cowzer, who, when they drew near enough, indicated that he had final instructions for them. But Crawford was not going to go through all that again, so telling Agnew to hold his course, he shouted across the water 'I have my orders. I am not going to take further orders. . . . If these orders are not signed by Sir Edward you can take them back to those who issued them, because you won't come aboard'. Cowzer established, with some difficulty, that they *were* signed by Carson, and only then were they accepted.[12]

'These instructions', ran the carefully worded message, 'the order of Sir E. Carson, and the order of Gen. Sir Geo. Richardson, are sent to you by Mr. Dawson Bates: —

'It has been found necessary to alter the arrangements for the arrival of the S.S. *Clydevalley* in the Musgrave Channel, and the following plan is substituted.

'The ship will just proceed to Larne, where General Sir William Adair is in command, who has with him Captain Spender and is assisted at the Larne Harbour by Messrs. Chaine and Jenks, and there she will discharge the whole of her cargo excepting 40 tons = 4,000 Mauser rifles for Bangor, to which port the ship will proceed with all possible dispatch when she has completed the transfer and discharge of her cargo at Larne.

It is not only of the utmost importance, it is vital that nothing interferes with the rapid loading and dispatch of the steamer *Innismurray* to Donaghadee, and the steamer *Roma* for Belfast, also that all cargo excepting the 40 tons of Mausers should be out of the *Clydevalley* to enable her to proceed to Bangor, and thus avoid ships being at sea in daylight....'[13]

At 8 p.m., just at the time Crawford was reading this document, the mobilization of the Belfast Division began, the company commanders having received their orders in the afternoon. The battalions paraded at their assembly points along with their ambulance sections. The men were in ordinary clothes, without arms or bandoliers, but they had been warned to bring greatcoats, blankets, haversacks, and water bottles.

East Belfast mobilized at 8.30 p.m., and by Couchman's orders 500 men were marched to Musgrave Channel where they took up their positions on the quayside about 8.45.[14] By 9 o'clock the other regiments were in position and ready to begin the patrolling of roads in their sectors. Stringent orders were issued that the volunteers were to keep well away from Nationalist areas and that no provocation was to be given to the police or any other citizen during the night.

At about the same time 1,000 of the North Belfast volunteers were marched to the Midland Railway Station; 400 formed a guard outside and the rest were drawn up at the No. 1 main line departure platform. They were not dismissed until 4.30 a.m., somewhat disappointed because they had not been entrained — the real object of their presence was to frustrate any attempt to send troops to Larne. One hundred men of the West Belfast Special Service section mounted guard at the Old Town Hall at 9.30.

For the rest the Volunteers remained as far as possible out of sight in their drill halls, except that at frequent intervals strong patrols marched along the main roads, light-heartedly singing

> *Who were you with last night?* and
> *The roses round the door*
> *Make me love mother more.*[15]

At Maryville Richardson and Hacket Pain were kept informed by the signallers and dispatch riders of every stage in the mobilization. Couchman took over command at Musgrave Channel, and his staff officer, Captain Scriven, sent his temporary telephone number to Headquarters. As an after-thought he added that if the General wished to speak to Colonel Couchman during the night, he should do so in Hindustani.[16]

The movements at the docks, combined with the extra-ordinary activity elsewhere in the city, had aroused a good deal of curiosity. The rumour spread in East Belfast that a ship with a large consignment of arms was expected in the Channel, and that she was probably the mystery ship about which there had been so much in the newspapers earlier in the month. Little groups of sight-seers began to collect at Queen's Road, and swelled into crowds. Soon after the volunteers were in position, there was a ripple of excitement as heavy transport began to arrive; large horse-drawn wagons, coal-carts, and motor lorries were carefully backed along the wharf, in accordance with some predetermined plan. Then a large force of police arrived, accompanied by the long-suffering City Commissioner.

After that things were very quiet for a long time. The night was raw and cold, and the volunteers, told to stand easy, whiled away the time by singing patriotic songs, and joking with the patient crowd. Long lines of pin-point lights from their cigarettes and pipes glowed in the darkness. About an hour before midnight the tension returned. The Customs officers had been informed that a tramp steamer was making her way up the Lough in the most furtive way possible. The volunteers were brought to attention; the officers scurried to and fro, and the Customs and police took up their positions. Eventually the ship (it was the *Balmerino*) appeared in the Channel, barely moving over the water. Mystifying lights flashed and winked from her decks as she manoeuvred from one side to the other. It seemed an endless time before she reached her berth and was made fast.[17]

The Customs officers armed with staves and lanterns im-mediately went on board but they found the captain vague and obstructive. He had mislaid his keys and could not produce the ship's papers. At 12.30 Couchman wrote his first report on a Workman and Clark docket and sent it off to Maryville. 'S.S. *Balmerino* arrived with anticipated cargo. Customs officer has asked us to declare what the cargo is, and they assume it is arms. We have declined to answer and have told them we shall give them every facility when the hatches are off to inspect the cargo. They want to know if they will be allowed to open any packages which may be there. We have told them I have no instructions on that point and must await your answer, and that I cannot telephone about these matters.'[18]

When the Customs officers suggested that the examination of the cargo could be left until next day, Couchman replied that he had no instructions about unloading. One of the junior officials told Captain Scriven that they had applied to the police for help, but it had been refused. The police contented themselves with taking the numbers of all the motor cars and motor cycles, and sending a telephone message (which the U.V.F. intercepted) to Carrickfergus, to the effect that they had a ship full of arms in the Channel. Carrickfergus commanded a view of the whole of Belfast Lough, and they asked for a sharp look-out to be kept.[19]

At 2 a.m. Scriven communicated again with Maryville. 'Commander Belfast Division wishes me to report that Customs Superintendent is getting very impatient, and wants to search vessel. We have informed him that we have not yet got authority to open the hatches. . . . Can you say how long it will be advisable to keep hatches on the ship?' Refusing to wait any longer, the Superintendent had meanwhile prevailed on the second officer to remove the hatches, and when Couchman promptly had them replaced the Customs man angrily accused him of 'obstructing him in the execution of duty'.

Throughout these proceedings Mr. Smith, the City Commissioner, and his men had behaved like benevolent spectators. He had been, Scriven reported, 'quite pleasant,' and had told Couchman frankly that he believed the whole incident was an elaborate bluff, and that the arms were being landed elsewhere. He simply wanted to know if this were the case, so that he could go home to bed, but all that Couchman would say was that they had not yet landed any arms, and they could give no information as to future movements. Wearily, Smith went away to telephone his wife. It was going to be a long night.[20]

At Larne, twenty-five miles away, the opening stages of the operation had gone with clockwork precision. Outwardly there had been no sign of unusual activity in the port that day but, under the surface, all had been made ready for the landing. Chaine, the commander of the 2nd Battalion of the Central Antrim U.V.F., was chairman of the company which owned the harbour and was therefore able to make the arrangements.

Jenks, his assistant in the planning, worked for the Shamrock Shipping Company and commanded the Larne Harbour section of the Volunteers. Most of these men worked at the harbour and they were assigned the task of unloading the ship. Jenks also arranged to 'requisition' the other boats in the harbour which would be needed.

Few of the people engaged in these preparations knew their purpose; it was enough for them that they were necessary. Among those who were allowed into the secret were three women, members of the Larne U.V.F. Nursing Corps. Early on Friday morning Mrs. Jenks told Lucy McNeill and Nora Rankin that the landing of the guns was expected that night, and that they had been asked to provide food for 300 men, and 300 white armlets for the force which was to hold the town. To obtain such a large quantity of food at short notice without arousing suspicion was difficult, but they decided to buy as many loaves as possible and make sandwiches. They also managed to purchase two hams and large quantities of eggs from nearby farms. A reliable woman cooked the hams for them, and they hard-boiled the eggs in large pans at home. Once or twice they came near to having to reveal that something extraordinary was afoot, since it all had to be done in such a hurry. Making the armbands was also a problem, and obliged them to buy a roll of calico and 'every safety pin in Larne'.[21]

On Friday afternoon mobilization orders were issued to the section officers of the entire Central Antrim Regiment. When the men assembled at their drill halls early in the evening they were marched to the grounds of Drumalis House, the residence of the Dowager Lady Smiley, where they were told off into companies and allotted their duties.

At 8 o'clock precisely the volunteers took control of the town, without any interference by the police, who were by now so accustomed to U.V.F. test mobilizations that they did not at first realize what was going on. McCalmont briskly assigned his men to their positions. A strong force invested the harbour and the railway terminal at the cross-channel steamer berth, and pickets of men wearing the white armbands were posted in the roads leading to the town. There a second force kept guard in the main streets and at key points. At the same time on the hills above the sea Lord Massereene threw a cordon of the South Antrim Regiment right round the town and set up check-points on all the roads leading into it. After that no one entered or left Larne except on business for the U.V.F.[22]

The evening was cold and overcast, and a drizzling rain began to fall as the volunteers took up their positions. While Adair and Spender waited anxiously in the Harbour Office the experts from the Signalling Corps got to work. At 9 o'clock all telephone communication with Belfast abruptly ceased. Two telegraph lines connected Belfast with Larne, one to the post office (which had already been closed for several hours) and the other to the Midland railway station. The railway telegraph went dead in the middle of a batch of excited code signals.[23]

Meanwhile the first of the motor cars had begun to arrive. Since the early afternoon cars had been converging on Larne without the drivers being aware of the reason, or that other drivers were involved. A huge concentration of cars and other transport had secretly assembled during the day at Castle Upton, Lord Templetown's estate at Templepatrick, including a large contingent of the Co. Tyrone Motor Car Corps under Captain A. St. Q. Ricardo, the Adjutant of the Tyrone Regiment. Towards evening this weirdly assorted convoy issued on to the roads leading north. In those days when the motor car still had a certain novelty, the sudden increase in traffic alarmed the country folk, and at Ballyclare many sought their neighbours' houses 'believing that war had broken out'.[24]

About thirty cars from the North Antrim Regiment were under orders to reach Larne at 1 a.m. Another large squadron of cars and lorries had been organized from Ballymena and its surrounding district. But, as Adair had written a few days earlier to Captain O'Neill, 'We are lamentable (sic) short in Co. Antrim and have not half the transport we want.'[25] For this reason the Belfast Motor Car Corps undertook to distribute the rifles to pre-arranged dumps and hiding-places in Co. Antrim, and almost every available car in Belfast was pressed into service.[26]

Few of the drivers suspected that they were involved in an operation on so massive a scale. One young volunteer, for example, was instructed to drive his father's 12 h.p. Rover with certain passengers to Larne that evening and to await orders there. He was allowed to know that 'something' was coming in by boat and guessed what it might be. In Larne, however, the town was quiet and when he looked across the empty harbour he was sure that the operation would be a failure. Then, just as darkness fell, he 'saw a snake of bright lights appear on the hills — a great cavalcade of motor cars with brilliant headlights'. As it came nearer all the electric lights in the harbour flashed on, teams of men emerged from the shadows, and Larne suddenly came awake.[27]

'The heel of an April evening was merging into night', wrote a more insouciant young man, 'when I met a friend who knew a friend who had a fast motor — a fast Ford of twenty horse power — and he casually, as he stepped aboard, suggested that I should come along. I did so with a light heart and not too heavy overcoat.' As they sped northwards along the Shore Road and on through Carrickfergus he saw U.V.F. signallers on every eminence, men in semi-military uniform at every cross-roads, while dispatch riders passed and re-passed in the loom of their acetylene headlamps.

At the village of Glynn they were halted by a line of men across the road, and again on the outskirts of Larne. Then, to their astonishment, as they turned to the right for the Curran Road and across the railway track, they found themselves obliged to get into a line of cars waiting, with engines throbbing, to move towards the harbour.[28]

Spender remembered an atmosphere of tense excitement at the harbour office when, just at dusk, a vessel appeared on the horizon, and the sense of relief when she replied to the lamp signal flashed to her in code. Shortly after 9 o'clock they could hear the throb of her engines across the water, though her masthead lights scarcely seemed to be moving. There followed 'a most anxious and trying time' before she arrived at the harbour. The *Mountjoy* had been slowed down by poor coal, and it was 10.30 before she glided into the harbour, with clouds of black smoke billowing from her single smokestack.

Although the harbour was brilliantly lighted, there was great difficulty in getting alongside. When at last she was made fast it was after 11 o'clock, and the operation was running two hours late. Ashore, where the waiting had imposed a cruel strain, there was every resolve to make up the time lost. Hardly were the hatches removed when bands of sturdy men stripped to their shirts swarmed on board to begin the unloading.[29]

According to the plan approximately 11,000 rifles were to be landed on the quayside, and transferred to the waiting cars, except for 3,000 which 'Mr. Jenks is disposing of'. While this was going on, the guns for Belfast and Donaghadee were to be loaded into the motorships *Roma* and *Innismurray* simultaneously.[30] The *Roma* immediately went alongside, and 'willing, though amateur, hands started to tranship the cargo of the forehold into her'. The cranes and derricks whirred and buzzed as the bundles were swung over her side, and as soon as she had taken on board her quota of 720 bundles she slipped swiftly and silently out of the circle of the harbour lights.[31]

With the *Innismurray*, however, there was trouble. The skipper could not, or would not, come alongside the *Mountjoy*. He first of all declared that he could not start the motor, and then when he did, he handled his ship in a thoroughly unseamanlike manner. Only at this point did the organizers realize what was wrong with the *Innismurray*: the captain and some of his crew were Nationalists. This, in Crawford's words 'was a bit of bad management', though it seems to have been the only mistake made in the U.V.F. plans at Larne.

The saboteurs were replaced by a volunteer crew of more reliable politics, but a delay was inevitable. Adair wanted to keep to the original plan of loading direct into the *Innismurray*, but Crawford, who was certain that the Navy would arrive at any minute, decided 'to dump all the cargo on the quay except that for Bangor'.[32] In spite of all this the ship was loaded before 4 a.m. and she reached Donaghadee at 6 a.m.

Meanwhile the transfer of eighty tons of rifles to the cars was going on with incredible rapidity. As the dock cranes swung ashore the long canvas bales, the line of cars moved slowly forward. Each car took as many bundles as it could hold, its load was checked, and then driven away into the darkness. A great many of the rifles were taken quickly to secret dumps not far from the town, including the old lead mine-workings in Antrim, and the cars returned to Larne to make a second and third trip. The arms from the dumps were distributed on the following night, mainly to areas where the population was predominantly Nationalist.

The motor squadrons from Tyrone, however, were loaded first and returned home directly. The last car left Larne at midnight and reached its destination eleven hours later. 'We got all our lot for Tyrone safely in', Captain Ricardo wrote next day, 'without any friction or bother, except four bundles we had to leave near Lurgan — but which will be collected to-morrow. The picketing of our road through Antrim and Armagh was beyond all praise — it was perfect. I sincerely hope everything else went off as satisfactorily.'[33]

After midnight the operation proceeded with increasing speed and the lost time was taken up. The U.V.F. nurses kept the men supplied with hot coffee and sandwiches. Later they had to go on board to attend to a volunteer who had fallen into one of the holds, but who was not seriously injured.[34]

As she unloaded her cargo the *Mountjoy* took on board eleven tons of coal. Her fresh water was finished, and, writes Captain Agnew, 'we were thankful to get some at once, but before the water tank was half full a car ran over the hoses'. A message was flashed to Bangor asking Mr. Kelly to arrange to have thirty tons of coal and fresh water waiting for them on the quay.[35]

By 2.30 a.m. all the cargo had been unloaded except for the forty tons destined for Bangor, and Agnew cast off at once. For the hundreds of weary men at the harbour it was difficult to realize that it was all over, so suddenly. From beginning to end there had been no interference of any kind from the police, coastguards, or Customs. The naval and military authorities knew nothing of what had occurred. As the *Mountjoy* drew away from the harbour and edged round Ferris Point, Agnew, Crawford and the crew stood to attention and gave three cheers for the volunteers. It was still raining.[36]

In Belfast it was just growing light when the Customs discovered that Couchman was no longer objecting to the removal of the *Balmerino*'s hatches. A message from Headquarters, which may or may not have been in Hindustani, had told him that all was well at Larne. By then the crowds had thinned considerably, but there were still some spectators hoping to be rewarded with a sensation as the Customs examination of the ship began. The *Balmerino*'s papers were perfectly in order, and, as the manifest stated, her cargo consisted of — coal. When they were dismissed many of the volunteers took lumps of it home with them as souvenirs of the occasion.

While the attention of the Customs and the police had been on the *Balmerino* the *Roma* had quietly tied up at Workman and Clark's wharf and unloaded 70 bundles of rifles. The Customs officers did eventually spot her, but when they put out a launch and tried to land at steps they were met by a determined U.V.F. guard. Later that morning a special order was issued relating to 'the arms and ammunition stored at Messrs. Workman and Clark's yard'. If any attempt was made to search for or seize them the horn would be blown to mobilize the East Belfast Volunteers.[37]

At Bangor in Co. Down the landing operations were in charge of Colonel McCammon, who selected Crozier as his C.S.O. McCammon left Maryville at a quarter to seven and reached Bangor by car just in time to see the tender go out to the *Clydevalley* hove to in the bay; the steamer then stood off to the north-east. Sam Kelly told him that she would be in Larne at 9 o'clock, and back in Bangor by 1 o'clock. 'On receipt of this information', says McCammon, 'I accelerated all movements in Bangor by one hour.'[38]

At 7.30 Crozier was dining at the Ulster Club 'with some R.I.C. officers and others, who had instructions to keep the guardians of the law merry and bright, and far from the telephone, till past midnight'. Promptly at 10 p.m. a car called for him and whisked him off to Bangor, where he found 'all approaches to the town picketed, the telephone wires temporarily out of action, the coastguard office in the hands of the gun-runners, reserves of the U.V.F. ready at hand, motor cars waiting ready to drive off with their loads to known destinations, and Colonel McCammon all expectant'.[39]

Units of the 1st Battalion, North Down Regiment had been moving into the town since just after nine o'clock, but it was assumed by the inhabitants that they had come to attend a benefit performance in aid of the U.V.F. at a local picture house. An apprehensive English visitor who asked a volunteer if Bangor was going to be taken, received the laconic reply 'Bangor's tuk'.

But they were to have a long and nerve-straining night of waiting. At 11 o'clock two motor cyclists who had been posted to observe Holywood Barracks arrived to report that at 10.40 a company of soldiers fully equipped had marched out of the barracks towards Holywood. They added apologetically that 'their bicycles were concealed in the bushes at the Misses Ireland's and that it took them about five minutes to light their lamps and get under way for Bangor'. They had not passed the troops on the road.

Shortly after midnight the message arrived from Larne asking Kelly to have thirty tons of coal on the quay, and to arrange for fresh water, and by 1 a.m. they were able to reply that this had been done. At 1.30 the Chief Boatman and two coastguards wanted to get through the U.V.F. cordon at Victoria Road to go on duty in the look-out station. Eventually the senior man was allowed through, as 'he appeared quite civil', and said that it would suffice if he reported in. Then two R.I.C. constables asked to get through at the same place; they were told they could not pass and they went away.

At 2.30 a.m. the motor-cars began to arrive, and shortly afterwards there came a message from Larne to say that the *Mountjoy* was about to leave, and at a quarter to four they were given her estimated time of arrival at Bangor as 5 a.m. McCammon then informed Headquarters that the 'sixteen motor cars for Banbridge and Donacloney' (which, having farthest to travel in Co. Down, would be loaded first) could not now hope to leave before 5.30 at the earliest, and that the U.V.F. occupation of Bangor would have to continue well into daylight.[40]

In fact the dawn was just breaking when the bows of the *Mountjoy* appeared out of the morning mist and she was alongside at 4.25. McCammon was understandably anxious about the time. For a variety of reasons Bangor was more vulnerable than any of the other landing places. Although it was not then the dormitory town for Belfast which it has since become, it was only fifteen miles from the city, and had a large suburban population which could not easily be controlled after the beginning of the working day. Between it and Belfast lay the Holywood Barracks and if the authorities acted swiftly they could block the roads and trap all the arms landed at Bangor and Donaghadee on the Ards Peninsula, to say nothing of the volunteers and the transport. Again Bangor was situated on Belfast Lough, and not like Larne and Donaghadee on the open sea, so that the ship could be captured as well.

Secret mobilization, earthed wires and picketed roads were, as Crozier observed, one thing during the hours of darkness, and quite another in daylight. Soon réveillé would be sounding at Holywood; there was not a moment to be lost. On the quay the men worked relentlessly, and in one hour and thirteen minutes exactly the forty tons of rifles had been unloaded and dispatched by car. The whole operation, McCammon reported, went very smoothly, except that the work had to be interrupted to allow the coal lorries to pass along the pier. At 6.12 he was able to inform Headquarters that all arms and ammunition had been cleared from the ship by 5.40, and that she had sailed for Fishguard with coal, water, and stores on board.[41]

Before her departure, however, the firemen went on strike and refused to go any farther with her. Agnew paid them off, and since no firemen could be found at such short notice, five men of the North Down Regiment volunteered to go on board as stokers. They had no time to collect their belongings or even send a message home. Agnew wanted Crawford to go ashore, but he absolutely refused, declaring that while there was any risk of the ship being captured he preferred to stay with them. Just as they cast off a man came running down the pier with a dramatic message that a fast destroyer was on its way from Lamlash to intercept them.[42]

Although they could see no sign of the Navy, it was high time for them to be away. By now it was broad daylight and Bangor was waking up in no little astonishment. Crozier was amused to hear 'the remarks of the old landladies and servant girls of this pleasant little summer seaside resort . . . as they pulled up the blinds and blinked their sleepy eyes, on seeing hundreds of fully armed men and countless motor-cars, whose arrival had been unheralded and unheard'. At 7.20 the last of the cars left the pier, the volunteers were marched off, and Bangor returned to its customary decorum. By 9 o'clock Crozier was back in Belfast having breakfast in his club.[43]

It was characteristic of James Craig that, having been responsible for so much of the planning of the operation, he should choose for himself the position of least prestige on the night itself. His post was the little Co. Down harbour of Donaghadee, and while waiting for zero hour, he 'sat placidly at home at Craigavon, smoking his favourite pipe and playing patience'.[44] He knew that all the arrangements were as complete as he could make them, and, when darkness fell, he drove to Donaghadee to superintend the landing there.

The local force had been drilled as usual that evening and

dismissed, but with orders to mobilize again at midnight. Meanwhile the 2nd Battalion of the North Down Volunteers, men from the Newtownards and Comber areas, had mobilized at 8 o'clock, equipped with food and warm overcoats, for they had been told that they would be out all night. Before leaving Newtownards they were armed with hickory 'picking sticks' about two and a half feet long from the factory looms. They were then marched out of the town by a quiet road, picked up by the motor car section and conveyed to Donaghadee.

On their arrival they placed a strong cordon across the entrance to the quay. Some rather anxious-looking men who were standing together about half way up the pier, turned out on investigation to be the District Inspector of police with two of his men and two coastguards. Lord Dunleath, who commanded the battalion, carefully posted a circle of volunteers round them and warned them to stay where they were.[45]

The heavy transport arrived and the lorries were backed down the quay right to the lighthouse and packed together as closely as possible, ready to move up one by one to the single crane and get away with the utmost expedition. When Craig arrived there was a small vessel lying alongside the quay, and her captain refused to move at that time of night. 'There's something special on,' Craig shouted down the companion-way. 'If you move up you can charge your own demurrages.' The skipper's head popped up like a jack-in-a-box. 'That's spoken like a gentleman,' he said, and then as he looked round at all the activity on the quay, 'Can I gi'e ye a hand?'[46]

At Donaghadee, as at the other landing points, the signallers had earthed the telephone and telegraph wires. They had indeed put out of action the entire telephone and telegraph system along both shores of Belfast Lough, and north to Larne. The coastguard station at Donaghadee, however, was connected by a direct submarine cable to the Coastguard Headquarters at Kingstown, near Dublin, a fact either unknown to, or overlooked by, the U.V.F. This cable remained live throughout the night, and the Donaghadee coastguards were able to report what was happening to Kingstown, which at once informed the authorities. A message was flashed to Belfast, to tell the police there what was happening on their own doorstep, but it arrived too late to be of any use.[47]

At 11.45 one of the coastguards, Herbert Edward Painter,

was sent with a dispatch to the house of his divisional officer Lieutenant Ducat, at Ballywilliam on the Bangor Road — the message presumably had some connection with these facts. When he arrived at the house he dismounted from his bicycle and left it leaning against the gate, but before he reached the door, he collapsed and died from a heart attack brought on by the over-exertion. He was not found until after 1 o'clock. Painter was only thirty-eight, and he left an invalid wife and two small children.[48]

Totally unaware of this occurrence, Craig and his men were waiting patiently at the harbour. The hours after midnight passed slowly, for the delay in getting the *Innismurray* away at Larne had set back the timetable. It was 3 a.m. before a signal arrived from Orlock Point to say that she would leave Larne at 4 a.m. and be in Donaghadee at 7 a.m. Craig tore a page from his pocket book and wrote to Headquarters. 'We will all stand fast. All quiet. Send more motors if possible.'[49]

The *Innismurray* reached Donaghadee at 6 a.m., and Craig reported that all was quiet and that he had begun unloading the rifles, 'Police, coastguards and Customs looking on,' he added, 'but not interfering.' Since the ship had arrived after dawn, all the unloading had to be carried out in broad daylight. This was not so dangerous because the port was small, and far from Belfast or any military establishment. The Vetterlis were expeditiously landed and taken by the transport to convenient hiding places, as it would have been too risky to take them farther during daylight, and they completed their journey the following night.

At 8.30 Craig sent the third and last of his laconic reports 'All cleared. All quiet. Many thanks for the motors. Am returning to Craigavon. Please wire Carson'.[50]

Not long afterwards in London a telegram boy was ringing the bell at 5 Eaton Place. When he tore open the telegram Carson saw, to his immense relief, that it contained a single word — LION. It was the code signal that all was well.[51]

17

DARKNESS AND SHADOWS

On Saturday, most of the London papers managed to get out extra editions with the first news of the gun-running, and they were bought by thousands of football supporters up for the Cup Final. *The Times* had unluckily chosen that day to devote two whole pages, with a large map of northern Ireland, to an inquest on 'The Plot that Failed', and had to find space for the Larne news as well, which stole some of the thunder. Much more detailed reports appeared on Monday, including the scoop by the *Daily Express* correspondent, who had travelled to Larne with the motor transport from Templepatrick. The *Express* also published a cartoon showing Asquith and Churchill as coastguards fast asleep while the *Mountjoy* sailed away on the horizon; the caption read 'The Coup Final'.

Asquith received the news on Saturday morning in a telegram from Birrell at the Irish Office. Another telegram from Lord Aberdeen urged the immediate arrest of Adair and McCalmont, and requested authority to proceed in spite of the fact that 'the persons named and other leaders will be prepared to resist'. This was considered by the Cabinet on Monday morning, and when the Commons assembled, Asquith, describing the events at Larne as a 'grave and unprecedented outrage', announced that the Government would take without delay appropriate steps to vindicate the authority of the law.

At first Asquith did intend to take strong measures. The Cabinet met on four successive mornings, and the Irish Law Officers suggested three methods of procedure, all of which were rejected in favour of the advice of Simon that the correct course was to prosecute by 'exhibiting an information' in Dublin. Redmond, who had always resolutely opposed the arrest of the U.V.F. leaders on the grounds that it could do nothing but harm, wrote to Asquith to urge him against any such action, and Birrell agreed with him. Ultimately their advice was accepted; when the Cabinet broke up on Thursday morning Asquith telegraphed to Birrell in Dublin 'Please do not sign informations until further notice', and there the matter ended.[1] No further action was taken beyond a routine locking of the stable door; a cruiser and eighteen destroyers were sent to patrol the coasts of Antrim and Down, at an estimated cost of £3,500 a day. The U.V.F. signallers saluted them, and the officers were hospitably entertained ashore.

The gun-running did at least enable the Government to regain the moral advantage lost in March. Since the week-end of the Curragh incident they had been under relentless attack in the Commons, and Asquith alone had answered some 700 questions on the subject and was understandably wearied of it. If Larne did not altogether divert the Opposition, it did at least (in the Irish sense of the word) divert the public, for the breathtaking audacity and the faultless planning of the operation provided copy for journalists for many days to come.

When the immediate bluster of righteous indignation had subsided, Asquith had still to face the hard facts of the situation. Ulster was armed, and the policy of 21 March could never be repeated. Some other way out of the Irish impasse had to be found, and evidence that it was being sought was not long in coming. On 28 April Austen Chamberlain had moved for a full and impartial inquiry into all the circumstances surrounding the Curragh affair. Churchill, replying for the Government, asked how the Opposition 'fresh from their exploits in Ireland' dared ask for a judicial inquiry into the conduct of those responsible for maintaining law and order. It would be like a vote of censure by the criminal classes on the police. The Government had been patient throughout the long preparations for rebellion, the planning of military operations, the arming of 100,000 men to shoot down the King's servants. In such circumstances they had every right to put 40,000 to 50,000 men into Ulster, to use the Fleet to support the Army, to begin the arrest of the leaders, the seizure of arms, and the prevention of drilling. For the past two years they had had to listen to threats of civil war. Did the Opposition think that if war came only one side would take action? Was it to be all brilliant gun-running *coups* on one side, and nothing but fiendish plots on the other? He wished to make it perfectly clear that if rebellion came the Government would put it down, and if it came to civil war they would do their best to win the war.

Then suddenly the big stick was changed into an olive branch. Taking up a typewritten paper, Churchill read a statement which made the Nationalist and Radical members boil with anger. Observing that Carson was running great risks for strife, he begged him to run some for peace. 'Let him ask for the amendments to safeguard the dignity and interests of Protestant Ulster and promise in return to use his influence and goodwill to make Ireland an integral unit in a federal system.' That night Redmond wrote an indignant letter to Asquith, but the Government was rapidly approaching the point where it was prepared to pay any price for an Irish settlement.[2]

Carson's reply came next day. He took full responsibility for what had happened at Larne, but his tone was moderate. 'Nobody', he said, 'supposes that at my age I prefer strife to peace.' If only the Government would take away the limitation of six years and put instead 'until this Parliament shall otherwise determine' he would be prepared to meet them. 'If Home Rule is to pass,' he continued, 'much as I detest it . . . my earnest hope . . . would be that the Government of Ireland for the South and West would prove and might prove such a success in the future, notwithstanding all our anticipations, that it might be even for the interests of Ulster itself to move towards that Government and come in under it and form one unit in relation to Ireland.' He would like to see Ireland as an integral unit in the federal scheme, but for himself, he only wanted loyally to carry out the promises he had made to those who trusted him, and get for them such terms as will preserve for them their dignity, and their civil and religious freedom.[3]

Taking heart at this improvement in the political atmosphere Asquith re-opened negotiations on 5 May. Nothing practical was achieved, but Carson's attitude was highly significant. 'Only a fool would fight if there is a hope of accommodation,' he declared, 'and what a great thing it would be if this long-standing controversy could be settled once and for all.' On 12 May Asquith explained to the Commons that he proposed to secure the third reading of the Home Rule Bill before the Whitsun recess, and he also promised that an Amending Bill would be introduced in the Lords.

The consequence of this revelation was another stormy day in the House. The Unionists, having failed to elicit from Asquith the nature of the proposals which the Amending Bill would contain, created such an uproar that the Speaker, in exasperation, asked the Leader of the Opposition if it had his assent and approval. 'I would not presume', replied Bonar Law, 'to criticize what you consider your duty, Sir, but I know mine, and that is not to answer any such question.' At that the Speaker adjourned the House, and a few days later he apologized for his error of judgement.[4]

In Ulster a state of extreme tension persisted from the night of the gun-running until Whitsun. On the evening of Sunday 26th Macready arrived in Belfast 'full of desire to make the Ulster Volunteer Force laugh on the wrong side of their mouths', but after some discussion with Gleichen he cooled down. He thought that either the police or the military should have known about the gun-running beforehand and done something about it, but Gleichen pointed out that the Commissioner had no authority outside Belfast, and that it was not the business of soldiers to stop smuggling and gun-running. Unconvinced, Macready felt that the only thing to do now was 'to fill Ulster up with troops'.[5]

The U.V.F. was very much on the alert, and the G.O.C. issued to Colonel Couchman precise instructions to be carried out if the leaders were arrested:

'(1) Wire at once to London "Udeleag".*

(2) Mobilize as strong as possible, and march the men at once, day or night, to the localities where rifles are, undo the packages and let every man carry his own rifle away.

(3) If possible section commanders should be instructed to be responsible for the rifles of the sections and keep them together.

(4) Battalions moving towards the rifle depots *must be as strong as possible*, and look after themselves if attacked, but do not fire the first shot.

(5) Warn outlying counties.'[6]

In fact no military moves were ordered, and in any case by Sunday it was already too late. On the night of the 25th the

* i.e. Union Defence League.

U.V.F. Motor Car Corps had without interference removed the arms from the dumps to armouries at or near battalion headquarters in areas designated by the Old Town Hall. The distribution was, of course, shrouded in secrecy, but it is indicated, with probable accuracy, by a list among the C.S.O.'s papers, dated 4 May, which shows that the bulk of the German rifles (about 15,000) went to Belfast, Antrim and Down, and the rest to Londonderry and Tyrone. The Vetterlis landed at Donaghadee were distributed in Armagh, Fermanagh, and Monaghan, with 1,000 going to Londonderry.[7]

On 9 May Hacket Pain issued special instructions for the proper care of the arms and ammunition. The canvas bales with no marks each contained five new Steyr magazine rifles, fitted with the short bayonet and 500 rounds of ammunition in clips. Bales with one long black mark lengthways contained five German magazine rifles with long bayonet and 500 rounds of ammunition. Bales with four black marks crossways contained four Vetterlis with bayonets and 850 rounds of ammunition. Battalion commanders were to be responsible for the care and storage of the rifles near the place of mobilization; in no circumstances were they to be buried, unless rendered damp-proof.[8]

No cache of U.V.F. arms was ever seized by the authorities in 1914, and the ingenuity employed in concealing the rifles provided many entertaining stories at the time, some of which are current in Ulster to the present day. Gleichen relates one from his own experience; a short time after the gun-running he was spending a week-end at Antrim Castle, and discovered to his great amusement when he went to fetch some tennis balls from the long box in the hall that 'their place had been taken by something much more reprehensible'.[9]

One result of the gun-running, apparently unexpected by the U.V.F., was the stimulus which it gave to the National Volunteers, who had by now enrolled as many men, and who had every intention of arming themselves as soon as possible and in the same way. A sizeable proportion of the National Volunteers belonged to Ulster, and while the U.V.F. were armed and the National Volunteers arming, the peace of the north rested upon a knife edge.

In the first week of May General Adair wrote to Headquarters to ask what action the U.V.F. should take with regard to the National Volunteers. 'In the meantime,' he added, 'I presume I may proceed with present arrangements for disarming the Nationalists on the first occasion of their giving the U.V.F. any trouble.'[10] He was told that the attitude towards the National Volunteers must be one of tolerance, and that 'if absolutely necessary in case of violence, threatenings or outrages, yes, they should be disarmed'.[11]

It was true that both volunteer forces had declared that their intention was not to fight each other but the British Government. Nevertheless, with feeling running high and the men often drilling within a few hundred yards of each other in some localities, there was always the risk of a collision which might have incalculable consequences.

Now that sufficient arms were available, the U.V.F. were contemplating the formation in each regiment of *bataillons de marche* — 'marching battalions' which would be prepared to move in any direction in an emergency.[12] Their real purpose would be to contain the National Volunteers in areas like North Antrim where there were isolated pockets of Roman Catholic population. Careful instructions were also issued with regard to action against the police. In the event of the police attempting to seize the arms, the U.V.F. were not to fire on them or use any extreme measures. Instead they must always be present in sufficient strength to render such an attempt hopeless, and to anticipate any movement by the police they must obtain information from 'constables in sympathy with the movement'. If the police produced arms, then armed volunteers would take the place of the unarmed. The same tactics were to be used if an attempt was made to arrest the leaders.[13]

As the time for the third reading of the Home Rule Bill drew near, the U.V.F. were warned to hold themselves ready for any emergency, and divisional commanders were authorized to take whatever steps they deemed advisable to maintain the peace and 'to prevent disloyal processions, burnings, bonfires, and other provocative actions or displays taking place in Unionist territory throughout their command'.[14] So tense was the atmosphere that even the smallest incident created danger. A company of the Norfolks on night manoeuvres near Craigavon on 15 May alarmed Headquarters into mobilizing two battalions of the East Belfast U.V.F. And although the Norfolks' C.O. published the future dates of his manoeuvres in the Press, the story that the leaders' houses had been surrounded migrated from the local papers to the *Daily Mail* and *Daily Express* and eventually led to questions in the Commons. A few days later when a motor car tyre burst in the suburbs of Belfast both the Ulster and National Volunteers of the district rushed to arms.[15]

Macready crossed to London and returned with instructions which Gleichen regarded as highly satisfactory since they reflected his own recommendations of the previous winter. They were that if Carson set up his Provisional Government the troops were to sit tight in Holywood and do nothing, that the Lord Mayor, and not the Government, was responsible for keeping order in Belfast, and could use the police and if necessary the U.V.F. for this purpose, but that he was not to call on the soldiers except in the last resort.[16]

The Home Rule Bill was passed on 25 May, and in Ulster the day came and went in peace. Afterwards the G.O.C. expressed his high appreciation of the discipline and common sense displayed by the Force, especially in Derry, 'a centre requiring special tact and discretion'.[17]

A strange calm now descended upon Ulster. The strain had been too intense and had lasted too long, and in a curious way, everyone seemed to be relieved that the Bill had passed. There had to be a truce before the final confrontation, a lull before the storm. The rival Volunteer Forces took stock of each other's armament, but almost as if comparing notes, and each took pride in its efficiency in keeping its own rowdies quiet.[18]

The cold and uncertain spring of 1914 had given way to a summer of rare splendour. As June came in with long days of unbroken sunshine, the U.V.F. held a series of reviews and parades at which many battalions were presented with colours. Carson came over at Whitsuntide and, while inspecting the West Belfast Regiment, including Crozier's Special Force, uttered a warning note. 'I recognize some of the *Mountjoy*'s cargo,' he told them, 'I rely on you to keep your arms with a view to keeping the peace.'[19]

From this point on Carson's attitude changed perceptibly, and his mood became pessimistic. The great object for which he had striven for two years, to which he had devoted so much of his time and energies, was to force Asquith to drop the Home Rule Bill, and in this he had patently failed. His hand had been called; it was time for him to put his cards on the table. But all along he had hoped that the Government would give way before the armed rebellion of Ulster became necessary.

He knew — no one better — that the U.V.F. would fight to the last ditch. They would never let him down, nor he them, but in his heart of hearts he could not feel the certain confidence of Craig and the Ulstermen that all would be well. Civil war in the United Kingdom, especially at a time of menace abroad, would be a catastrophe; humanity as well as policy demanded that a way out be found, and how was it to be found without the sacrifice of principle, the breaking of his sworn word?

The next date which loomed menacingly ahead was 12 July, on which the Orangemen held their Boyne celebrations and parades, a day of maximum danger for civil tumult in Northern Ireland. Carson had absolute control of his followers, they hung upon his every word, but this time, when conditions were so critical, he was prey to a neurotic anxiety as the date approached. The Government had meanwhile announced the terms of the Amending Bill, which Lord Crewe introduced in the House of Lords on 23 June, inviting amendments to it. To the disappointment of the Unionists it merely repeated the offer of March 9, and the peers immediately substituted for county option and the six-year limit the permanent exclusion of the whole of Ulster. Thus amended, the Bill passed its third reading on 14 July and was sent down to the Commons.

Carson went to Belfast on the 10th for a specially convened session of the Ulster Unionist Council. Was the Rubicon to be crossed at last? On the previous day Craig had issued to the Press the preamble and some of the articles of the constitution of the Provisional Government, until now a closely kept secret. One article stated that the administration would be taken over 'in trust for the constitution of the United Kingdom', and that 'upon the restoration of direct Imperial Government, the Provisional Government shall cease to exist'.[20] All along this had been the main Unionist defence for extra-legal action, and an ingenious theory was even advanced that, in attempting to enforce Home Rule upon the whole of Ireland, the Liberals were clearly insane, and that reasonable men had therefore a duty to carry on the functions of administration while this aberration continued.

The Unionists took comfort in the fact that Professor A. V. Dicey, acknowledged as the greatest expert on the Constitution, had signed the British Covenant, and strongly supported their resistance. But Dicey was careful to point out to Milner that if the Home Rule Bill passed, defiance of it would be 'crime and probably treason', and that though some defence might be argued for the Ulstermen, he doubted if this were so for Englishmen.[21] Milner, ignoring this advice, went on studying ways in which Ulster might take the initiative and assume the prerogatives of sovereignty before the Home Rule Bill left the Commons. On 12 May he had written to Carson: 'I have heard of the plan to get the Ulster magistrates to set the ball rolling, and it seems to me such an excellent one, that I am only afraid that it may be "turned down" by people here without adequate consideration ... of course you know much better than I whether the scheme is feasible. If you thought it an impracticable one, I should not have a word to say. But I should be slow to put it out of court if it smiled to the Ulstermen. Something has got to be done, and I cannot think of any forward move, which would be less open to objection.'[22]

Milner's plan, in short, was that the lieutenants, deputy-lieutenants and magistrates of Ulster, 'or as many of them as are trustworthy', should convene and form a 'provisional committee', which would pass resolutions calling upon all good citizens to give them every assistance and support. The committee would thereby call the Provisional Government into existence for the limited purpose of assisting the magistracy to keep the peace; it would not assume any administrative powers. The Cabinet would then be in a dilemma. 'If it did nothing, which was the most probable course, it would be seriously shaken in the House of Commons, and it could not prevent the provisional committee rapidly extending its authority and so making things much easier for the subsequent taking over of the administration by the Provisional Government.'[23]

The whole point of this ingenious scheme was, as far as possible, to make the Government rather than the rebels appear in the wrong. However Carson was in no hurry to take the final step, and throughout May and June he had kept his cards very close to his chest.

One curious aspect of the Ulster Provisional Government, which ought to be mentioned here, was its attitude to women's franchise. Carson had promised in September 1913 that in Ulster women would be admitted to the vote, and that there would be a woman on each of the committees of the Central Authority. Craig was known to be an advocate of women's suffrage, but not all his colleagues agreed with him. In March 1914, when a suffragist deputation reminded Carson of his promise, he had to admit that the Ulster members were divided on the matter, and that he could not allow division in the ranks as long as the Home Rule question was before them. Much dissatisfied with this reply, the women formally declared war on the Ulster movement. On 10 April windows were smashed in the Old Town Hall, and a few days later as Carson was waiting for his train after inspecting the Central Antrim volunteers he was attacked by two suffragettes who loudly accused him of 'betraying the women of Ulster'. They were escorted from the platform by the U.V.F. guard. A wave of minor incendiarism swept over the province, and in Ballymena two Australian ladies who were on a motoring tour of Ireland were mistaken for suffragettes and surrounded by a hostile crowd. Eventually they took refuge in a shop, and the local U.V.F. had to be called out to help the police escort them to their hotel.[24]

But such incidents were entirely overshadowed by the major crisis. The Unionist Council's session on 10 July was secret, but Ronald McNeill, who was a member of the Provisional Government, gives us an account of it. Carson spoke for forty minutes, explaining the gravity of the situation. 'Nothing remained for them in Ulster but to carry out the policy they had resolved upon long ago, and to make good the Covenant. After his speech a quiet and business-like discussion followed. Plenary authority to take any action necessary in emergency was conferred unanimously on the executive. The course to be followed in assuming the administration was explained and agreed to, and when they separated, all the members felt that the crisis for which they had been preparing so long had at last come upon them. There was no flinching.'[25]

The 'Twelfth' came and went without incident, Carson's presence being, in the words of one of his admirers 'worth twenty battalions in keeping order'. As it fell that year upon a Sunday, the parades were held on the following day. On the Saturday Carson had reviewed the U.V.F. at Larne and publicly thanked Crawford who was on the platform. 'The lesson of that night', he told them, 'has taught you what discipline means: it has taught you what can be achieved, not by any rowdy spirit or rowdy element, but by carefully thought-out plans and by obedience to orders.' But the melancholy which weighed on Carson's spirits was now publicly uttered. 'I see no hopes of peace,' he said, 'I see nothing at present but darkness and shadows . . . we must be ready. In my own opinion the great climax and great crisis of our fate, and the fate of our country, cannot be delayed for many weeks . . . unless something happens — when we shall have once more to assert the manhood of our race.'[26]

18

'THE KAISER'S ULSTER FRIENDS'

When the *Mountjoy* steamed out of Bangor harbour on 25 April Agnew turned her head north-east, in the precise direction from which the fast destroyer might be expected. Once again she became the innocent collier *Clydevalley*, and except for her strange crew there was nothing about her to arouse suspicion. But the alarm was false; no warship appeared out of the morning mist to intercept her, and five miles out Agnew changed course and headed down the Irish Sea.[1]

Crawford had now decided that it would be dangerous to make for Fishguard, and Agnew agreed to land him at Rosslare, along with one of the volunteers who did not want to go any farther, and then take the ship on to Hamburg. The two men were put ashore but Crawford was later identified by a coast-guard who apparently tried to blackmail him. Followed on board the Dublin train, he had, in the best secret service tradition, to switch compartments and disguises and, to his grief, to tear up the precious orders signed by Sir Edward. Eventually he made his way to Belfast where he went into hiding for a few days in Cunningham's house at Glencairn, before returning to Hamburg. Carson had advised that he should stay on the Continent until all the fuss had died down.[2]

Meanwhile the *Clydevalley* was making eight knots an hour in calm weather, which Agnew thought good since none of his firemen had ever been in a ship's stokehold before. 'Sweat poured off us in streams,' one of them recalls, 'and we drank gallons of water in the week's voyage to Hamburg. When we looked in a mirror there we hardly recognized ourselves. All of us had lost so much weight that we looked like skeletons.'[3]

Off the German coast the sea was like glass, and an eerie white fog closed down upon them as they neared the mouth of the Elbe. The *Clydevalley* slipped along in furtive silence, with fog-horns sounding all around her, and tied up in Hamburg on the last day of April. Early next morning Agnew went to seek Spiro, but he was not at his office. He did find Schneider, however, who arranged for an agent to look after the ship. Her papers were sent to the British consul, but her notoriety had reached him first, and he angrily demanded that Agnew should come and see him at once. Instead Agnew went to the station to meet Crawford and his wife arriving from Belfast.

His next action was to engage a motor launch and search the port for the *Fanny*. When at last he located her he learned that Captain Falck, contrary to his instructions, had written home and received letters and newspapers from his wife. He had discovered that he was a very unpopular man in Norway for having acted against the interests of a friendly power. He was so upset that he locked himself in his cabin, alleging that Captain Luke, the chief mate, and the engineer had all combined against him. On Agnew's arrival he emerged, with the ship's log under his arm, and declared that he was taking it to the Norwegian consul. Agnew took it from him and he never got it again.[4]

All these activities could hardly have gone on without the knowledge of the Hamburg authorities and of the German Government. Crawford was under police surveillance during February while the rifles were being packed, but, technically at least, there was no reason for the police to intervene for the transaction was perfectly legal and Spiro took the responsibility of seeing that regulations were not infringed. There is nothing, in the evidence which the author has seen, to suggest that at any stage the purchase of the guns was other than a straightforward business deal.

Nevertheless it would be difficult to shake the popular belief that Germany connived at the gun-running in order to foment Irish troubles, and there are some curious aspects of the affair which lend colour to it. One is the coincidence that while Crawford's rifles were being loaded into the lighter, other derricks in Hamburg were 'swinging huge crates of rifles and other munitions aboard the ships *Ypiranga*, *Bavaria*, and *Kronprinzessin Cecilie*, their destination Vera Cruz'.[5] This was a consequence of German intervention in the affairs of Mexico, and was part of a deliberate challenge to American and British influence there. Although the Ulster gun-running was on a smaller scale, it is hard to believe that it did not form part of the same plan or policy, and would at least be well-known to the German Government.

The Kaiser was undoubtedly interested in the Ulster crisis; it had, indeed, been brought to his attention by the Ulstermen themselves, who, at an early stage of the agitation, had briefly considered him as a latter-day substitute for William III. In January 1911 Craig had spoken of a feeling in Ulster that Germany and the German Emperor would be preferred to 'the rule of John Redmond, Patrick Ford and the Molly Maguires',* and Crawford himself said in a speech at Bangor in April 1912 that 'if they were put out of the Union . . . he would infinitely prefer to change his allegiance right over to the Emperor of Germany, or anyone else who had got a proper and stable government'.[6] Such sentiments scandalized the Liberals, and the Ulster Liberal Association published a pamphlet on the subject under the title of *The Kaiser's Ulster Friends*.

Tongues were set wagging again in 1913 when Carson met the German Emperor at a luncheon party in Homburg in August 1913. The conversation ran upon gardens, and the latter, who had seen a photograph of the gardens at Mount Stewart,† said that they must be very beautiful. Carson assured him that they were, and the Kaiser remarked wistfully that the management of gardens was very like that of States. He thought that Britain did too little to consolidate her Empire. 'We have our own ideas', replied Carson, 'and we give them self-government.' The Kaiser then confided that he would have liked to go to Ireland, but that his grandmother, Queen Victoria, had not let him, adding with a smile: 'Perhaps she thought I wanted to take the little place.' 'I think, sir,' replied Carson, 'you are well out of it,' at which there was general laughter. But when the German ruler, pressing on indomitably, asked about Ulster, Carson adroitly changed the subject.[7]

The influence of the Irish crisis on German policy has generally been underestimated. A month after the Kaiser's meeting with Carson, the German strategist General von Bernhardt wrote an article for the *Berlin Post* entitled 'Ireland, England and Germany' in which he declared 'it is not without

* Ford was a veteran of the Fenian Movement. 'Molly Maguires' was the popular name for the Hibernians.

† The seat of Lord Londonderry in Co. Down.

interest to know that if it ever comes to war with England, Germany will have allies in the enemy's camp, who in given circumstances are resolved to bargain, and at any rate will constitute a grave anxiety for England, and perhaps tie fast a portion of the English troops'.[8]

Nor was Germany the only country interested in England's Irish difficulties. After the Curragh incident Wilson had had to make a special visit to Paris to assure General de Castelnau that the affair was less serious than it seemed, and in July 1914 the Belgian minister at Berlin had told his government that England was paralysed by internal dissensions and her Irish quarrels.[9]

There is some evidence to suggest that the Ulster situation received serious attention in Austria. On 26 July Dr. E. J. Dillon, a special correspondent in Vienna, telegraphed his newspaper that one of the reasons why Austria expected a free hand in dealing with Serbia was that the British Government was absorbed 'in forecasting and preparing for the fateful consequences of its internal policy in regard to Irish Home Rule, which may, it is apprehended, culminate in civil war'.[10] The Chief of the General Staff of the Austrian army, Field-Marshal Conrad von Hötzendorff, refers directly in his memoirs to the effect of Home Rule on British policy, and mentions both the raising of the U.V.F. and the Curragh incident.[11]

It is reasonable to assume that Germany had secret agents in Ulster in 1914. During the spring and summer a number of German journalists came over to report on events,[12] and afterwards people remembered that some German geologists had just then been very interested in the rock formation of Co. Antrim. The American ambassador in Berlin, James W. Gerard, wrote later in his memoirs that 'The raising of the Ulster army by Sir Edward Carson, one of the most gigantic bluffs in all history, which had no more revolutionary or political significance than a torchlight parade during one of our Presidential campaigns, was reported by the German spies as a real and serious revolutionary movement, and, of course, it was believed by the Germans that Ireland would rise in rebellion the moment that war was declared.'[13] Whether Gerard or the German secret service was farther out in assessing the importance of the U.V.F. it is difficult to say, but experienced foreign observers in Berlin and Vienna certainly believed that the

Central Powers calculated upon England's being unable to take any active part if war should come.

The strangest episode of all was the visit which the Counsellor at the German Embassy in London, Richard von Kühlmann, was alleged to have made to Belfast on 12 July 1914. Unfortunately this brilliant and cultivated diplomatist says nothing at all about the Ulster situation in his memoirs, although they do contain detail about his day-to-day interest in British politics and his contacts with leading figures in the Government. When the war broke out, Kühlmann was cast in the role of villain by a section of the British press, which alleged that he had gone behind the back of the German ambassador Lichnowsky in advising Berlin on the situation in Britain. Between 6 July and 2 August he was at home in Germany, and the rumour was later current that he had visited Ulster incognito during this time to see how things were for himself. In her autobiography Margot Asquith, who knew Kühlmann very well indeed, recounts that she discussed the trip with him on his return, and several writers mention it with circumstantial detail.[14]

The matter was brought to a head by Dillon in the House of Commons in 1917, when, in the course of an attack on Carson, he declared: 'We shall want to know what brought Baron Kühlmann over to Ulster on the eve of the war. We shall want to know what were the relations between the leaders of the Ulster party and the chief spy of the Kaiser in Ireland. We shall want to know about the dispatch which Baron Kühlmann sent from Ulster to Berlin, and which was seen by a friend of mine in Vienna, where it was sent, and on receipt of which dispatch the Emperor determined to go on with the war.'[15] After the war Kühlmann emphatically denied ever having been in Ireland in his life, and one of his English friends, Thomas Rhodes, in a book which he wrote to vindicate him, said that Mrs Asquith's statement was 'without a shadow of foundation'.[16] In any case there was little that Kühlmann could have learned in Belfast which he was not able to find in the columns of *The Times* and the *Morning Post*, which he read over his breakfast every morning.[17]

What *is* clear is that it was part of his duty to study the Ulster situation. J. A. Spender, the great Liberal journalist, who met him almost daily at this time, later wrote that Kühlmann 'seemed very well-informed about the Ulster movement, indeed better-informed than I was myself, and he used to tell me that I underrated its seriousness'.[18] Kühlmann deliberately cultivated Spender because the latter was always in a position to hear information from Asquith or members of the Cabinet.[19]

It was against a rapidly darkening international background that Asquith made his final attempt to bring the Irish parties to agreement. On 20 July, when he was expected to introduce the Amending Bill in the Commons, he announced instead that the King had called an all party conference at Buckingham Palace for the following day. Asquith and Lloyd George represented the Government, Lansdowne and Bonar Law the Opposition. Carson and Craig spoke for the Ulster Unionists and Redmond and Dillon for the Nationalists.

The King addressed them briefly before they began their deliberations. 'For months', he said, 'we have watched with deep misgivings the course of events in Ireland. The trend has been surely and steadily towards an appeal to force and to-day the cry of civil war is on the lips of the most responsible and sober-minded of my people. We have, in the past, endeavoured to act as a civilized example to the world, and to me it is unthinkable, as it must be to you, that we should be brought to the brink of fratricidal strife upon issues apparently so capable of adjustment as these you are now asked to consider, if handled in a spirit of generous compromise.' Having wished them Godspeed the King left, and the Speaker took the chair.[20] The discussion was soon centred upon the question of area. Redmond insisted that if any part of Ireland was to be excluded from Home Rule, it must not include areas which were predominantly Nationalist, whereas Carson asked for the 'clean cut' of the whole of Ulster, declaring that if this were done generously Ulster might, within a reasonable time, be willing to come in to a united Ireland.[21]

For the next few days the conference, in Churchill's words, 'toiled round the muddy byways of Fermanagh and Tyrone' without reaching the firm ground of compromise. Asquith, as a last resort, proposed the definite exclusion of the six north-eastern counties which now form Northern Ireland, but neither Carson nor Redmond would accept this and the conference broke down. The Prime Minister reported its failure to the Cabinet on July 24, and as the meeting ended Sir Edward Grey was handed a document from the Foreign Office. It was the Austrian ultimatum to Serbia. In his book *The World Crisis* Churchill recalls that as he listened to the Foreign Secretary's measured tones, he found it difficult to disengage his mind from the tedious debate which had just closed. Then he began to perceive that the ultimatum was one which no State in the world could accept. 'The parishes of Fermanagh and Tyrone faded back into the mists and squalls of Ireland, and a strange light began immediately, but by perceptible gradations, to fall and grow upon the map of Europe.'[22]

But Ireland, which had held the stage for so long, was not to leave it for another week, and not without a characteristic sensation. On the afternoon of 26 July the Irish National Volunteers, following the Ulster pattern, landed a quantity of rifles at Howth harbour near Dublin. This time, however, the operation was carried out in broad daylight, no attempt was made at concealment, and the volunteers, including the young Eamonn de Valera, marched off with the rifles on their shoulders.

Unlike his Northern counterparts, Mr. David Harrel, the Assistant Commissioner of Police, was not prepared to stand idly by while the guns were taken away. He telephoned Sir James Dougherty, the Under-Secretary in Dublin Castle, but he neglected to tell him that he was not only calling for more police, but also, through General Cuthbert who commanded the infantry brigade in Dublin, for two companies of the King's Own Scottish Borderers.

The volunteers found their route back to Dublin barred by the troops. About twenty rifles were seized, and in the scuffle two of the soldiers were shot in the legs, but the Volunteers escaped with the rest of the guns to Dublin, where all kinds of rumours now began to circulate. On their return to the city the troops were jeered at and stoned by a huge crowd as they marched along Bachelor's Walk on the quayside of the Liffey. When almost every one of the soldiers had been hit, Major Haig, the officer in charge, changed his rearguard and ordered it to hold the road with fixed bayonets and rifles at the ready. Though he later stated emphatically that he gave no orders to fire, firing broke out. Three people were killed and thirty-eight wounded.[23]

There was an immediate outcry throughout Nationalist

Ireland, and Bachelor's Walk took its place in the Irish martyrology. A shocked and dismayed Government made Harrel the scapegoat, and Asquith privately expressed his disillusion with the Irish Administration in Dublin Castle. 'I am tempted to regret', he wrote bitterly, 'that I didn't make the "clean cut" six months ago, and insist upon the booting out of Aberdeen . . . and the whole crew. A weaker and more incompetent lot were never in charge of a leaky ship in stormy weather; and poor old Birrell's occasional and fitful appearances at the wheel do not greatly improve matters.'[24]

At the very end of July war in Ulster seemed certain, and only the outbreak of the war in Europe averted it. The fierce light which has been directed on the German war has thrown the preparations for that other war into the shadows, but they were, in fact, extraordinarily elaborate. In Ulster the U.V.F. was completely ready for the *coup d'état* and waited only for Carson to telegraph 'Go ahead' or 'Hold back in the meantime'. On 29 July Craig had written to him, 'you may take it that immediately you signify by the pre-arranged code that we are to go ahead, everything prepared will be carried out to the letter unless in the meantime you suggest any modification. All difficulties have been overcome and we are in a very strong position'.[25]

Craig anticipated a blockade and was trying to arrange for sympathizers in Glasgow to send a shipload of flour, meal, tinned beef, tea and sugar. He thought that Milner's organization might do something in Liverpool and the other ports. The residences which had since been earmarked as clearance and base hospitals were now made ready, according to a carefully worked out plan, and the U.V.F. medical corps prepared to cope with thousands of hypothetical casualties.

A very elaborate scheme had been drawn up for the evacuation of women and children to England and Scotland. It was considered desirable that certain categories of refugees should be sent away before the actual outbreak of hostilities. They were (1) the wives and families of the U.V.F. Special Force, whose assured protection would set free the men to fight where and when required, and (2) women and children in exposed or outlying districts where they could not easily be safeguarded. These were not merely paper plans; the names of the people concerned had been entered into huge ledgers at Headquarters, refugee officers appointed, and transport arranged, while on the English side rest stations at Eaton Hall and elsewhere were being got ready to receive them.[26]

Meanwhile Milner was trying to arrange a currency for the rebel government. Moreton Frewen, a former M.P. for North-east Cork and a financial expert, sent him a specimen of a 'clearing house certificate' which had been used in the New York Bank crisis of 1907, and suggested that it could be used as a model upon which the Ulster Provisional Government might base its own paper currency. Eventually these certificates would replace sovereigns and banknotes in Ulster, and 'force the legal currency into the banks of Belfast, thus strengthening the financial resources of the Ulstermen'.

Milner wanted the Ulstermen to set up their Provisional Government at once. 'He is altogether against Ulster waiting any longer to suit Asquith's convenience,' Wilson noted, 'and is urgently in favour of a strong forward policy.' When Milner asked him what the Army would do, Wilson replied 'I think if Carson and his Government were sitting in the City Hall and we were ordered down to close the Hall, we would not go'.[27]

On the morning of 30 July Asquith was in the Cabinet room 'with a map of Ulster and a lot of statistics about populations and religions, endeavouring to get into something like shape my speech on the Amending Bill' when Bonar Law telephoned, asking him to go and see him and Carson at his house in Kensington. He had sent his car and Asquith got into it feeling that he might be about to be kidnapped by a section of Ulster Volunteers. The two Unionist leaders proposed that, in the interests of the international situation, the second reading of the Amending Bill should be postponed, in order not to adver-tise the country's dissensions at so grave a time. To this Asquith eventually agreed, after consulting his colleagues and Redmond, and announced his decision in the Commons that afternoon.[28]

On that sunny August bank holiday week-end when the world fell to pieces Carson and other members of the Opposition were the guests of Sir Edward Goulding at Wargrave over-looking the Thames. There Captain Spender came to seek him on the Sunday, on the urging of his friends in the Committee of Imperial Defence, to get a decision on the future of the U.V.F. Carson at once stated that 'a large body of Ulster Volunteers will be willing and ready to give their services for Home Defence and many will be willing and ready to serve anywhere they are required'.[29]

Next day, in spite of the intense feeling aroused by Bachelor's Walk, Redmond made a similar gesture in the House. The Government, he declared, could take their troops out of Ireland, and, 'if it is allowed to us, in comradeship with our brethren of the north, we will ourselves defend the coasts of our country.'

Redmond had spoken after the solemn statement in which Grey had explained why Britain must stand by her obligations to Belgium. At one point, with a sudden lift in his voice, the Foreign Secretary had said: 'The one bright spot in the very dreadful situation is Ireland. The position in Ireland — and this I should like to be clearly understood abroad — is not a consideration among the things we have to take into account now.'[30]

By the evening of August 4, Britain was at war with Germany, and Lord Kitchener of Khartoum, just as he was about to board a Channel steamer on his way to Egypt, was recalled to become War Minister, an office which Asquith had held since Seely's resignation in March. Three days later Kitchener sent for Colonel Hickman and said, 'I want the Ulster Volunteers'.[31] Hickman told him he must see Carson and Craig. Kitchener did see them, but the interview was less than amicable, for he had the poorest opinion of politicians, and took the line that Carson and Redmond were a pair of silly schoolboys who ought to have their heads knocked together. His opening remark 'Surely you are not going to hold out for Tyrone and Fermanagh?' was infelicitous to say the least, and drew from Carson the retort 'You're a damned clever fellow telling me what I ought to be doing'. Carson and Craig wanted the U.V.F. kept together as a fighting unit, and suggested that the word 'Ulster' should follow the name of the Division it was proposed to raise, but Kitchener would not hear of this, and the meeting ended inconclusively.[32]

Having all along insisted on the fervent loyalty of Ulster as his trump card, Carson was now in a difficult position. Already most of the officers of the U.V.F. had been recalled to their regiments; and Kitchener's eagerness to get the volunteers for his citizen army was more than matched by their keenness to enlist. But what if, when the U.V.F. was taken away, the Prime Minister should bring in the Home Rule Bill as it stood? In vain Carson sought an assurance from him that this would not be done. It looked as if Asquith's procrastinating tactics were, after all, to be successful in the most unexpected way.

On 10 August, to the dismay of the Unionists, Asquith announced that his promise to drop all controversial legislation was not to prevent him from advising the King to sign the Home Rule Bill. Carson's indignation was intense, and he feared that the Ulstermen would feel he had betrayed them. But Craig, always a reservoir of practical good sense, saw what had to be done. 'However much we curse and damn the Prime Minister in the House,' he told Carson, 'we must all say the same, that we will do our best under the circumstances for the Army and the country; then come over here and face the music. . . .'[33]

Meanwhile the news from France was bad, and before going over to Belfast to 'face the music' the leaders again saw Kitchener and offered him without conditions 35,000 of the volunteers, whereupon Kitchener agreed to the inclusion of 'Ulster' in the designation of such units as might be formed, and Hickman and Craig were appointed chief recruiting officers for the Ulster area. On leaving the War Office Craig took a taxi to the firm of Moss Brothers, which had previously supplied U.V.F. equipment, and ordered 10,000 complete uniforms.[34]

On 3 September, Carson presided at a meeting of the Ulster Unionist Council in Belfast, at which his arrangements with the War Office were approved. 'England's difficulty is not Ulster's opportunity,' he told the delegates, to frantic cheers. 'However we are treated, and however others act, let us act rightly. We do not seek to purchase terms by selling our patriotism.'[35]

Asquith had been playing for time. He had adjourned the House of Commons for a fortnight, and when it reassembled, obtained a further adjournment of ten days. 'The Irish on both sides are giving me a lot of trouble just at a difficult moment', he confided to his diary, 'I sometimes wish we could submerge the whole lot of them and their island for, say, ten years under the waves of the Atlantic.'[36]

At last, on 15 September, he announced to the House that the Home Rule Bill would become law on the 18th. In the hope of appeasing both Irish parties, he stated that it would be accompanied by a bill to suspend its operation until the end of the war, and that an Amending Bill would be introduced in the next session to give Parliament a full opportunity of 'altering, modifying, or qualifying its provisions'. At the same time Asquith paid tribute to the patriotic spirit of the U.V.F. which had made the coercion of Ulster 'unthinkable'.

In a stinging reply Bonar Law declared this a poor recompense for the Government's lack of faith. They had taken advantage of the Unionists in order to betray them, yet to squabble over this domestic quarrel in the hour of national danger would be indecent. He thereupon walked ostentatiously out of the Chamber, followed by Carson and the entire Opposition. Three days later the last scene of the Home Rule drama was enacted. There were only eight Unionists present, and Carson was not one of them.[37] On the previous day he had been married quietly to Miss Ruby Frewen in the village of Charlton Musgrave in Somerset.

By the time Carson announced in Belfast that an Ulster Division would be formed from the U.V.F. many of the young men, impatient at the politicians' delay, had already enlisted. They were possessed by the fear that the war might be over before they reached the Front. In Tyrone, however, Captain Ricardo had anticipated the formation of the division by raising two companies from the Tyrone U.V.F. which ultimately became the nucleus of the 9th Battalion of the Royal Inniskilling Fusiliers.[38]

In Belfast the recruiting officers took over a building at 60 Victoria Street, near the Old Town Hall, and as each man was attested he went from one building to the other, where he was fitted out with his uniform and full equipment at the expense of the U.V.F. Unlike other recruits elsewhere he was spared weeks of drilling in civilian clothes and inadequate boots.[39] The 36th (Ulster) Division was swiftly organized; three infantry brigades were formed — the 107th from the Belfast Volunteers, the 108th from Antrim, Down, Cavan, and Monaghan, and the 109th from Tyrone, Londonderry, Donegal, and Fermanagh, with one Belfast battalion. A pioneer battalion was raised in Co. Down, and two field companies of Royal Engineers and a Signal Company in Belfast.[40]

It was decided that, owing to his seniority of rank, General Richardson could not take command of the Division, but

Colonel Hacket Pain became C.O. of the 108th Brigade.*
Richardson stayed in Belfast as G.O.C. of the volunteers, and
another Indian Army officer, Major General C. H. Powell took
command of the Division. Craig, until his health broke down
completely in 1915, was its Assistant Adjutant and Quarter
Master General, and Spender became its G.S.O.2.

Training began at once under canvas, then in hutted camps
at Clandeboye, Ballykinler, and Newtownards in the east, and
at Finner on the coast of Donegal. The Division was kept a long
time in Ireland, to the great discontent of the men. It was not
until July 1915 that they were moved to Seaford in Sussex, and
October before they crossed to France.

But before they went, they held one more parade in Belfast.
On 8 May 1915, a fine, clear day, the buildings were decked
with flags and bunting, and special trains brought in relatives
and sight-seers from every part of the province. With bands
playing and colours flying, the volunteers marched through the
streets of their city for the last time, and those who watched
them go are haunted still, after half a century, by the memory of
their eager faces. 'There be of them, that have left a name
behind them, that their praises might be reported. And some
there be, which have no memorial; who are perished, as though
they had never been.'

* He was subsequently transferred to the Northern Command in Ireland,
a strange position for the former Chief of Staff of the U.V.F. to find himself
in.

19

THE WAY THROUGH THE WOOD

This story has an epilogue, which everyone in Ulster knows. The battle for which the U.V.F. so long and so diligently prepared was not denied them. It opened on 1 July 1916 at 7.30 a.m. and is known to history as the Battle of the Somme.[1] On that morning the 36th (Ulster) Division, as part of the X Army Corps, held a section of the British front from the north-east corner of Thiepval Wood to the point called the Mary Redan. The line was intersected by the deep-cut and impassable River Ancre, astride which the Division was to attack. In front rose the crest of the impregnable Schwaben Redoubt, guarded by lines of German trenches and masses of barbed wire; on the right flank lay the fortified village of Thiepval, on the left the strongholds of Beaumont Hamel and Y Ravine.

During the night the artillery on both sides had fallen ominously silent, and in the complete lull before dawn the 107th Brigade, assembling behind the lines, could hear a solitary nightingale singing in Aveluy Wood. As they listened, Colonel Crozier and Colonel Bernard, who commanded the 9th and 10th Battalions Royal Irish Rifles respectively, were discussing their orders. Bernard pointed out that if the 32nd Division on their right failed to take Thiepval their flank would be in the air, and they secretly agreed to change their orders if on emerging from Thiepval Wood they found that the village was still in German hands. They decided also to ignore the order that battalion officers should not accompany their men in the first assault. Bernard's last remark, as he finished his coffee and walked away, was: 'I hope this war will settle the Irish question.'[2]

At 7.30, the time chosen as zero, it had already been light for four hours. 'The dawn came with a great beauty', wrote Philip Gibbs, then a war correspondent at the front, 'there was a pale blue sky flecked with white wisps of cloud. But it was cold, and over all the fields there was a floating mist which rose from the moist earth and lay heavily on the ridges, so that the horizon was obscured.'[3] After fifty years, the men who were there remember chiefly 'the weather, bright and fair after two days rain — and the stillness of the summer dawn'.[4] As they waited in the cruel silence, some could see in imagination the sun slanting on green hills in Antrim, or on the islands set in the grey waters of Strangford; some thought back to the night they brought the guns in at Larne, others could only think 'in a few hours I shall be dead'. A few made jokes, but the laughter that came from parched throats was short and unnatural; many prayed, and sought comfort in scraps of well-remembered hymns and psalms. At dawn the padre had read to them: 'Thou shalt not be afraid for the terror by night nor the arrow which flieth by day. A thousand shall fall by thy side, and ten thousand at thy right hand, but it shall not come nigh thee.'[5] Sweating and sick, their faces white and grim under their steel helmets, they longed for the artillery to break the intolerable strain.

It was let loose at 6 a.m. and by 7.15 it had risen to a hurricane bombardment that seemed to be tearing the sky apart. The gunners claimed proudly that it was the heaviest concentration of shellfire in history and that nothing could live under it. 'Shells were rushing through the air as though all the trains in the world had leapt their rails and were driving at express speed through endless tunnels in which they met each other with dreadful collisions.'[6] Around the tightly-packed infantry the muddy trenches quaked and heaved.

Under the cover of smoke barrages some of the troops were formed up in 'No Man's Land', facing their objectives, and at 7.15 they moved through the gaps torn in the British wire and raced to within one hundred and fifty yards of the German trenches, reaching them in fact before the German defenders had left the shelter of their bunkers to re-occupy them.[7]

At zero the artillery lifted off the first line, bugles sounded, officers blew their whistles, and long lines of men sprang up and advanced at a marching pace towards the enemy positions. It was the original anniversary of the Battle of the Boyne, and as they scrambled over the parapet they shouted the old battle cries 'No Surrender' and 'Remember 1690'. Many wore Orange ribbons, and one sergeant of the Inniskillings had on his Orange sash.[8] 'I stood on the parapet between the two centre exits to wish them luck . . .' wrote Ricardo, who commanded the 9th Inniskillings, 'They got going without delay; no fuss, no shouting, no running, everything solid and thorough — just like the men themselves.' Colonel Macrory of the 10th Inniskillings saw his men 'moving forward, with rifles sloped and the sun glistening upon their fixed bayonets, keeping their alignment and distance as well as if on ceremonial parade, unfaltering, unwavering'.[9]

At 8 o'clock Crozier emerged from Thiepval Wood 'at the head of the pick of Belfast', and saw at once, from the 'heaped up masses of British corpses suspended on the German wire', that Thiepval was still held by the enemy. At the edge of the wood they came under some shell-fire. A splinter flew past Crozier's shoulder and struck the leg of the leading man behind, and he heard his men call out 'you're well out of it, Jimmy, good luck to you, give 'em our love, see you later'. The wild dash from the wood to the sunken Thiepval Road was accomplished just before the enemy got the range, but once there they were enfiladed by machine-gun fire from the village.

Crozier now went to look for Bernard on his right, only to discover that the colonel and most of his two leading companies had been killed by mortar fire as they came out of the wood. The remnants of the battalion had gone to ground in desperation, and refused to move until he drew his revolver and threatened to shoot.[10]

To the north of the Ancre the 9th Fusiliers (Armagh, Monaghan and Cavan Volunteers) swept through the enemy front line trenches at zero, though with terrible losses. On the left the 12th Rifles (the Central Antrim Volunteers who unloaded the *Mountjoy*) were repulsed at the unbroken wire of the German salient, three times reformed, and all but wiped out. Among the casualties was Captain Jenks of Larne Harbour, who was mortally wounded. By 8 o'clock the enemy had retaken all of his front line north of the river.

South of the river the assault was technically successful, despite appalling losses. The Ulstermen took the second line of German trenches at precisely 7.48 as planned, and the third

line, including a corner of the Schwaben Redoubt, at 8.48. By
10 o'clock runners came back to report that the third line had
been taken, and a last desperate attack, the order for which had
already been countermanded, brought a handful of survivors as
far as the fourth line, where the trenches were full of German
reserves. Here Craig's brother Charles, M.P. for South Antrim,
was wounded and taken prisoner. But while Thiepval remained
in German hands, and not a yard was gained on either flank,
these advances could only result in the Division pushing a deep
and untenable salient into the German lines.[11]

By the afternoon 'No Man's Land' had become 'a ghastly
spectacle of dead and wounded'. The battalions which had
come out of Thiepval Wood had walked through a hail of
machine-gun fire that was almost solid, and whole companies
were wiped out in the space of minutes. Many of the wounded
began to crawl slowly back towards their lines and were hit
again as they did so, but the majority lay out all that long hot
day 'sun-baked, parched, uncared for, often delirious and at any
rate in great pain'. Because of the breakdown on the trench
tramway through shell-fire the stretcher bearers had sometimes
to carry wounded right down from Thiepval Wood and across
the Ancre at Authuille.[12]

At 3 p.m. fresh reinforcements from the 49th Division were
brought in to attack Thiepval village under a barrage. The
attack failed, again because of the terrible machine-gun fire,
and was immediately followed by a German counter-attack.
Meanwhile the situation of the rapidly-thinning numbers who
were grimly holding on to the trenches deep in the German
lines was now desperate; the men were exhausted, there was no
water or ammunition and no way of sending it up. In the dusk,
as yet another enemy counter-attack was launched, they gave
up inch by inch what had been gained at so vast a cost. At
10 p.m., says Crozier, the curtain rang down on hell. Of the
700 men of his West Belfast Battalion, 'the Shankill boys,' he
had seventy left.[13]

Early next morning as he stood by his dugout, smoking a
cigarette, he saw that Thiepval Wood, too, had disappeared.
About the same time Spender, his eyes smarting from the acrid
fumes of the shells, sat down to write a letter that was to become
an historic eye-witness account of the action. 'I am not an
Ulsterman,' he wrote, 'but yesterday, the 1 July, as I followed

their amazing attack I felt that I would rather be an Ulsterman than anything else in the world.

'My position enabled me to watch the commencement of their attack from the wood in which they had formed up, but which long prior to the assault was being overwhelmed with shell-fire, so that the trees were stripped, and the top half of the wood ceased to be anything but a slope of bare stumps with innumerable shell holes peppered in the chalk.

'It looked as if nothing could live in the wood, and, indeed, the losses were heavy before they started, two companies of one battalion being sadly reduced in the assembly trenches.

'When I saw the men emerge through the smoke and form up as if on parade, I could hardly believe my eyes. Then I saw them attack, beginning at a slow walk over 'No Man's Land' and then suddenly let loose as they charged over the front two lines of enemy trenches, shouting 'No Surrender, boys'.

'The enemy's gun-fire raked them from the left, and machine guns in a village enfiladed them on the right, but battalion after battalion came out of the awful wood as steadily as I have seen them at Ballykinler, Clandeboye or Shane's Castle. . . .'[14]

That day what was left of the 107th Brigade was again thrown into battle to relieve British troops who, at dawn, were seen to be holding out still in the first two lines of German trenches. In two days the Division lost 5,500 officers and other ranks, killed, wounded and missing, and won four Victoria Crosses. Their attack, wrote Gibbs, was 'one of the finest displays of human courage in the world'. In terms of ground it gained practically nothing.[15]

The newspapers in Belfast, as elsewhere on 3 July, reported the opening of the Somme offensive, and spoke of brilliant successes. It was several days before the casualties were known, and as day by day the lists in the papers grew longer, a hush of mourning fell upon the whole province. No Division was more closely-knit, because its core was the U.V.F., and, besides, the Ulster community was small and compact. In the trenches, writes Captain Falls, 'the talk, not only of men from Belfast and the larger towns, but of those from the country villages, would be of streets . . . of farms and lanes of which those present had known every detail from childhood'.[16]

In the long streets of Belfast mothers looked out in dread for the red bicycles of the telegram boys. In house after house blinds were drawn down, until it seemed that every family in the city had been bereaved. The casualty lists were full of familiar names, and always after them in brackets appeared the U.V.F. unit to which they had belonged. That year there were no Orange processions on 12 July, and the Lord Mayor requested the total suspension of business for five minutes at noon. In a downpour of rain, the traffic was halted, and passers-by stood silent in the streets.

The volunteers had sealed their covenant in blood, but they had not, of course, a monopoly of Irish courage and sacrifice. Irish losses in France were heavy, and included two well-liked Nationalist Members of Parliament, Professor Tom Kettle and Redmond's brother William, both of whom, though over military age, insisted on being in the front line, and volunteered to go into action again and again. But the war did not, and could not, settle the Irish question, and, however repugnant it might be to Ulster, other Irishmen had sealed a covenant in blood in the Easter Rising of 1916. The thundercloud of civil war which had gathered in 1914 eventually burst over Ireland in the years after 1918, and at once assumed a form more vicious and brutal than anything envisaged in the days of the volunteers.

In 1920, when it spread to Ulster, Spender was asked by Carson and Craig to re-recruit the U.V.F. as an unpaid organization to maintain order, and the Larne guns were used to arm them.[17] After the Treaty of 1921, the six Ulster counties with substantial Protestant populations achieved their object of remaining in the United Kingdom, ironically by a form of 'Home Rule' which gave Northern Ireland a Parliament of its own at Belfast. In time an impressive Parliament building was constructed at Stormont on the Holywood Hills overlooking the city, and on the terrace above its mile-long approach stands a statue of Carson, in a typically defiant pose. Craig became the new state's first prime minister, and Spender, who during the war had been awarded the D.S.O. and M.C., became the first secretary to its Cabinet, and eventually head of the Northern Ireland civil service. He died in Hampshire in 1960.

Ten years after the gun-running Crawford and Spiro met once again in Berlin, where Crawford and some of his friends had gone in connection with a reparations claim on the

Clydevalley, which had been seized in Hamburg at the outbreak of the war. To celebrate the reunion, Spiro invited the whole party to dinner in the Adlon on the *Unter den Linden*. He was delighted to see Crawford, but talked sadly about the war, inflation and the changes in Germany.[18] It was their last meeting, though they kept up a correspondence for another decade, and in 1934 exchanged some interesting letters about the rifles. (See Appendix.) A year later, Spiro's firm was 'Aryanized' by the Nazis, and he was sent to a concentration camp, where he committed suicide.[19] Crawford lived on until 1952, volunteering for active service in the second world war, an offer which the Government regretfully declined.

APPENDIX

One of the strangest aspects of the Larne gun-running is the uncertainty about the exact number of rifles landed. Newspaper reports at the time varied from 30,000 to 50,000, but it was naturally difficult to get authoritative confirmation. It soon became accepted that the number of rifles was either 30,000 or 35,000, along with 3,000,000 rounds of ammunition, and one or other of these totals is given in most accounts of the Larne gun-running, even in recent works. The Unionist Council did not deny these figures; it was naturally to the advantage of the U.V.F. that they should be over-estimated, and this is what in fact happened. The actual quantity of rifles landed was considerably less than is usually stated.

It would be reasonable to assume that Crawford knew exactly how many guns were aboard the *Clydevalley*, but curiously it is in Crawford's statements that the error would appear to have been born. Crawford's story is briefly as follows: he accepted Spiro's third offer of 15,000 brand new Austrian (Steyr Männlicher) rifles and 5,000 ex-German Army (Mauser) rifles, with 2,000,000 rounds of 7·9 mm (·303 in.) Standard Männlicher ammunition in clips of five, suitable for both weapons. He also states, however, that at the time of the negotiation Spiro 'already held about ten thousand Vetterli rifles and bayonets and a million rounds of ammunition which we had previously purchased'. These were now packed and put on board the lighter along with the rest of the consignment.

Crawford therefore thought, at least when he wrote his narrative, that the *Fanny*'s cargo consisted of 30,000 rifles and 3,000,000 rounds of ammunition. (Crawford D. 1700.)

The agreement which Spiro made with 'J. W. Graham' on 26 February 1914 reads: 'I agree to let you have 20,000 rifles, amongst which 11,000 new ones, Steyr make, calibre 7·9, and two million rounds of ammunition at a total sum of £45,640.' (Including the estimated cost of the steamer, crew, coal and Schneider's expenditure for packing, Spiro calculated a grand total of £50,927. In the end the whole transaction cost somewhere between £60,000 and £70,000.) Thus at the time of the agreement the number of rifles was still 20,000, although the proportion of Austrian and German guns may have changed. (D. 640.27.)

The only problem, in fact, concerns the exact number of Italian rifles which Crawford brought with him. Clearly he had a fixed impression that he had 10,000 Vetterlis, but this is not borne out by the U.V.F. records of the landing. For this purpose the most useful document is the order for the unloading of the *Clydevalley* issued by Colonel Hacket Pain on 24 April 1914. (In all the U.V.F. records the Austrian and German guns are referred to indiscriminately as 'Mausers'.) 'In unloading the *Clydevalley*', the order runs, 'the cargo should be discharged into the *Innismurray* and the *Roma* simultaneously, and . . . the cargo for Larne, viz. 8,000 Mauser rifles for Antrim, Tyrone and Derry, and the 3,000 which Mr. Jenks is disposing of, should be landed on the quay, and Mr. Jenks' lot then placed in the boats he has collected for the purpose. The *Clydevalley* will therefore discharge as follows:

LARNE. 8,000 Mauser rifles = 80 tons = 1,600 bundles.
DONAGHADEE. 4,600 Vetterlis = 60 tons = 1,430 bundles
(per   1,400
Innismurray)   6,000
BELFAST.   3,600 Mausers = 36 tons = 700 bundles (per *Roma*).
BANGOR
(per
Clydevalley)   4,000 Mausers = 40 tons = 800 bundles.

At first this does not appear to add up correctly, but if we include 'the 3,000 which Mr. Jenks is disposing of' at Larne, we arrive at a total of 20,000 'Mausers' and 4,600 Vetterlis. The *Innismurray*'s cargo for Donaghadee consisted of 4,600 Vetterlis and 1,400 'Mausers' (D.1327/3/8). A U.V.F. order issued on 9 May 1914 points out that the Vetterli bundles each contained *four* rifles and bayonets, and not five as in the case of the 'Mausers'; this explains the number of bundles assigned to Donaghadee (1,150 Vetterli + 280 'Mauser' = 1,430). In a letter to the G.O.C., written on 25 April 1914, Sir William

Adair states that 'about 4,600 Vetterlis were landed on the quay and then reshipped on board *Innismurray*' (D.1327/3/8).

The total number of rifles landed was thus 24,600.

Nevertheless, the mystery of the Vetterlis does not end there. Twenty years later Crawford wrote to Spiro to ask him how many rifles he had purchased from him. Spiro's reply, written on 28 April 1934, was surprising: '. . . according to your wish I have looked up everything in my books, and I found there had been shipped for the account of my old friend, Mr. John Washington Graham, whom you know so well,

10,900 quite new Männlicher rifles, model 1904,
cal. 7·9 mm, with short bayonets, and
9,100 Mauser rifles model 88, cal. 7·9 mm,
with longer bayonets, and with
2,000,000 cartridges, cal. 7·9, in clips of five
to fit both kinds of rifles.

These figured in my books under the date of March 26, 1914, and there are figuring,

1,000,000 cartridges, article II.

(I suppose these were the Vetterli-Vitali cartridges) under the name of C. Matthews, under the date of June 25, 1913, but I believe that these cartridges had been shipped together with the lot of 20,000 Mauser/Männlicher rifles and their two millions of cartridges'. (D.1700.) He says nothing at all about Vetterli *rifles*. This must have puzzled Crawford, and he was not a man to give up easily. We find Spiro writing again on 14 May 1934 'I am making full investigations but as far as I could find out in the meantime I found only one lot of 1,000 Vetterli-Vitali rifles . . . as having been sold to Thomas Valentine, 25 August 1911, destined for you . . . I remember of one lot having been confiscated while you saved the bayonets but I suppose those were none (*sic*) from me as I never shipped such a lot as 10,000 to London'.

The last sentence undoubtedly refers to the Hammersmith seizure, and confirms Crawford's statement that the bayonets were saved. On 26 May 1934 Spiro sent a list of twelve small consignments of rifles, ammunition, and spare parts, nine of which were of Vetterlis or other 'old rifles' consigned to Hunter & Son of Belfast between September and December 1913. The total number of rifles involved was under 400, and the largest lot was of 250 rifles in eight cases, dated 3 December 1913.

These cases were seized by the Customs at Belfast, and were the subject of an action by Hunter to test the legality of the Arms proclamations. Finally on 31 May 1934 Spiro wrote that he had gone back in his books to 1908, but could find nothing connected with Crawford apart from the lots already mentioned, and he reminded Crawford that he had originally bought some 'goods' through a British firm. (D.1700.)

In spite of this, it is impossible to believe that the rifles in the Hammersmith store were not purchased from Spiro, for they were undoubtedly Vetterlis, and reporters noticed that the cases removed to Scotland Yard were stamped with the letters S. and B. and the word Hamburg. Spiro may have had some good and sufficient reason for denying knowledge of the Vetterlis in 1934, but it is more likely that they were not entered in his books, and that he had forgotten about them. Only Crawford says that there were *ten thousand* Vetterlis, and he is frequently hazy about numbers and dates. He says that 6,000 or 7,000 rifles were seized in Hammersmith, but the newspapers at the time said that the police had found about '4,000 rifles and bayonets'. The Proof Act applied only to the guns, and therefore, according to Crawford, Spiro was able to recover the bayonets, which later came to Ulster in the *Mountjoy*. Adgey, however, gives a quite different account of the Hammersmith bayonets. He says that they were left in the store, and the police kept watch on the entrance. Some time later, after making a careful reconnaissance, he and Hunter managed to rent the yard next to the store, and one night they made a hole in the wall and neatly removed the bayonets from under the noses of the police. (Adgey, pp. 16–18.)

On the face of it, it seems more likely that it was the rifles, and not the bayonets, which Spiro was able to recover by legal means. In his letter of 14 May 1934 he says 'you saved the bayonets', and on 26 May 1934 he explicitly mentions that he had 'made an allowance' on 4,800 (*sic*) Vetterli-Vitali bayonets though the reference is not very clear. We do know that 4,600 Vetterli-Vitali *rifles* were landed on 24 April 1914, and the only hypothesis which seems to fit all the evidence is that these were the rifles originally impounded at Hammersmith.

In July 1914 Headquarters requested returns of arms from every county division. When added up, these returns show that the official total of rifles and carbines possessed by the U.V.F. was 37,048, made up as follows:

Mauser/Männlicher	18,173.
Vetterli-Vitali	6,422.
·303 rifles (British)	3,123.
·303 carbines (British)	9,330.

As the figure for the 'Mauser' shows, these totals are on the low side (there were no 'Mausers' in Ulster before Larne, but a considerable number of Vetterlis and ·303 rifles). They indicate, however, that the total armament consisted of not much over 40,000 rifles, of which the Larne guns made up at least half. There were in addition a few machine-guns. (D.1327/4/13.)

Although rifles of all kinds were desperately needed in the early months of the war, Craig not surprisingly refused to allow them to go out of Ulster, in particular turning down a request that they should be used to equip the Belgian Army. Large quantities of ammunition, however, were transferred to the military in Belfast.

A new problem arose after the Easter Rebellion in Dublin in 1916. The Government decided that the civilian population must be disarmed, but did not see how they could enforce the regulation in the south of Ireland while the Ulstermen still held *their* rifles. During the emergency, the U.V.F. had been armed and partially mobilized; a proportion of the rifles were in the hands of the rank and file, and the rest in U.V.F. armouries. The military authorities approached the U.V.F. leaders to request that the guns should be handed in to stores which would be under the Army's control. They were told that any attempt to seize the rifles would be resented and obstructed, but eventually Lord French, the G.O.C., arranged with the Head-quarters Staff that all the rifles should be concentrated in stores under military protection, chiefly in Belfast and Londonderry, and receipts issued stating that they were being held in trust for their owners.

The situation in Ireland deteriorated so rapidly after the war that it was considered advisable to continue this arrangement, and in 1920, when Spender raised a special constabulary from members of the U.V.F., the rifles were used to arm them. Some of them disappeared during 'the troubles', hidden away by those who were determined that the loyalists would not again be dis-armed and left defenceless, or dumped into lakes to prevent their capture by the I.R.A. But the bulk of them remained in police barracks as the stock armament of the B Specials.

A colourful legend current in Ulster tells that, in some remote and inaccessible part of the globe, the tribesmen are armed with German Mausers bearing the words 'U.V.F. For God and Ulster'. The truth is almost as exotic. When peace returned to Ireland, the existence of a large quantity of ageing rifles became something of an embarrassment, and eventually, just before the outbreak of the second world war, a large proportion of them were sold in London. But before they went, the U.V.F. stamp was carefully obliterated from each rifle. They turned up again in 1941, in — of all places — Ethiopia, where they were used, along with some millions of rounds of Männlicher ammunition captured from an Italian ship, to equip the Ethiopian patriot levies who, under British officers, played a vital part in restoring the Emperor Haile Selassie to his throne.

Those rifles which remained in Ulster were issued to the Home Guard in 1940, and after Dunkirk formed part of the out-of-date equipment with which Britain waited for the onslaught of the *Wehrmacht*. Few weapons can have given such sterling service as these heavy rifles, which were already obsolescent at the time of their purchase in 1914. Quite a few of them are to be found in Ulster still, preserved for sentiment rather than use, including those with small inscribed plates set into the stock, which Crawford presented to those who had helped him in his enterprise.

SOURCES

I. UNPUBLISHED

This account of the Ulster crisis has been written largely from original documents deposited in recent years in the Public Record Office of Northern Ireland. The most important source for this purpose is the collection of the papers of the Ulster Unionist Council, one section of which (D.1327/4) consists entirely of the records of the Ulster Volunteer Force. The numbers which follow the sources listed below are those of the classification in the P.R.O.N.I. In the notes, where reference is made to the Ulster Unionist Council papers, only the P.R.O.N.I. number is given, but other collections are identified by name also.

1. *Ulster Unionist Council Papers*. D. 1327/1–9.
2. *Spender Papers*. D.1295.
   Papers and correspondence of Lieut.-Col. Sir Wilfrid Spender.
   Manuscript account of the origins of the 36th (Ulster) Division.
   Microfilm of a narrative of the Larne gun-running by W. B. Spender. (MIC. 103.)
3. *Diary of Lady Spender*. D. 1633. Volumes for 1913 and 1914.
4. *Craigavon Papers*. D.1415/B.1–43.
   i. Miscellaneous papers of Lord Craigavon.
   ii. Typescript of long extracts of Lady Craigavon's Diary, which includes copies of correspondence.
5. *Craigavon press-cutting books*. D.1415/A7 and A8.
6. *Crawford Papers*. D.640 and D.1700.
   Papers and correspondence of Lieut.-Col. F. H. Crawford, including the manuscript of 'Record of the Home Rule Movement' (his account of his career and gun-running adventures).
7. *Hall Papers*. D.1540.
   Papers and correspondence of Captain Roger Hall relating to the 2nd Battalion South Down U.V.F.
8. *Kilmorey Papers*. D.1268.
   Papers and correspondence of the Earl of Kilmorey and Captain Roger Hall, relating to the U.V.F. in South Down.

9. *Kilmorey press-cutting book.* D. 1268.
10. *O'Neill Papers.* D.1238.
    Papers and correspondence of Captain the Hon. Arthur O'Neill relating to the North Antrim Regiment, U.V.F.
11. *Richardson Papers.*
    Photostat copies of papers of General Sir George Richardson in the National Army Museum. (T.2180.)
    Miscellaneous papers of General Richardson. D. 1498.
12. *Miscellaneous records of the U.V.F. in Down, Fermanagh, Londonderry and Tyrone.* D.1263, D.1244, D.1402, D.1414, D.304 and T.1784.

II. PUBLISHED

ADGEY, R. J. *Arming the Ulster Volunteers, 1914.* Privately printed, n.d.

AMERY, L. S. *My Political Life.* 3 vols. Hutchinson, 1953.

ARMOUR, W. S. *Armour of Ballymoney.* Duckworth, 1934.

ASQUITH, Margot. *Autobiography.* Faber & Faber, 1962.

BARKLEY, J. M. *A Short History of the Presbyterian Church in Ireland.* Church House, Belfast, 1959.

BATES, Jean V. *Sir Edward Carson, Ulster leader.* John Murray, 1921.

BAYLY, Admiral Sir Lewis. *Pull Together!* Harrap, 1937.

BEAVERBROOK, Lord. *Politicians and the War, 1914–16.* Thornton Butterworth, 1928.

BECKETT, J. C. *A Short History of Ireland.* Hutchinson, 1952.

BLAKE, Robert. *The Unknown Prime Minister.* Eyre & Spottiswoode, 1955.

CALLWELL, Major-General Sir C. E. *Field-Marshal Sir Henry Wilson, his Life and Diaries.* 2 vols. Cassell, 1927.

CHURCHILL, Winston S. *The World Crisis.* 4 vols. Thornton Butterworth, 1923–1929.

COLLIER, Basil. *Brasshat: a Biography of Field-Marshal Sir Henry Wilson.* Secker & Warburg, 1961.

COLVIN, Ian. *The Life of Lord Carson.* 3 vols. (Vol. 1 by Edward Marjoribanks.) Gollancz, 1934.

CONRAD VON HÖTZENDORFF, Field-Marshal Count Franz. *Aus Meiner Dienstzeit, 1906–1918.* Rikola Verlag, 1921.

CRAWFORD, Lt.-Col. F. H. *Guns for Ulster.* Graham & Heslip, 1947.

CROZIER, Brigadier-General F. P. *A Brasshat in No Man's Land,* Cape, 1930.

—— *Impressions and Recollections.* Werner Laurie, 1930.

—— *Ireland for Ever.* Cape, 1932.

—— *The Men I Killed.* Michael Joseph, 1937.

ERVINE, St. John. *Craigavon, Ulsterman.* Allen & Unwin, 1949.

FALLS, Captain C. *The History of the 36th (Ulster) Division*. McCaw, Stephenson & Orr, 1922.

FERGUSSON, Sir James. *The Curragh Incident*. Faber & Faber, 1964.

FRENCH, Major the Hon. Gerald. *The Life of Field-Marshal Sir John French, First Earl of Ypres*. Cassell, 1931.

GARDNER, Brian. *The Big Push*. Cassell, 1961.

GERARD, J. W. *My Four Years in Germany*. Hodder & Stoughton, 1917.

GIBBS, Sir Philip. *The War Dispatches*. Anthony Gibbs & Phillips, 1964.

GLEICHEN, Major-General Lord Edward. *A Guardsman's Memories*. Blackwood, 1932.

GOLLIN, A. M. *Proconsul in Politics: a study of Lord Milner in Opposition and Power*. Anthony Blond, 1964.

—— *The* Observer *and J. L. Garvin, 1908–14*. Oxford University Press, 1960.

GOUGH, General Sir Hubert. *Soldiering On*. Arthur Barker, 1954.

GREEN, Alice Stopford. *Ourselves Alone in Ulster* (pamphlet). 1918.

GWYNN, Denis. *The Life of John Redmond*. Harrap, 1932.

HALDANE, Richard Burdon. *An Autobiography*. Hodder & Stoughton, 1929.

HALEVY, Elie. *A History of the English People, 1815–1914*. Vol. 6. The Rule of Democracy, 1905–1914. Benn, 1934.

HOLT, Edgar. *Protest in Arms*. Putnam, 1960.

HYDE, H. M. *Carson*. Heinemann, 1953.

JEFFERSON, Herbert. *Viscount Pirrie of Belfast*. Wm. Mullan & Son, n.d.

JENKINS, Roy. *Asquith*. Collins, 1964.

KÜHLMANN, Richard von. *Erinnerungen*. Verlag Lambert Schneider, 1947.

LONG, Walter, Viscount Long of Wraxall. *Memories*. Hutchinson, 1923.

LYONS, F. S. L. *The Irish Parliamentary Party, 1890–1910*. Faber & Faber, 1951.

MACDONAGH, Michael. *The Home Rule Movement*. The Talbot Press and T. Fisher Unwin, 1920.

—— *The Irish on the Somme*. Hodder & Stoughton, 1917.

MACREADY, General Sir Nevil. *Annals of an Active Life*. 2 vols. Hutchinson, 1924.

MAGNUS, Philip (Sir Philip Magnus-Allcroft). *Gladstone*. Murray, 1954.

—— *Kitchener*. Murray, 1958.

MANSERGH, Nicholas. *The Government of Northern Ireland*. Allen & Unwin, 1936.

—— *The Irish Question, 1840–1921*. Allen & Unwin, 1965.

MARTIN, F. X. *The Irish Volunteers, 1913–1915: recollections and documents.* James Duffy & Co., 1963.

MAURICE, Major-General Sir Frederick. *Haldane, 1856–1915.* Faber & Faber, 1937.

MAXWELL, Henry. *Ulster was Right.* Hutchinson, 1934.

McNEILL, Ronald. *Ulster's Stand for Union.* Murray, 1922.

MIDLETON, The Earl of. *Ireland—Dupe or Heroine.* Heinemann, 1932.

MOLES, Thomas. *Lord Carson of Duncairn.* Carson Presentation Committee, n.d.

MORRISON, H. S. *Modern Ulster.* H. R. Allenson, 1920.

NEVINSON, H. *More Changes, More Chances.* Nisbet & Co., 1925.

NICOLSON, Harold. *King George the Fifth.* Constable, 1952.

OXFORD AND ASQUITH, The Earl of. *Memories and Reflections.* 2 vols. Cassell, 1928.

RHODES, Thomas. *The Real von Kühlmann.* Noel Douglas, 1925.

ROBERTSON, Field-Marshal Sir William. *From Private to Field-Marshal.* Constable, 1921.

RYAN, A. P. *Mutiny at the Curragh.* Macmillan, 1956.

SALVIDGE, Stanley. *Salvidge of Liverpool.* Hodder & Stoughton, 1934.

SEELY, J. E. B. *Adventure.* Heinemann, 1930.

SHAW, George Bernard. *The Matter with Ireland* (Collected writings on Ireland). Rupert Hart-Davis, 1962.

SHEARMAN, Hugh. *Not an Inch: a study of Northern Ireland and Lord Craigavon.* Faber & Faber, 1942.

SPENDER, J. A. *Life, Journalism and Politics.* Cassell, 1927.

TAYLOR, H. A. *The Strange Case of Andrew Bonar Law.* Stanley Paul, n.d.

TREGUIZ, Louis. *L'Irlande dans la crise universelle.* Librarie Felix Alcan, 1917.

TUCHMAN, Barbara W. *The Zimmermann Telegram.* Constable, 1959.

WINTERTON, Earl. *Orders of the Day.* Cassell, 1953.

WRENCH, Sir (John) Evelyn. *Alfred, Lord Milner.* Eyre & Spottiswoode, 1958.

—— *Geoffrey Dawson and Our Times.* Hutchinson, 1955.

The Annual Register.

Hansard, *Parliamentary Debates,* 5th series, House of Commons.

White Papers, Cd. 7329 and 7318. Correspondence relating to Recent Events in the Irish Command.

The Belfast Newsletter.

The Belfast Evening Telegraph.

The Unionist (Recollections of Sir Wilfrid Spender, February–June 1949).

NOTES

Abbreviations

BNL.   Belfast Newsletter.
BET.   Belfast Evening Telegraph.
CC.   Confidential Circular.
CM.   Circular Memorandum.
UVFO.   Ulster Volunteer Force printed orders.

1. PRELUDE

1. Michael MacDonagh, *The Home Rule Movement*, pp. 261–264; Hansard, *Parliamentary Debates*, 5th Series, LXVI, cols. 1018–1019.
2. P. Magnus, *Gladstone*, p. 332.
3. ibid., p. 354.
4. W. S. Churchill, *Lord Randolph Churchill*, ii, 59.
5. R. R. James, *Lord Randolph Churchill*, p. 223.
6. BNL. 23 Feb. 1886.
7. James, p. 234.
8. Magnus, p. 357.
9. ibid., p. 361.
10. ibid., p. 362.

2. THE ORANGE CARD

1. For detail of the Scottish colonization of Antrim and Down see C. Maxwell, *Irish History from Contemporary Sources*, pp. 298–307.
2. J. M. Barkley, *A Short History of the Presbyterian Church in Ireland*, p. 8.
3. J. C. Beckett, *A Short History of Ireland*, p. 101.
4. N. Mansergh, *The Government of Northern Ireland*, p. 225.
5. W. F. Marshall, *Ulster Sails West*, pp. 44–45.
6. Castlereagh to Addington, 21 July 1802, *Castlereagh Corres.* iv, 223.
7. Dr. Alexander Haliday to Lord Charlemont, 13 July 1797, *Charlemont MSS*, 13th Report, ii, 303.

8. H. Shearman, *Anglo-Irish Relations*, p. 151.
9. Report of the Ulster Unionist Council for 1911 (*U.U.C. Year-book*, *1912*, p. 52).

3. DRAMATIS PERSONAE

1. Earl Winterton, *Orders of the Day*, p. 36.
2. A. P. Ryan, *Mutiny at the Curragh*, p. 18.
3. Blake, *The Unknown Prime Minister*, p. 28.
4. Ryan, p. 20.
5. Blake, pp. 20–22.
6. H. M. Hyde, *Carson*, p. 1.
7. A school report for 1884 is among the Craigavon Papers, D.1415/B/1B.
8. Diary of Lieut. James Craig. D.1415/B/2.
9. D.1415/B/5.
10. St. John Ervine, *Craigavon, Ulsterman*, p. 135.
11. G. B. Shaw, *The Matter with Ireland*, p. 79.
12. Lord Riddell, *More Pages from my Diary*, p. 52.

4. STORM WARNING

1. Ervine, p. 185.
2. R. McNeill, *Ulster's Stand for Union*, pp. 49–51.
3. ibid., p. 53.
4. ibid., p. 56.
5. I. Colvin, *Carson*, ii, 87.
6. For the careers of Armour and Pirrie, and their part in the Home Rule controversy, see W. S. Armour, *Armour of Bally-money* (chaps. XII and XIII); H. Jefferson, *Viscount Pirrie of Belfast* (pp. 133–141); and for White see his autobiography, *Misfit*.
7. Quoted McNeill, p. 64 from *The Times*, 18 January 1912.
8. Colvin, ii, 89.
9. ibid., ii, 92–93.
10. Major-General Lord Edward Gleichen, *A Guardsman's Memories*, p. 361.
11. Colvin, ii, 92. The car is now in the Ulster Transport Museum.
12. Gleichen, p. 362.
13. Minute book of the Demonstration Sub-Committee, 26 Feb. 1912 (D.1327/3/1); Ulster Unionist Demonstration of 1912, official programme; BNL. 10 April 1912.
14. Blake, p. 129.

5. THE COVENANT

1. Parl. Deb., 5th Series, XXXVI, col. 1452.
2. Gwynn, *The Life of John Redmond*, p. 202.
3. Parl. Deb., 5th Series, XXXIX, col. 773.
4. Colvin, ii, 126.
5. BNL. 1 July 1912.
6. The Castledawson and shipyard incidents continued to reverberate throughout 1912 and 1913 as the press reported in full the cases of claims for compensation.
7. BNL. 16 Sept. 1912.
8. McNeill, pp. 103.
9. ibid., pp. 104–105.
10. The step from which the Covenant was read still bears an inscription to this effect. Craigavon has been since 1915 a U.V.F. hospital.
11. Colvin, ii, 140–141.
12. One of Ulster's most uncompromising supporters was Lord Charles Beresford, a redoubtable old sea-dog whose customary breakfast greeting at this time was: 'Good morning, one day nearer the German war.' At the beginning of September he wrote to Craig: 'I have just heard from Mrs. Burgess Watson, widow of a dear friend of mine. . . . She owns the Orange standard, carried by one of the Admiral's (her late husband's) ancestors at the Battle of the Boyne, who was the King's standard bearer. Mrs. Watson would be very glad to lend the standard for the great meeting or procession on the 27th or 28th September in Ulster, but her position is this: she has two sons in the Navy. You know how unscrupulous the present Government are, and now that mulatto, Fisher, is back supreme at the Admiralty, vengeance would surely be wreaked on the boys if it were known that their mother had lent the famous standard to Ulster. . . . I have told her that her name need not appear at all. . . .' (quoted Ervine, p. 234). The letter well illustrates the political bitterness of the time. A Catholic Belfast newspaper commented, 'If that flag ever saw the Battle of the Boyne, all we can say is that the man who manufactured it deserves undying fame for the strength and durability of the material' (Ryan, p. 61).
13. quoted Ervine, p. 236. A cinematograph film of the scenes on Covenant day was made by Wilson Hungerford. It was shown on B.B.C. television in 1962.
14. in the *Spectator*. Quoted Ervine, p. 237.
15. BNL. 30 Sept. 1912.
16. S. Salvidge, *Salvidge of Liverpool*, pp. 120–121.

17. Parl. Debates, 5th Series, XLIII, cols. 2041–2054; 2088–2089.
18. Annual Report of Ulster Unionist Council, 1914.

6. AN ARMY WITH BANNERS

1. McNeill, pp. 57–58; almost certainly the idea was taken up first by the lodges in Co. Down. cf. Tréguiz, p. 51. '*L'idée d'une Special Constabulary orangiste, lancée le 14 Novembre 1911 par la Lecale district loyal orange lodge (No. 2) de Downpatrick . . .*'; and see Hall Papers D.1540/3.
2. The decision was not made public at the time, but see the report of the annual meeting of the Ulster Unionist Council, BNL. 20 Jan. 1914.
3. Plan of the organization of the Ulster Volunteer Force. Hall papers, D.1540/3.
4. The county returns, dating from 13 Dec. 1912, are in D.1327/4/18.
5. Hall Papers, D.1540/3/5.
6. ibid., D.1540/3/6.
7. ibid., D.1540/3/10.
8. Gwynn, p. 224.
9. Gleichen, p. 367.
10. BNL. 17 May 1913.
11. Gleichen, p. 367.
12. McNeill, p. 161.
13. Even Bonar Law was critical of Carson, and Leo Maxse went so far as to suggest that he and Smith had been retained in order to silence them in the Commons. Smith defended himself in *The Times* but Carson ignored the criticisms. 'I know I was right in my action,' he told Lady Londonderry, 'I am unrepentant.' J. H. Campbell appeared as counsel for *Le Matin*. Hyde, pp. 329–334; Blake, pp. 140–144.
14. Carson to Edward Sclater. Printed and sent to the secretaries of the Unionist clubs, 7 Aug. 1913. Hall papers, D.1540/3/9.
15. Hyde, pp. 340–341.
16. Typed agenda D. 1327/4/14.
17. McNeill, pp. 156–157.
18. McNeill, p. 162.
19. Notes taken at the meeting of 2 Sept. 1913, D.1414.
20. ibid., p. 163.
21. BNL. 29 Sept. 1913.

7. THE OLD TOWN HALL

1. Harold Nicolson, *King George the Fifth*, pp. 222–225.
2. ibid., p. 226.

3. Ryan, pp. 79–80.
4. Hyde, p. 339.
5. ibid., p. 342.
6. ibid., pp. 342–343.
7. Gwynn, p. 232.
8. Ryan, p. 86.
9. D.1327/4/14.
10. In December 1911 the city corporation agreed to rent the Old Town Hall building to the Unionist Party for two years. Minutes of Demonstration Joint Sub-committee, D.1327/3/1.
11. File: Headquarters Staff. D.1327/4/12.
12. J. A. Spender, *Life, Journalism and Politics*, i, 5 n. 1.
13. Summary of particulars of case, to accompany Captain Spender's letter to the War Office. 4 May 1913. Spender Papers, D.1295; Spender, *Unionist*, February, 1949.
14. ibid.; and correspondence with the War Office. Spender Papers, D.1295.
15. Spender, *Unionist*, February, 1949.
16. 11 December 1912. Spender Papers, D. 1295.
17. 9 June 1913. Spender Papers, D. 1295.
18. File of U.V.F. orders 'A.Q.M.G.' D. 1327/4/3; Spender, *Unionist*, March, 1949.
19. ibid.
20. ibid.
21. File of U.V.F. orders. D.1327/4/3.
22. McNeill, pp. 37–38.
23. UVFO. 1 November 1913. D.1327/4/3. There is also a complete file on the medical organization of the U.V.F. in the O'Neill Papers. D.1238.
24. UVFO. 20 October 1913. D.1327/4/3. A box of these badges, and several armbands in their pristine state are among materials in D.1327/4.
25. Equipment of a volunteer. Hall Papers. D.1540/3.
26. Mobilization orders. Hall Papers, D.1540/3.

8. THE GUN-RUNNERS

1. F. H. Crawford, 'Record of the Home Rule movement'. Crawford papers, D. 1700. Except where otherwise stated, the essential facts in this chapter, and in chapters 14 and 15, are from this source, which is more detailed than the published version, *Guns for Ulster*.
2. D. 1327/4/12.
3. F. H. Crawford, *Guns for Ulster*, p. 8.

4. Dictionary of National Biography *under* William Crawford and Adair Crawford.

5. See entry under 'F. H. Crawford' in the Belfast Town Book. Crawford's copy, with corrections in his own hand, is in the Linenhall Library, Belfast.

6. Crawford always referred to Spiro as 'Benny Spiro', but this was really the name of Spiro's father, who founded the weapon and armaments firm in 1864. The son's first name was Bruno. *Benny Spiro, Waffen, Munition und Militär-Effekten (1864)* had offices in Hamburg, *Adolphsbrücke 9/11*, and in Berlin, *An der Heerstrasse, 85.*

7. Rev. C. Brett Ingram, two articles in the *Belfast Telegraph* 27 April, 4 May 1963.

8. BNL. 4 June 1913.

9. ibid., 7 June 1913.

10. ibid., 11 June 1913.

11. ibid., 16 June 1913.

12. ibid., 12 July 1913.

13. Information supplied by the late Lt.-Col. Frank Hall.

14. R. J. Adgey, *Arming the Ulster Volunteers, 1914*, p. 19.

15. ibid., p. 20.

16. ibid., p. 24.

17. Information supplied by Mr. W. P. Johnston.

18. Adgey, p. 52.

19. CC. D.1327/4/8.

20. D.1327/4/21.

21. CC. D.1327/4/8.

22. Correspondence of 6, 19, 21 November 1913. D.1327/4/8.

23. D.1327/4/8.

9. COUNCILS OF WAR

1. Denis Gwynn. *Life of John Redmond*, p. 242.

2. Ryan, p. 92.

3. His article 'The North Began' in the journal of the Gaelic League called for the formation of Irish Volunteers on the same pattern. (Printed in F. X. Martin, *The Irish Volunteers, 1913–15*, pp. 57–61.)

4. Gwynn, p. 244.

5. Annual Register, 1913, p. 251.

6. J. A. Spender and C. Asquith, *Life of H. H. Asquith*, ii, 37. For a full account of the negotiations, and the correspondence between Asquith and Carson see Colvin, ii, 260–271.

7. Ryan, p. 97.

8. R. B. Haldane, *An Autobiography*, p. 185.

9. Sir C. E. Callwell, *F. M. Sir Henry Wilson, his life and diaries*, i, 130.
10. ibid., i, 131.
11. ibid., i, 132.
12. White paper. Cd. 7318, p. 2. Memorandum of an interview between the Secretary of State for War and the General Officers commanding in chief, 16 Dec. 1913.
13. ibid., p. 2.
14. Notes on conference in London, 17 Dec. 1913. (Four large typed sheets with answers in pencil) D.1327/4/21.
15. ibid.
16. Notes on conference at Craigavon, 19 Dec. 1913. D.1327/4/21.
17. General Richardson's notes. D.1327/4/21.

10. NEW YEAR RESOLUTIONS

1. BNL. 2 Jan. 1914.
2. ibid. 1 Jan. 1914.
3. B. W. Tuchman, *The Zimmermann Telegram*, pp. 46–47.
4. Memorandum of Sir William Adair. O'Neill papers. D.1238.
5. Hacket Pain to Crawford, 17 Jan. 1914. Crawford papers. D.640/22.
6. Crawford to Hacket Pain, 19 Jan. 1914. D.1327/4/21.
7. D.1327/4/21.
8. Spender, *Unionist*, April 1949.
9. ibid.
10. ibid.
11. Mobilization of transport. Spender papers. D.1295.
12. BNL. 22 Dec. 1913.
13. BNL. 19 Jan. 1914.
14. Motor Car Corps. 14 Feb. 1914. D.1327/4/3.
15. Notes on conference in London, 17 Dec. 1913, par. 3; notes on conference at Craigavon 19 Dec. 1913, par. 6. D.1327/4/21.
16. Idea of a Special Service Force for Belfast. D.1327/4/21.
17. Spender, *Unionist*, March 1949; information supplied to the author by Mr. R. G. D. Hamilton.
18. Crozier, *Impressions and Recollections*, pp. 136–140.
19. Crozier, *Ireland for Ever*, p. 34.
20. Crozier, *Impressions and Recollections*, p. 143.
21. ibid., p. 149.
22. Headquarters Defence Scheme. Spender papers. D.1295.
23. 'The No. 1 Scheme.' D. 1327/4/21.
24. D.1327/4/20. Lists of commanding officers, with number and strength of regiments. Captain O'Neill, the father of the present prime minister of Northern Ireland, was the first Member of

Parliament to be killed in action on the Western Front, in November 1914.

25. Several writers mention aeroplanes as part of the U.V.F. armament. The source for this would appear to be Gleichen, p. 375. He says that Colonel Repington, the military correspondent of *The Times* told him that the U.V.F. had 'machine guns, transmission troops (excellent), aeroplanes and ambulances . . .'. But there is no reference to aeroplanes in the U.V.F. records.

26. Lady Spender, Diary, 10 March 1914.

27. ibid. 17 March 1914.

11. LORD MILNER INTERVENES

1. The letter is printed in Colvin, ii, 241–242 and in Sir Evelyn Wrench's *Alfred, Lord Milner*, p. 280.

2. Colvin, ii, 242.

3. Wrench, *Milner*, pp. 280–281.

4. A. M. Gollin, *Proconsul in Politics*, p. 184.

5. L. S. Amery, *My Political Life*, i, 440, and see the comment by Gollin, p. 184, n. 1. 'Amery often supplied the detailed plans, even the ideas.'

6. Amery, i, 440.

7. Wrench, *Milner*, p. 282.

8. Amery, i, 440–441.

9. BNL. 29 November 1913; 9 December 1913.

10. D.1327/4/2 enclosure.

11. Colvin, ii, 243.

12. From information given to A. M. Gollin by the late Lord Winterton (Gollin, p. 176). See also Lord Winterton, *Orders of the Day*, p. 38.

13. Viscount Long of Wraxall, *Memories*, p. 201; Gollin, p. 185.

14. Amery, i, 441.

15. Gollin, p. 186.

16. Wrench, *Milner*, p. 283.

17. Gollin, p. 182; Long, p. 203.
    The first issue of *The Covenanter* appeared in May. (BNL. 20 May 1914.)

18. Gollin, p. 188.

19. Wrench, *Milner*, p. 287.

20. Gollin, p. 188.

21. ibid., p. 190; Blake, 175–181.

22. Callwell, i, 139.

23. Gollin, pp. 199–200.

24. ibid., p. 190.

25. Blake, p. 178.
26. BNL. 18 March 1914.
27. Kilmorey papers. D.1268.
28. BNL. 9 March 1914.
29. BNL. 8 Oct. 1913.
30. BNL. 2 March, 6 April, 6 May 1914.
31. BNL. 3 March 1914.
32. Debates of the House of Commons, Dominion of Canada, CXIV, p. 1785.
33. ibid., CXIV, p. 2178.
34. ibid., CXIV, pp. 1902, 2085.
35. Parliamentary Debates, Commonwealth of Australia, LXXI, p. 1621.
36. BNL. 9 March 1914.
37. BNL. 7, 27 May 1914.
38. Parliamentary Debates, Commonwealth of Australia, LXX, p. 1477. Home Rule was debated in the Senate on 25 June 1914 and a resolution was passed approving it (LXXIV, pp. 2537–2542).
39. BNL. 18, 20 May 1914.
40. BNL. 15 April; 20 July 1914.
41. It would be tedious to try to enumerate all the contributions but their volume may be gauged from these random examples in the spring and early summer of 1914; £612 from Scottish Orange lodges, £423 from Toronto loyalists, £100 from Ulster and Loyal Irishmen's Society of Victoria, £102 from Ontario West Orangemen, £100 from Montreal County loyal Orange lodge; £400 from the Grand Black Chapter of Regina, £500 from the University of Melbourne, £100 from the Transvaal Ulster Fund, another £1,000 from Sir Samuel McCaughey . . . (BNL. March–July, *passim*. See also the list of guarantors to the £1,000,000 Indemnity Fund, D.1327/3/6).
42. Wrench, *Milner*, p. 286.

12. ENTER CONSPIRATORS

1. The text of the memorandum is printed in Gwynn pp. 256–258.
2. Colvin, ii, 298.
3. White Paper, correspondence relating to recent events in the Irish Command (in continuation of Cd. 7318) Cd. 7329 Part I, No. 2.
4. ibid., No. 3.
5. ibid., No. 4.
6. Gleichen, p. 371.
7. White Paper, Part I, No. 5.
8. ibid., No. 6.

9. Sir James Fergusson, *The Curragh Incident*, p. 46.
10. Sir Nevil Macready, *Annals of an Active Life*, ii, 157.
11. Fergusson, pp. 46–47.
12. White Paper, Part I, No. 7.
13. Gleichen, p. 375.
14. Text of orders issued to the 5th Division on 19 March 1914, Fergusson, Appendix A, pp. 219–221.
15. F. P. Crozier, *Impressions and Recollections*, p. 151; Spender, *Unionist*, May 1949.
16. Gleichen, p. 371.
17. Fergusson, Appendix A, p. 220.
18. Ryan, p. 121.
19. Spender, *Unionist*, April 1949.
20. Fergusson, pp. 51–52.
21. White Paper, Part II, No. 2.
22. ibid., No. 4.
23. ibid., No. 1.
24. ibid., No. 5.
25. ibid., No. 3.
26. Callwell, i, 139.
27. Parl. Deb., 5th Series, LIX, cols. 2271–2278; Colvin, ii, 316.
28. Colvin, ii, 311.
29. Spender, *Unionist*, May 1949.
30. CC. 18 March 1914. D.1327/4/8.
31. CC. 19 March 1914. D.1327/4/8.
32. BNL. 20 March 1914.
33. Spender, *Unionist*, May 1949.
34. Lady Spender, Diary, 20 March 1914. D.1633.
35. Crozier, *Ireland for Ever*, p. 38.
36. BET. 21 March 1914.
37. Lady Spender, Diary, 21 March 1914. D.1633; Spender, *Unionist*, May 1949.
38. Crozier, *Ireland for Ever*, p. 40; *Impressions and Recollections*, pp. 143–144.
39. Crozier, *Ireland for Ever*, p. 41.
40. Crozier, *Impressions and Recollections*, p. 144.
41. Fergusson, pp. 67–69; White Paper. Cd. 7329. III. Paget's statement.
42. Fergusson, pp. 69–70; Sir Hubert Gough, *Soldiering On*, p. 101.
43. Fergusson, pp. 76–78.
44. Spender, *Unionist*, May 1949. The C.O. was Lieut.-Col. Bols, later, as General Sir Louis Bols, Allenby's Chief of Staff.
45. Hyde, p. 352.
46. UVFO. 28 March 1914.
47. BNL. 21 March 1914.

48. Captain Andrew Agnew, Log of the S.S. *Fanny*, 24 March 1914.
49. Lady Spender, Diary, 20 March 1914.
50. Spender, *Unionist*, May 1949; Lady Craigavon, Diary, 20 March 1914.
51. Lady Spender, Diary, 20 March 1914.
52. Crozier, *Ireland for Ever*, p. 42.
53. Lady Craigavon, Diary, 20 March 1914.
54. Colvin, ii, 322–323.
55. Quoted in BNL. 21 March 1914.

13. PLOT AND COUNTERPLOT

1. White Paper, Cd. 7329, Part I, 17.
2. ibid., p. 19.
3. Field-Marshal Sir William Robertson, *From Private to Field Marshal*, p. 194.
4. Fergusson, pp. 74–75.
5. ibid., pp. 80–81; Gleichen, p. 376.
6. Fergusson, p. 193.
7. Lady Spender, Diary, 21 March 1914. D.1633.
8. Fergusson, pp. 102–3.
9. Papers marked 'Intelligence'. No. 4. D.1327/4/21.
10. Fergusson, p. 124.
11. Papers marked 'Intelligence' No. 3. D.1327/4.
12. Crozier, *Ireland for Ever*, p. 43.
13. ibid., pp. 43–44; *Impressions and Recollections*, p. 148.
14. Crozier, *Ireland for Ever*, pp. 42–45; Memo of Sir William Adair, 'Verbal instructions by Sir Edward Carson, 21 March 1914.' O'Neill Papers, D.1238.
15. Crozier, *Ireland for Ever*, p. 42.
16. Gleichen, p. 377.
17. Fergusson, p. 138.
18. J. E. Wrench, *Geoffrey Dawson and Our Times*, p. 98.
19. The subject has been fully and brilliantly treated in Mr. A. P. Ryan's *Mutiny at the Curragh* (1956) and Sir James Fergusson's *The Curragh Incident* (1964).
20. General Sir Hubert Gough, *Soldiering On*, p. 107.
21. Fergusson, p. 147.
22. Ryan, p. 152.
23. ibid., p. 153.
24. Fergusson, p. 149.
25. White Paper, Part I, 39; 'It was typical of Seely's complacency that he thought himself licensed to tamper with a Cabinet paper. The amazing thing is that Lord Morley, as he admitted in the

House of Lords two days later, connived and even assisted with
the framing of the two paragraphs . . .', Fergusson, p. 150. How
so experienced a minister as Morley consented to the re-
drafting has never satisfactorily been explained. See also
Jenkins, *Asquith*, p. 312.
26. Major the Hon. Gerald French, *The Life of Field-Marshal Sir
John French, First Earl of Ypres*, p. 193.
27. ibid., p. 194.
28. Fergusson, p. 158.
29. Maurice, *Haldane*, i, 344–345.
30. Gough, p. 110.
31. Colvin, ii, 352–353.
32. Ryan, pp. 162–164; Wrench, *Milner*, p. 288.
33. UVFO. 4 April 1914.
34. Macready to Spender, 16 June 1913. Spender Papers, D.1295.
35. Macready, who took his responsibility very seriously, travelled
extensively in Ulster, and was shadowed day and night by
U.V.F. dispatch riders (Spender, *Unionist*, May 1949).
36. Macready, p. 182.
37. Colvin, ii, 349–350.
38. BNL. 17 April 1914.
39. Cf. Fergusson, p. 204, 'No categorical answer can be given until
the relevant files of the War Office and the Admiralty are laid
open to the historian, and even then it may not be complete';
and Blake, p. 205, 'No direct evidence of a "plot" has ever
emerged, but that is scarcely surprising. If there had been any
such orders drafted in the War Office or the Admiralty, they
could — and certainly would — have been suppressed.'
40. Gleichen, p. 382.

14. DAYBREAK AT LANGELAND

1. Crawford Papers. D.640/28.
2. Crawford, D.1700.
3. Crawford Papers. D.640/27.
4. ibid. To one of Spiro's letters she has added in pencil, 'Take care
that my address is always carefully written. The letter of this
morning was not carefully enough written and the Post Office
had to seek me.' Frau Kanzki (Frau Thiesswald by her second
marriage) was living at the same house, *17 Poseldorferweg*, at
the time of her death in 1959. Crawford described her as 'a
marvellous woman . . . one of the cleverest ladies I ever met'.
(D.1700.)
5. Crawford Papers. D.640/27. The paymaster for the gun-running
was Craig. Crawford writes: 'James Craig got me all the money,

how I do not know.' It is fairly certain that it came from the Carson Defence Fund and the Union Defence League. The Carson Fund was launched in January 1912, and provided the resources for the buying of arms in 1913. A letter from Carson to the Treasurer, included in minutes for 6 March 1914, states: 'This year, however, will be exceptional and will be the climax of all that we have been aiming at. We are now going to make good in action all that we have been saying and preparing for during the past two years. The struggle before us is a very grave and a very difficult one, involving action almost unprecedented, at all events in recent history.' This letter was duplicated and sent to subscribers, with another stating, 'To maintain properly our organization a very large sum is *urgently and immediately required*.' — a strange departure from the elaborate secrecy surrounding the whole operation. (Minute book of the Carson Defence Fund, 6 March 1914. D.1327/3/4.) In a letter to Carson on 4 March Craig wrote: 'To come to another matter, we must have a cheque for £20,000 here by return of post. There is a big move on into the details of which I need not venture, and it will require the whole of this sum to see us through.' He goes on to say that 'it has been sprung upon us here in connection with the Special Force the General is now getting well forward', but Carson replied next day, 'As to the money, I gave C. a cheque for £15,000 so with another now for £20,000 that will be £55,000 and I thought our limit was £50,000. (Lady Craigavon, Diary, D. 1415.) Crawford states in his diary that on 27 March he had to see Walter Long 'about the finances of the business' and make final arrangements for paying very large cheques. (Crawford Papers. D.1700.)

6. Spiro to Crawford, 28 April 1934. See Appendix.

7. Throughout his narrative Crawford refers to the master of the *Fanny* as 'Captain Falke', but a letter written by the captain in 1922, complaining that the *Fanny* affair had brought him 'to the brink of ruin', is signed 'Marthin Falck'. (Crawford Papers, 640/29.) A plate photograph of the ship among Crawford's effects also gives the master's name as M. Falck.

8. Crawford to C. C. Craig, 27 Jan. 1937. (Crawford Papers, D.640/30.)

9. Diary, 26 March 1914. 'Left tonight by God's help to carry out the enormous duties my fellow-citizens in Ulster have placed upon me.' (Crawford Papers, D.1700.)

10. In his narrative Crawford writes that he distinctly heard a voice say: 'Go with the guns tonight, and don't lose sight of the rifles till you have handed them over in Ulster,' and that this message was thrice repeated. But his diary, written shortly after

the events, says nothing about mysterious voices. (Crawford Papers, D.1700.)

11. Diary, 28 March 1914. (Crawford Papers, D. 1700.)

15. THE CRUISE OF THE *FANNY*

1. *The Times*, 1, 2 April 1914.
2. This incident is recorded by Agnew in the log, but for Thursday, 26 March. (*Guns for Ulster*, p. 66.)
3. Spender, *Unionist*, June 1949.
4. ibid.
5. The original is among General Richardson's papers in the National Army Museum at Sandhurst. Photostat copy in P.R.O.N.I. (T.2180); Holograph copy made at the time in D.1327/4/16.
6. The facts concerning Spender's adventure have been taken from an account written by Spender for Ronald McNeill (Lord Cushendun), but not used by him in *Ulster's Stand for Union* (MIC. 103), and from Spender, *Unionist*, June 1949.
7. 'Agreement between Captain Spender and Mr Schneider', 9 April 1914. D.1327/4. Found among the leaves of a file of U.V.F. orders.
8. The old inn at Rhiconich is now a police station, about one hundred yards from the present Rhiconich Hotel. Before the first world war it was part of the estates of the Duke of Sutherland. (For information about the inn I am indebted to Mr Peter Grant, son of the innkeeper in 1914, and to Mr John McLeod of the present Rhiconich Hotel.)
9. Agnew, log, 8–12 April. (*Guns for Ulster*, pp. 70–72.) Carbon copies of the instructions Cowzer brought are in D.1327/4/21.
10. Crawford, D.1700; Lady Craigavon, Diary, undated but before 20 April; Colvin, ii, 357–358.
11. Agnew, log, 19 April. (*Guns for Ulster*, p. 75.)

16. OPERATION LION

1. Spender, *Unionist*, April 1949; Spender to R. McNeill, MIC.103.
2. Crawford, D.1700. 'It was eventually agreed that I should run her up the Musgrave Channel. I arranged to do so on the Friday following.'
3. BNL. 14, 15 and 16 April 1914.
4. Crawford, D.1700.
5. Secret summons to motor car owners. D.1250; Gen. Adair to Capt. the Hon. Arthur O'Neill, 21 April 1914. O'Neill papers, D.1238.

6. Spender speaks of Carson consulting his 'eleven leading advisers', *Unionist*, April 1949.
7. D.1327/3/21.
8. Spender, *Unionist*, April 1949.
9. O'Neill papers, D.1238.
10. Adair to O'Neill, 21 April 1914. O'Neill papers, D.1238.
11. D.1327/3/8.
12. Crawford, D.1700.
13. Order for unloading the S.S. *Clydevalley*. D.1327/3/8.
14. Col. G. H. H. Couchman to Col. W. Hacket Pain, 24 April 1914; orders of Major Tempest Stone to South Belfast regiment U.V.F.; mobilization orders to West Belfast regiment; (D.1327/3/8). BNL. BET. 25 April 1914.
15. Article by 'George Dickson' (R. G. D. Hamilton) in BNL, 22 April 1964.
16. Memo from Capt. J. Scriven to C.S.O. 24.4.14. D.1327/3/8.
17. BNL. BET. 25 April 1914; eyewitness accounts.
18. Couchman to H.Q. D.1327/3/8.
19. ibid.
20. Scriven to H.Q. D.1327/3/8.
21. Information supplied by Mrs. R. Kirkpatrick (Lucy McNeill).
22. BET. 27 April 1914.
23. Spender to McNeill. MIC. 103; *The Times*, 27 April 1914.
24. BNL. 27 April 1914.
25. Adair to O'Neill, 21 April 1914. O'Neill papers. D.1238.
26. MIC.103.
27. Article by 'George Dickson' in BNL, 22 April 1964.
28. 'Onlooker', BET. 25 April 1914.
29. MIC.103; Crawford D.1700.
30. Order for unloading the S.S. *Clydevalley*. D.1327/3/8.
31. BET. 25 April; Crawford D.1700.
32. Crawford D.1700.
33. Capt. A. St. Q. Ricardo to Col. Hacket Pain, 25 April 1914. D.1327/3/8.
34. Mrs. Kirkpatrick.
35. Agnew, Log. 24 April 1914; Col. T. V. P. McCammon, 'Report on the operations at Bangor, 24/25 April 1914.' D.1327/3/8.
36. BET. 25 April 1914.
37. CC. Special Instructions, 25 April 1914. D.1327/4/8.
38. McCammon's report. D.1327/3/8.
39. Crozier, *Impressions and Recollections*, pp. 152–153.
40. McCammon's report. D.1327/3/8.
41. ibid.; Crozier, op. cit., p. 153.
42. Crawford, D.1700; Agnew, log. 25 April 1914.
43. Crozier, op. cit., p. 153.

44. Lady Craigavon's diary. D.1415/B.
45. Information supplied by W. P. Johnston.
46. Colvin, ii, 375.
47. BNL. 28 April 1914.
48. Report of the inquest. BNL. 27 April 1914. The same edition printed a letter from Lord Dunleath stating that it was proposed to open a fund for the coastguard's family.
49. Craig's notes. D.1327/3/8.
50. ibid.
51. McNeill, p. 220.

17. DARKNESS AND SHADOWS

1. R. Jenkins, *Asquith*, pp. 316–317.
2. Parl. Deb. 5th Series, LXI, cols. 1575–1591; Gwynn, p. 306. The Federal scheme which lay at the back of Churchill's proposals was the ingenious product of the group of young disciples of Milner, who called themselves the *Round Table*. It gave a measure of Home Rule to England, Scotland, Wales, Ireland, and Ulster, and would, they claimed, solve not only the Irish question but a number of others as well. Milner, in his mood of that time, was not prepared to listen to them, but they gained the ear of Lord Roberts, and also succeeded in convincing Churchill during a cruise on board the Admiralty yacht *Enchantress*. For the influence of the *Round Table* at this time see Gollin, pp. 209–213.
3. Paul. Deb., 5th series, LXI, cols. 1750–1751.
4. Colvin, ii, 387.
5. Gleichen, p. 386.
6. CC. 26 April 1914.
7. Distribution of rifles, 4 May 1914, D.1327/4/13.
8. CM. 9 May 1914.
9. Gleichen, p. 387; Macready, i, 185; O.S. maps among the U.V.F. papers have the location of some of the *caches* in Co. Armagh marked in red ink.
10. Div. Commander, Co. Antrim to C.S.O. 6 May 1914. O'Neill papers, D.1238.
11. C.S.O. to Div. Commander, Co. Antrim. May 1914. O'Neill papers, D.1238.
12. CM. 7 May 1914; UVFO. 22 May 1914.
13. CM. 14 May 1914.
14. CM. 18 May 1914.
15. BNL. 18 May 1914; Gleichen, pp. 388–389.
16. Gleichen, p. 388; Macready, i, 190–192.
17. UVFO. 29 May 1914.

18. Gleichen, p. 392.
19. Colvin, ii, 401.
20. McNeill, p. 226.
21. Gollin, p. 198.
22. ibid., pp. 217–218.
23. ibid., pp. 215–216.
24. McNeill, p. 145; BNL. 9 March, 10 April, 9 June 1914.
25. McNeill, p. 226.
26. Colvin, ii, 403.

18. 'THE KAISER'S ULSTER FRIENDS'

1. Agnew, log, 25 April 1914. (*Guns for Ulster*, pp. 77–78.)
2. Crawford, D.1700.
3. Information supplied by Mr. C. G. Hume, quoted from an article by 'George Dickson' in BNL. 22 April 1964.
4. Agnew, log, 5 May 1914. (*Guns for Ulster*, pp. 79–80.)
5. B. W. Tuchman, *The Zimmermann Telegram*, p. 47.
6. Gwynn, pp. 205–206.
7. Colvin, ii, 193; Hyde, pp. 337–338.
   A slightly different account of the meeting is given by Thomas Rhodes in *The Real Kühlmann* (see below). The story was told to him by Sir Frank Lascelles, the British ambassador, and was as follows: 'There was an English lady living in Homburg with whom the Emperor invariably lunched on the occasion of his annual visit to that city. It was her wish to bring the Kaiser and Sir Edward together, but year after year Sir Frank had dissuaded her from attempting it. At last, however, he not only gave way but said, "And forget all the etiquette you ever learnt and put Carson next to the Kaiser." ' The two got on very well, and Carson 'told some of his best tales'. 'Then they came to serious talk about Ireland, in the course of which the Kaiser said "You mean you won't be ruled by the priests?" Carson assented!' (p. 31.) Not long after this, adds Rhodes, 'a German occupying a high position in the industrial world' asked him if he knew Sir Edward, saying that Carson had made a deep impression on the Kaiser, and that he himself would like to know more about him. (p. 31.)
8. Quoted BNL. September 1913.
9. Callwell, i, 146; Gwynn, p. 349.
10. Gwynn, p. 350.
11. F. M. Count Franz Conrad von Hötzendorff, *Aus Meiner Dienstzeit*, iii, 73–74, 676.
    'Wie sich England im Falle kriegerische Konflikte verhalten würde war schwer abzusehen. . . . Auch mochten die inneren

Unruhen nicht ohne Einflusz auf seine Entscheidungen sein'. (p. 73.)

Ulster . . . brachte zirka 10.000 (*sic*) Freiwillige unter die Waffen und drohte mit dem Bürgerkrieg gegen Irland. Die dagegen zum Einschreiten befohlene englische Kavalleriebrigade Gough versagte dem Gehorsam. Ihre Offiziere weigerten sich, gegen Ulster die Waffen zu gebrauchen. (p. 74.)

12. H. Nevinson, *More Changes, More Chances*, pp. 403–404.
13. J. W. Gerard, *My Four Years in Germany*, p. 63. He also says that the German Foreign Office and most people in the capital believed that the British were 'so occupied with the Ulster rebellion and unrest in Ireland that they would not declare war'. p. 91.
14. Margot Asquith, *Autobiography*, p. 91, and see (for example) Tréguiz: 'M. von Kühlmann parcourait l'Ulster, hôte d'honneur des réunions élégantes chez les chefs orangistes à qui il offrait sa photographie avec dédicace.' p. 139, n. 1.
15. Parl. Deb., 5th Series, XCI, col. 1841.
16. T. Rhodes, *The Real von Kühlmann*, p. 28. Rhodes prints letters which he received from Kühlmann between 6 July and 2 August 1914.
17. Richard von Kühlmann, *Erinnerungen*, p. 303. For a description of Rhodes see p. 307, and of the Asquiths, pp. 309–310.
18. J. A. Spender, *Life, Journalism and Politics*, ii, 5. Spender was a cousin of Wilfrid Spender, but violently opposed to the Ulster movement.
19. Kühlmann, p. 305.
20. Nicolson, pp. 242–243.
21. Colvin, ii, 416.
22. W. S. Churchill, *The World Crisis*, i, 193.
23. Gwynn, p. 347.
24. Jenkins, p. 322.
25. Colvin, ii, 419–420.
26. File of papers of the Refugee Committee, D.1327/4/5; information supplied by Sir Wilson Hungerford.
27. Gollin, *The* Observer *and J. L. Garvin*, p. 421; Callwell, i, 148.
28. Jenkins, p. 323.
29. Colvin, iii, 17; the wording is from Carson's statement in *The Times* 1 August 1914.
30. Parl. Deb., 5th Series, LXV, cols. 1824–1829.
31. C. Falls, *The 36th (Ulster) Division*, p. 3.
32. Colvin, iii, 27.
33. Hyde, p. 379.
34. Falls, p. 4.
35. Colvin, iii, 33.

36. Hyde, p. 379.
37. Parl. Deb., 5th series, LXVI, cols. 882–893.
38. Falls, p. 5.
39. BNL. 9 September 1914.
40. Falls, p. 7.

19. THE WAY THROUGH THE WOOD

1. The action described is officially known as the Battle of Albert, but those who took part call it Thiepval (see Falls, p. 298).
2. Crozier, *A Brasshat in No Man's Land*, p. 97; *The Men I Killed*, p. 81.
3. Sir Philip Gibbs, *The War Dispatches*, p. 98.
4. Article by 'George Dickson' in BNL. 1 Sept. 1962.
5. ibid.; Brian Gardner, *The Big Push*, p. 1.
6. Gibbs, p. 99.
7. Falls, pp. 51–52; Gardner, p. 83.
8. M. Macdonagh, *The Irish on the Somme*, p. 37.
9. ibid., p. 41; Falls, p. 52.
10. Crozier, *Brasshat*, pp. 103–104; *Impressions and Recollections*, p. 174.
11. Falls, pp. 54–56.
12. ibid., p. 61.
13. Crozier, *Brasshat*, p. 110; Falls, p. 57.
14. W. B. Spender, 2 July 1914. Spender papers. D.1295.
15. Falls, p. 59; Gibbs quoted in Ervine, p. 325; D. 1327/3/21. Papers relating to the Ulster Division and the Somme. A letter of Major H. Singleton describing 1 July ends: 'Casualties; Officers 222, Other ranks 5,300.' The censor has carefully ringed this with blue pencil and written opposite 'Omit'.
16. Falls, p. 59.
17. Spender Papers, D.1295.
18. An account of the dinner was given to me by Mr. Norman Canning who was present. The *Clydevalley* was purchased by a firm of coal importers, and returned frequently to Larne with more innocent cargoes. During the war she crossed the Atlantic to St. John's, Newfoundland, and according to *Lloyd's Register* she was still afloat in 1965.
19. Information supplied by Mrs. Doreen Penson.

INDEX